DEATH
IN THE
FIELDS

A graduate of Bristol University and the Royal Military Academy Sandhurst, Jonathan Trigg served as an infantry officer in the Royal Anglican Regiment, completing tours in Northern Ireland and Bosnia, as well as the Gulf. He is the author of over a dozen books of military history. His book on the destruction of Hitler's Axis allies in Russia, *Death on the Don*, was nominated for The Pushkin Prize for Russian history in 2014.

For other work by the author
visit www.jonathantrigg.co.uk

DEATH IN THE FIELDS

The IRA and East Tyrone

JONATHAN TRIGG

MERRION
PRESS

First published in 2023 by
Merrion Press
10 George's Street
Newbridge
Co. Kildare
Ireland
www.merrionpress.ie

© Jonathan Trigg, 2023

9781785374432 (Paper)
9781785374449 (Ebook)

A CIP catalogue record for this book is
available from the British Library.

Unless otherwise stated, all images are courtesy of the author.

Typeset in Minion Pro 11.5/17 pt

Cover design by Fiachra McCarthy.

Merrion Press is a member of Publishing Ireland.

CONTENTS

For Rachel, Maddy and Jack – for always

'They [the British] have been killing people in Tyrone for hundreds of years, they have been killing Irish people in these fields for over a thousand years, but we will teach them the lesson that no matter how many people they kill … others will pick up and follow on.'

Belfast Sinn Féin councillor Máirtín Ó Muilleoir's oration at the funeral of IRA volunteer Tony Doris, Coalisland, 1991

AUTHOR'S NOTE

This book is the product of a whole series of interviews with veterans from all sides in the conflict: former Provisionals, Loyalists (members of pro-unionist paramilitary organisations), British Army, UDR, RUC, Special Branch and the British security service. Some are quoted by name, but most are not, unsurprisingly preferring anonymity. So many have helped me but I would like to express my particular thanks to Jay Nethercott – thanks for everything, Jay. I would also like to record a heartfelt thank you to all my interviewees for their candour and honesty in telling their stories. I hope I have done you all justice.

On a separate note, I'd like to thank Toby Harnden, Aaron Edwards, Patrick Mercer and Henry Robinson for their advice and guidance, and Conor and Patrick at Merrion Press – thank you.

A couple of points on the text. I have opted to use the Irish Historical Studies (IHS) convention when referring to Derry for the city and bishopric, and Londonderry for the county and parliamentary constituencies. I have also opted to use several terms as shorthand to describe the Provisional IRA, including the IRA, the Provisionals, PIRA and the Provos. I am aware that the volunteers themselves preferred to refer to themselves as 'the Army'; however, as I use the word Army in the book to refer to the British Army I feel that mixing the two could be confusing for the reader, hence my decision. When referring to the East Tyrone Brigade of the Provisional IRA I use an upper case 'E', but when referring to the population of east Tyrone or the geographical area itself, I use a lower case 'e'.

As reference for the dates and details of those who lost their lives in the war I have used Ulster University's excellent CAIN Archive, and specifically Malcolm Sutton's Index of Deaths from the Conflict in Ireland, including the designations and affiliations of those same individuals.

Last, but not least, I often refer to the conflict as 'the war' as well as 'the Troubles'. I know that the latter is the accepted term, but I believe for those who fought in the struggle from all sides, it felt like a bloody war.

PREFACE

Saturday, 13 June 1981 was a wet and windy day in east Tyrone, and Sammy Brush was in a hurry. A postie in Dungannon, he was keen to finish up his round and head over to the local Ulster Defence Regiment's (UDR) Open Day in the town. A proud member of the regiment himself, Brush was going to pick up his young son and then join in the fun, despite the weather. But first he had one last delivery 'for a Mrs Mary McGarvey, Cravney Irish, Ballygawley', as Brush would later recount. There were no other letters for the road that day, and in truth Mrs McGarvey's was only being delivered 'because it had been sent First-Class'. Pulling up outside the house in his red Post Office van, he walked to the front door and popped the delivery through the letter box. As he turned to go 'a gunman wearing a balaclava appeared ... he fired the first shot and it hit me here [upper left chest], it was like being kicked by a donkey, and it spun me around'. Brush's life was only saved by the body armour his UDR company commander – Ken Maginnis – had insisted he wear on his rounds a bare six weeks earlier. Then a second gunman appeared and 'the next shot missed the body armour and went straight through my right lung and came out in the centre of my back'. Adrenalin flooded Brush's system, somehow enabling him to pull his personal protection weapon – a pistol – from its shoulder holster and return fire. 'My right hand was out of action – I didn't know at the time but the bullet had cut the nerves to it – so I used my left hand and just turned and fired two shots at one of them.' In the confusion 'I got back in the van, reversed out and drove to Ballygawley police station about a mile and a half away, and just sat there and blew the horn until George Gilliland [an RUC officer at the station] came out.' Miraculously Brush survived, but looking back on the attack he believed he'd been set up: 'That letter was deliberately sent, it was a notice about the Benburb Sunday event but wasn't from the Benburb Priory.'

The attempt on Sammy Brush's life was just one of hundreds of operations carried out by one of the deadliest units the Provisional IRA ever produced – its East Tyrone Brigade. In British Army circles at the time the saying went that 'in Belfast the Provos are trying to make the 6 o'clock news, in east Tyrone they're trying to kill you'.

The Provisional Irish Republican Army (PIRA) – the Provos – were birthed in the violence and mayhem of 1969 as the Troubles erupted and the old-style, or Official Irish Republican Army (OIRA), was found wanting in terms of its ability to protect local Catholic populations under attack from Protestant unionist (people pro the union with Great Britain) mobs. Given it was in the cities where the violence was most pronounced, this was where the infant Provos first made their mark, forming themselves into the Belfast and Derry Brigades. As for rural Northern Ireland, it was initially stony ground for the Provos, but within a few years the new organisation had spread across the entire north, local units springing up to take on the British Army and Northern Ireland's police force – the Royal Ulster Constabulary (RUC).

Not structured, trained or equipped like a standard army, nonetheless individual Provisionals saw themselves as soldiers – Volunteers – and fashioned themselves into companies and battalions that usually operated close to home. Above that level the Provisionals across the bulk of Northern Ireland were fairly loosely organised, with Tyrone and Fermanagh, north Armagh, south Londonderry and, at times, east Donegal, structured as an amorphous 'Mid-Ulster Command', which proved itself too unwieldy to be truly effective. Only South Armagh – unsurprisingly an exception – kept its distance and quickly became a recognised brigade alongside Belfast and Derry.

As for counties Fermanagh and Tyrone, the Provisionals there were dominated by a series of local hard men – many from families with staunchly republican backgrounds – who imposed themselves on their areas and, to an extent, fought their own almost private wars. This was especially true of Tyrone, a county with a keen sense of its own history and a distinct feeling of exceptionalism.

At first, the Tyrone Provisionals found themselves up against state security forces that were just as unprepared for the war as PIRA was itself. Scrambling to respond, British government policy shifted to one of 'Ulsterising' the war as the saying went. That meant wrestling the lead role in combating the Provisionals away from the Army and giving it to the RUC, and establishing a different type of military force to anything the British had up until then: the Ulster Defence Regiment. Locally recruited, its ranks filled with a mix of full- and part-time members, UDR soldiers patrolled their own streets and fields and weren't liable for service outside Northern Ireland. As such the UDR was a very different beast from the rest of the regular Army and posed a unique problem for the Provisionals.

With the RUC taking the lead, the non-uniformed men of RUC Special Branch (SB) – known simply as 'the Branch' – came into their own, recruiting and running 'sources' – individuals providing information from within the organisation – who soon peppered the Provisionals. As the 1970s ended and the war entered its second decade it was clear PIRA needed to change before it drowned under the weight of its own informers. The mayhem of the first years of the campaign ended, to be replaced by the Long War strategy, devised by Gerry Adams to slowly but surely defeat the British and force them out of Northern Ireland. The new strategy was to be delivered by a new IRA, one based on small cells of volunteers to minimise the threat from informers – these were PIRA's Active Service Units, their ASUs. Along with them came two new rural brigades: Fermanagh and East Tyrone, which would become pivotal to PIRA's war, and none more so than East Tyrone. Across its claustrophobic patchwork of farms, fields, villages and towns, sweeping east from Ballygawley and the republican strongholds of Cappagh mountain and Pomeroy, through Cookstown, Coalisland and Dungannon, down to Ardboe on the shores of Lough Neagh, the East Tyrone Brigade held sway. Its members may not have been professional soldiers but they were dedicated and extremely active, as one former IRA volunteer proudly stated: 'East Tyrone was the Provos' engine room.'

That engine room went up a gear after the signing of the Anglo-Irish Agreement in 1985, as the Brigade attempted to seize the initiative and decisively turn the tide of war in favour of the Provisionals. Then, on a warm spring night in early May 1987, as millions sat in front of the TV to watch the latest episode of the *Wogan* chat show, East Tyrone PIRA's war was ripped asunder. In a few short minutes a Special Air Service (SAS) ambush in the north Armagh village of Loughgall killed eight of its most committed and experienced volunteers – its so-called A Team – and that was just the start.

Over the next five years East Tyrone PIRA suffered a bloodletting like no other. The Brigade wasn't helpless and the deadly traffic was far from being one-way, but in operation after operation the forces at the cutting edge of Britain's war with the Provos exacted a heavy toll. By the time the peace process began to get into gear one Tyrone republican commented ruefully to the Irish journalist Ed Moloney that 'we [East Tyrone PIRA] had nobody left'.

But if the history of militant Irish republicanism teaches anyone anything, it's that there's always someone left – always.

East Tyrone PIRA didn't materialise out of thin air; they sprang from a tradition they believe goes back centuries, to a time of Norman knights and Gaelic warriors, the Plantations of the 1600s and on through the 1916 Easter Rising and Anglo-Irish War – the Tan War as it is known across Ireland – and the Border Campaign of the 1950s and '60s. That is their back story and they see themselves as simply the latest incarnation of an ongoing struggle – a struggle they have not forsaken. This is the story of the men and women, from all sides, who lived and breathed the Troubles in the villages and fields of Tyrone until an imperfect peace finally took hold in 1994. Long may it last.

The Counties of Northern Ireland

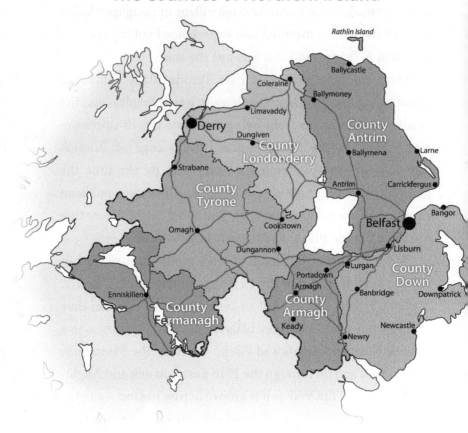

East Tyrone

County Londonderry

West Tyrone

Dunnamore

Cookstown

Coagh

Pomeroy

Stewartstown

LOUGH NEAGH

Cappagh

Coalisland

Donaghmore

Dungannon

Ballygawley

Moy

County Armagh

County Fermanagh

Aughnacloy

County Monaghan

Caledon

1

A HISTORY OF WAR
AND BLOODSHED

John de Courcy, Lord Kingsale and premier baron of Ireland, was a man of considerable girth who disdained cider as having the unpleasant effect of bursting the veins in his nose, and proudly exclaimed to all and sundry, '[I am] prepared to lend my hand to absolutely anything, however dirty or unpleasant.'[1] True to his word, de Courcy once personally installed a gents' urinal in his local pub in exchange for a couple of weeks of free meals. The 35th Baron Kingsale eventually passed away penniless in sheltered housing in 2005. His namesake – the very first Baron Kingsale – was an altogether different proposition. Somerset-born like his erstwhile descendant, the first John de Courcy was the second son of a noble lord in an age where that meant the path to riches lay either through a career in the Church or at the point of a sword; he chose the latter. At a time when most other second sons of the Anglo-Norman nobility headed east to France in search of wealth, de Courcy instead turned his face west and sailed to Ireland in 1176. So began a military and political career spanning three decades that, at one point, saw him minting his own coinage and titling himself *princeps Ultoniae* – 'master of Ulster'.

Starting out with a small force of some twenty-two knights and 300 foot soldiers, de Courcy, 'a tall, blond man with long bony limbs ... physically very strong and of exceptional courage', marched north from Dublin in the bitterly cold first weeks of January 1177 to attack the kingdom of Ulaid in eastern Ulster. Successful from the start, de Courcy – 'a valiant man of war' – launched a series of campaigns that spilled over into the Northern Uí Néill's territory of Tír nEógain – Tyrone. Relatively untouched by earlier Viking incursions, Tyrone now found itself inexorably drawn into the maelstrom of conflict between the Anglo-Normans and the native Gaels.

After a century and a half of intermittent warfare, the Normans and their English levies were hit hard by the advent of the Black Death in the 1340s, and the resulting decimation led to their retreat to the Pale of Dublin and its hinterland. The ensuing native Irish resurgence held sway for over two hundred years until the English Catholic Tudor Queen, Mary I, began the Plantation of Ireland with English and Scottish settlers granted land in Laois and Offaly.

This wholly new phenomenon in Ireland continued under successive Tudor monarchs, reaching its zenith in the reign of the Anglo-Scot James I with the Plantation of Ulster – the north-eastern of Ireland's four provinces, the other three being Munster, Leinster and Connacht. James's decision was triggered by the so-called Flight of the Earls in 1607, when Hugh O'Neill, 2nd Earl of Tyrone, and his compatriot Rory

O'Donnell, 1st Earl of Tyrconnell, sailed for mainland Europe under a September harvest moon to try and enlist Catholic Spanish support for their ongoing war with the English Crown. With them went much of the old Gaelic order, and the vacuum was filled by a combination of servitors – Anglo-Scots veterans of the Irish wars – the Protestant Church of Ireland, and English and Scottish landowners who agreed to import some of their existing tenants to the new estates granted to them from confiscated Irish land. James insisted that all these new settlers be Protestants as well as English-speaking, and preferably whole families, rather than single men, to discourage intermarriage with the native Irish population as had happened to the Norse and Anglo-Normans. As a result there were perhaps as many as a hundred thousand newcomers living in Ulster by the 1630s. In both east Tyrone and north Armagh the settlers formed a majority; however, many of them preferred Tyrone's growing towns to life on the farm, leaving the new landlords with little choice but to entrust much of their holdings – particularly their least productive acres – to native Irish tenants contrary to the terms of their original land grants.

At the same time Tyrone itself began to be recognised as one of the new northern counties, a title also given to Monaghan, Cavan, Fermanagh and Donegal. As such Tyrone became the largest county in the north of Ireland, sharing borders with Donegal in the west, Londonderry to the north, Armagh and Fermanagh to the east and southwest respectively, and with northern Monaghan jutting into its heart. Traditionally covered in dense forests that were often home to bandits and brigands, it was commonly referred to as 'Tyrone among the bushes', although the arrival of the Protestant settlers saw widespread forest felling to make way for crops and cattle. Those same settlers tended to concentrate in certain areas of the county, with large numbers of Presbyterian Scots moving into the townships of Cookstown in the east, and Strabane and Newtownstewart to the west, while many of their Anglican co-religionists favoured the farmland that stretched southwest from the bottom of Lough Neagh to the well-to-do villages of the Clogher valley, aptly captured in the local rhyme; 'Augher, Clogher, Fivemiletown, Sixmilecross and seven-mile round.'

The new county had much in common with neighbouring Armagh; both were rural, with the pace of life mirroring the changing of the seasons, and both had their Protestant incomers, but while in Tyrone those incomers were mainly concentrated in the south, in Armagh the settlers congregated in the north, leaving the south almost wholly Catholic. None of Tyrone's towns – Omagh being the county seat – were of any great size and tended to keep themselves to themselves, whereas Armagh City preferred to wear her position as the seat of All Ireland's Catholic and Protestant faiths with scrupulous pride. As for her people, after so many years as the beating heart of Ulster resistance to English incursions, it was inevitable that the native Irish of Tyrone would be imbued with a strong rebellious streak, expressed locally by the term 'Tírghrá', loosely translated into English as meaning 'love of one's county'. But whereas in nearby south Armagh this same feeling produced a more or less closed local community – immune to outsiders – the intermixing in Tyrone of Protestant and Catholic, settler and native Irish, made the same outcome almost impossible except in a few upland areas like Carrickmore and Cappagh.

However, conflict was only ever just beneath the surface, and the upheavals of the Ulster Plantation were followed by the 1641 Rebellion where massacres of Protestants, such as the Portadown killings in November of that year, played to the worst fears of the incomers and sparked outrage in Britain. Hysterical pamphlets appeared in London proclaiming that bloodthirsty Catholics were spearing Protestant babies on pitchforks and that as many as 200,000 settlers had already been murdered, a wild exaggeration that nonetheless helped fuel the fires of revenge for Scottish Covenanters who committed tit-for-tat atrocities during the ensuing English Civil War, or more correctly the Wars of the Three Kingdoms.

The fighting devastated Tyrone, with thousands dead and thousands more homeless, destitute and starving. The legacy of those years was a bitterness tied to the land itself, the poison from neighbour fighting neighbour leeching into the very ground. Three hundred years later that hatred still festered as the Provo-turned Gardaí (Garda Síochána – the Irish national police service) informer Sean O'Callaghan – himself a country boy from County Kerry – realised only too well: 'To stand with an old farmer on a hillside in Pomeroy while he pointed out Protestant farms "stolen from us by them black bastards [derogatory slang for Protestants]" is to understand the emotive power of blood and earth.'[2]

By the early twentieth century Tyrone still felt like a frontier state in Ireland's complex social and political life. In 1911 Catholics were a slim majority of the county's 140,000-odd population, with the growth of the linen trade transforming the likes of formerly Protestant Dungannon – ancient stronghold of the O'Neill's – into a magnet for Catholics from the surrounding countryside, radically altering its character as they moved into town. In the countryside, higher rents forced some Catholics off their land, while others were actively buying up Protestant landholdings, intermixing the communities even more. But what hadn't changed was the balance of power, with the gerrymandered electoral boundaries drawn up by British officials back in 1898 shamelessly working in favour of Unionists. This meant both Dungannon's urban and rural district councils were still dominated by Unionists, despite Protestants being visibly outnumbered, and that outcome was replicated in Omagh, Cookstown and even Catholic Castlederg, with Strabane being the only urban council in the county with a Catholic nationalist majority.

By then, Home Rule was the clarion call of the day, and as Ireland once again took centre stage in Westminster politics, the north–south split that would come to define the next century of the island's history was beginning to take shape. Ancient Protestant fears of a return to the settler massacres of the seventeenth century merged with the dread of losing political and economic dominance, to foment a powerful brew across Ulster's now-nine counties where the overwhelming majority of Ireland's Protestants lived, despite the Plantation attempts in Munster, Connacht and the like. While 'Home Rule' proved a powerful rallying cry for Irish Catholics, so fear of 'Rome Rule' did much the same for Ireland's Protestants. Nowhere was this feeling stronger than in Tyrone where over a third of all Protestant adult males were members of the Orange Order at the time, the Order being very much a bulwark of Unionism and the existing Protestant Ascendancy.

Alarmingly, both sides proved all too willing to turn to the threat of force to achieve their goals. For Tyrone's Catholics their previous allegiance to the moderate, constitutional nationalism of the Irish Parliamentary Party and Ancient Order of Hibernians, began to disintegrate as supporters drained away to the strident militancy of Sinn Féin and the Irish Volunteers. This growing radicalisation among Tyrone's Catholics was matched by their Protestant neighbours who, spurred on by the likes of the inflammatory Dublin barrister Sir Edward Carson, also embraced a paramilitary option by flocking to the newly established Ulster Volunteer Force (UVF). Indeed, by the summer of 1914, Tyrone's UVF could boast 8,000 men in its ranks, facing off against 5,000 of their neighbours in the Irish Volunteers.

Carson, meanwhile, was increasingly turning his rhetoric towards partition as the only answer for Ireland's troubles. In January 1913 his first proposal was that all nine of Ulster's counties be excluded from Home Rule, but despite the large Protestant minorities in Cavan, Monaghan and Donegal – a full quarter in the first two and one in five in the latter – it was clear that their inclusion would mean there would be no in-built Protestant majority in any new northern mini-state. What was also clear was that those counties' Catholic majorities would never accept such an arrangement either. Come autumn of that same year Carson performed a *volte face* and jettisoned his demand for all nine Ulster counties to be excluded, instead arguing that the remaining six: Tyrone, Fermanagh, Londonderry, Armagh, Antrim and Down were 'the irreducible minimum'. Suddenly, Donegal's 3,000 UVF volunteers found themselves cast adrift, a victim of Ireland's often Machiavellian politics.

Many in unionism were aghast at what they saw as a naked betrayal of their co-religionists, with that Tyrone scion of the Ascendancy, Sir James Henry Stronge, 5th Baronet, later declaring in a letter to his friend and fellow Tyrone grandee, Hugh Montgomery, that the politicians in Belfast had thrown the Protestants of Cavan, Monaghan and Donegal 'to the wolves, with very little compunction', to which the hard-nosed Montgomery had succinctly replied the decision wasn't 'a question of ethics and honour, but a question of arithmetic'.[3]

As the blisteringly hot summer of 1914 burned on across Europe, Great Britain seemed almost unaware of the growing drumbeat for war on the European Continent and was instead focusing much of its political energy on the continuing crisis in Ireland. Herbert Asquith, the Liberal prime minister of the day, opened the Buckingham Palace Conference on Tuesday, 21 July hoping to reach an agreed position across the political spectrum on the partition question. It became clear remarkably quickly that while the exclusion from Home Rule of Counties Down, Antrim, Armagh and Londonderry was not disputed, the same could not be said for Fermanagh and Tyrone. Asquith, a serial letter writer notoriously indiscreet with his pen, wrote to a friend that he 'rarely felt more helpless in any particular affair, an impasse with unspeakable consequences, upon a matter which, to English eyes, seems inconceivably small and to Irish eyes immeasurably big'. He followed up this missive with another to the prominent socialite and object of his infatuation, Venetia Stanley, describing Tyrone as 'that most damnable creation of the perverted ingenuity of man'.[4] Three days after it began, the Conference closed with no sign of agreement, and when Britain declared war on Imperial

Germany less than a fortnight later, Churchill – rarely happier than when making a statement for posterity – declared that 'the parishes of Fermanagh and Tyrone faded back into the mists and squalls of Ireland'.[5]

As it was, the First World War initiated a significant burying of the hatchet between Ireland's Catholics and Protestants – and not in each other – but rather towards a common cause as young Catholics and Protestants alike stepped forward and willingly took the King's shilling – conscription never being introduced across Ireland. Catholics were mainly incorporated into the 10th and 16th (Irish) Divisions, while Protestants usually found themselves in the 36th (Ulster) Division, but there were men of both denominations in all three. Not that there was an almighty flood of volunteers, particularly from the rock upon which the Buckingham talks had floundered, with only some 2,123 men coming forward from Tyrone in the seventeen months from August 1914 to mid-January 1916. Observers could be forgiven for thinking that the men of Tyrone were keeping their powder dry for a post-war showdown of their own.

As it happened that particular showdown didn't wait for peace but exploded into life with the Easter Rising in 1916. Under instructions from Patrick Pearse and James Connolly – the latter as commander of the Irish Citizen Army – Tyrone was set to play a key role in the revolt with its nationalist volunteers ordered to assemble in Coalisland then march *en masse* to Belcoo in neighbouring Fermanagh. Once there they were to join Liam Mellows's Connacht contingent and position themselves on the River Shannon ready to aid the hoped-for Imperial German Army landing on the coast. How anyone could believe that the Germans would be able to evade the serried ranks of the Royal Navy and successfully disembark a force in Ireland – let alone do so when the Kaiser's forces were being bled white fighting the French at Verdun – is moot, but the reality was succinctly captured by the Irish historian Fergal McCluskey: 'The 1916 Rising in Tyrone was a fiasco.' It's hard to argue with him. Detailed preparations and communications – or rather the lack of them – resulted in dither and drift. Even before the Rising began, Patrick McCartan – a leading Tyrone republican – wrote to his friend and fellow republican Joseph 'Joe' McGarrity, baldly stating, 'We have failed in Tyrone – miserably failed – but it is not the fault of Tyrone but of Dublin.'[6] As McGarrity had been living in Philadelphia for over twenty years there was little he could do, but as a fellow Carrickmore-man he sympathised with McCartan's lament. Perhaps the most significant aspect of the damp squib that was the Rising in the North was the appearance in Coalisland at the time of 150 volunteers from Belfast. In 1916 the driving force of the republican effort in the North was supposed to be Tyrone, and not Belfast – after 1916 this was never again the case.

The failure of the Rising seemed to consign militant republicanism to the ashes, only for it to be reborn phoenix-like from the smoking barrels of the British firing squads that executed the leaders of the revolt. Tyrone even had its own martyr when the bespectacled Tom Clarke was shot on 3 May. The son of a British Army non-commissioned officer (NCO), Clarke had been born in genteel Hampshire but he'd called Dungannon home since the age of seven.

Two years later victory in the Great War was a triumph for Britain and her Empire, but it left the country exhausted and near bankrupt, and she was ill-prepared for a resumption of strife in Ireland that quickly escalated to new heights of violence. Once more it was Winston Churchill who caught the mood of the political class with his penmanship: 'Great empires have been overturned. The whole map of Europe has been changed ... But as the deluge subsides and the waters fall short we see the dreary steeples of Fermanagh and Tyrone emerging once again. The integrity of their quarrel is one of the few institutions that have been unaltered in the cataclysm that has swept the world.' In a campaign that would have disturbingly similar echoes half a century later, the newly created Irish Republican Army (IRA) established a number of territorially based units in the north, with the bulk of Tyrone designated the operational area of the 2nd Northern Division and coming under the care of Eoin O'Duffy, previously the IRA's commander in Monaghan. The appointment started a collaboration between the two counties' republicans that has lasted ever since, but at the time O'Duffy was far from happy about it, with his new charges – in his own words – ignoring 'reasonable orders' and being far too 'easy going'. O'Duffy left IRA high command in no doubt that he wanted his old Monaghan job back instead. Unsurprisingly he wasn't popular in Tyrone, whose men much preferred their own local leaders rather than someone they viewed as an outsider foisted on them against their will.

Regardless, O'Duffy's division comprised two brigades, the stronger being No. 1 Brigade centred on the republican heartlands in the east stretching from Coalisland and Dungannon across the uplands to Carrickmore and Greencastle. Meanwhile, No. 2 Brigade covered Omagh and central Tyrone including the nationalist enclaves around Dromore, Fintona and Trillick. The division's zone of operations didn't correspond entirely to the county's borders, with Strabane and the west coming under the neighbouring 1st Northern Division, much of the Clogher valley coming under the 5th Division, and Frank Aiken's South Armagh command taking on Brantry. However, the rather grandiose military titles used by the IRA at the time didn't conform to anything any Great War veteran would recognise. O'Duffy's 2nd Northern could field 1,350 volunteers in October 1921, whereas a corresponding division in any European army of the day numbered anywhere between 10,000 and 20,000 men. If the number of volunteers was a problem for the IRA, it was small beer compared to the lack of arms, with the Cookstown contingent not having a single gun, while the entire division could only muster a hundred or so rifles between them.[7]

Outnumbered more than two to one by the locally raised and better armed Royal Irish Constabulary (RIC), Tyrone's IRA engaged in a strategy pioneered by the Irish Republican Brotherhood (IRB) back in the Fenian Rising of 1867, and one it would regularly revisit over the next six decades and more: the destruction of isolated RIC stations (traditionally called barracks) to facilitate parallel IRA control of the countryside. The attacks began in Easter 1920, with six barracks burnt down by the end of June, including Donaghmore and Castlecaulfield. By late summer the IRA had set up their own courts dispensing 'country-justice', with a typical case being that of four local men accused of breaking into a pub in Gortin to steal all the drink they could carry off. Admitting their guilt the miscreants agreed to pay the landlord for what they'd stolen and were then released with shamed faces. Boot-leggers were also targeted with one unlucky poteen distiller forced to watch in misery as eighty gallons of his finest spirit was emptied into a nearby river. Then, a volunteer was killed when Cookstown barracks was attacked and the offensive stalled. In the hiatus the RIC took the initiative and reopened nine hitherto closed barracks by the new year of 1921. The renowned Independence War historian Charles Townshend believed that the offensive in Tyrone failed in large part because the divisional structure was 'just too big' and 'too ambitious for their [Tyrone IRA's] actual resources'. He also laid a good portion of the blame on O'Duffy himself, saying that for the independently minded Tyrone men 'persuasion and goodwill worked better than the direct exercise of authority'.[8] This was a lesson that would resurface in later campaigns.

As Tyrone became something of a backwater in the War, so its political importance once again came to the fore. Northern Unionists were now reconciled to the loss of Cavan, Monaghan and Donegal in the upcoming partition and with the signing of the Anglo-Irish Treaty on 6 December 1921 they abandoned some 70,000 of their brethren on the implicit understanding that Tyrone and Fermanagh were part of Carson's 'irreducible minimum'. For republicans there was horror at the compromises made by Michael Collins and his negotiating team. However, Article 12 of the Treaty stated that a Boundary Commission would be established if Northern Ireland chose to secede – which it did a bare two days after the Free State's inception on 6 December 1922. Collins claimed that he had received certain assurances that the Commission would oversee the transfer of 'large territories, not merely a boundary line' and on that basis he 'had already promised to bring into the Free State almost half of Northern Ireland, including the counties of Fermanagh, Tyrone, large parts of counties Armagh and Down, Derry City, Enniskillen and Newry'.[9]

Given that transfers on anything like this scale would leave the infant Northern Ireland an uneconomic dwarf state incapable of maintaining its existence there was no real hope of that outcome in the face of strident unionist opposition. It therefore seems unlikely that the British government ever thought that wholesale boundary changes were realistic, and the fact that haggling over the Commission's membership and scope went on for two years before it was finally established equally points to the Commission as being stillborn. Nevertheless Collins hung his hat on the Commission but didn't live to see that same hat fall ignominiously to the ground. With civil war raging in the Free State, the Commission didn't start sitting until late 1924, and even then its composition was controversial as the new government in Stormont refused to appoint a representative to a body it believed was designed to strip it of territory. Its chairman, the tall South African-born patrician Richard Feetham, was handed a poison chalice from which he and his fellow commissioners, the Free State's Education Minister Eoin MacNeill and the unionist barrister and newspaper editor, Joseph R. Fisher, had little option but to drink heartily. Dogged by all manner of disputes, when the final report was leaked to the London *Morning Post* newspaper in November 1925 it was condemned by all sides and promptly buried. William T. Cosgrave – head of the Free State government at the time – immediately recognised the Commission's report as a dead letter and agreed to keep the border as was in return for cancellation of his country's share of Great Britain's enormous pile of war debt. Little wonder that Éamon de Valera declared acidly that Cosgrave had 'sold Ulster natives for four pound a head'. The Commission's actual report was finally released into the public domain in 1969, whereupon the Unionist politician John Taylor wistfully said of it, 'we'd have gotten some really nice places like Letterkenny [County Donegal] and gotten rid of places like south Armagh'. Taylor would become MP for South Tyrone in the short-lived Northern Irish Commons before being shot five times in the head and neck by an OIRA gunman in Armagh on 25 February 1972 as he sat in the front seat of his car – he survived.

There's an old republican saying, coined by the renowned Irish rebel Wolfe Tone, that 'England's difficulty is Ireland's opportunity', so when Britain faced another war against Germany in 1939, for some in the IRA it seemed an opportunity had arisen. The IRA's Chief of Staff at the time was the Dublin-born hardliner Seán Russell, who came up with the so-called Sabotage or S-Plan, which would focus IRA efforts on a bombing campaign in England. Controversially, Russell turned to Nazi Germany for aid before dying from a burst gastric ulcer aboard a German U-boat en route home from the Third Reich. The only Tyrone connection of note in the S-Plan was the involvement of Patrick McCartan's old Irish-American friend Joe McGarrity who used his Clan na Gael (Irish-American sister organisation to the IRB) connections to raise funds to support it. There were a small number of attacks in Northern Ireland itself from 1942 onwards, but by 1944 a determined crackdown by Dublin and Belfast on both sides of the border had left the IRA a hollowed-out shell.

Tyrone's role in the next incarnation of IRA activity was of greater import. Raids on several armouries, including Gough barracks in Armagh and Felsted School's Officer Training Corps in Essex, had enabled the IRA to rearm to a significant degree by the mid-1950s and encouraged its then Chief of Staff, Tony Magan, to sell the family farm in County Meath to help fund the launch of yet another campaign of violence – Operation Harvest. More commonly known as the Border Campaign, this new phase of the Irish war began on the night of 12 December 1956 with simultaneous attacks on a number of targets in border areas across Northern Ireland. Fermanagh soon became the cockpit of the struggle, albeit only after Tyrone had made its mark in a wholly unexpected way.

The village of Pomeroy, sitting atop a large hill with views for miles across the surrounding bog and heath lands, has produced many a republican diehard, but few have been as committed to the cause as Liam Kelly. Born just before the Free State came into being, Kelly was drawn to republicanism and into the ranks of the IRA, becoming a senior figure in the organisation in Tyrone before he was thirty. Dismayed by what he regarded as a lack of militancy, Kelly led an attack in Derry in 1951 without the approval of the IRA's ruling Army Council, an act for which he was expelled from the organisation. It is a running joke within republicanism that at every meeting the first topic for discussion after agreeing the minutes of the last meeting is the next split, and so it was perhaps unsurprising when, undeterred by his expulsion, Kelly founded his own group, Saor Uladh (Free Ulster), taking with him almost every activist in east Tyrone to continue his attacks on customs posts and police barracks. A man who liked making a splash, in Easter 1952, the year after founding Saor Uladh, he and his men sealed off Pomeroy and declared it 'liberated' in front of clicking cameras. The following Easter he delivered the keynote speech in nearby Carrickmore, declaring to the large and appreciative crowd, 'I will not give allegiance to the foreign queen of a bastard nation. Do I believe in force? The answer is yes. The more the better, the sooner the better.' With the launch of Operation Harvest, Kelly put Saor Uladh at the disposal of the IRA, but his old comrades weren't the forgiving type and he remained *persona non grata*. He eventually emigrated to the United States in 1959 when his nephew, Patrick Joseph Kelly, was only two years old. Young Patrick would grow to pick up where his uncle had left off in east Tyrone.

Of even greater importance for the future East Tyrone PIRA Brigade than the involvement, or not, of the Kelly clan, was the participation in the Border Campaign of one Kevin Mallon. Mallon was born just outside the republican stronghold of Coalisland, a town built on the discovery of a nine-foot seam of the black stuff that promised huge wealth if it could be mined successfully. As it transpired that was a real problem, and what was worse was the difficulty, once mined, of shipping the coal to market in Dublin. The Catholic workers drawn to the new township by the promise of paid work mostly stayed on, digging the local clay and sand for the building trade, but it failed to live up to its promise as a mining boom town. Economically down on its luck, republicanism found a fertile recruiting ground in its careworn streets and among the 10,000 inhabitants. Just twenty years old when the Campaign was launched, Mallon – 'tall, rangy … a born leader [with] the kind of presence that would fill a room' – began his IRA career on Saturday, 17 August 1957 when a call to the local police was made from the public telephone box next to the village school in Edendork – halfway between Dungannon and Coalisland – reporting 'suspicious activity' at a house in nearby Brackaville. Constable William Dickson from the Coalisland station said, 'We got a call ... about a bomb and I went up to the address with the Army [two soldiers accompanied Dickson] while Sergeant Ovens travelled from Dungannon and arrived before us.'[10]

Arthur J. Ovens was a forty-three-year-old local policeman of no little experience. He'd arrived at the house and seen a light, but on knocking there was no answer and the place looked deserted – indeed it looked semi-derelict. Ovens was searching the house when Dickson arrived, and had found an internal door that seemed jammed shut. Dickson again, 'I recall it vividly as the two soldiers with me had just entered the place, and I was about to go in, when the house just blew up.' The telephone call from Edendork had been a 'come-on' – a call designed to lure the security forces into a trap – and it worked. The building was almost obliterated. 'Arty Ovens was killed, and the two soldiers were badly injured in the blast.' It took a half hour to find Sergeant Ovens's remains amidst the rubble. In a testament to the times, the killing shocked public opinion in Tyrone. Thousands attended Ovens's funeral, with the Reverend Gray describing his murder as 'deliberate and callous'. The Stormont government responded, posting a huge £5,000 reward – more than £100,000 in today's money – for information leading to a conviction. Kevin Mallon – recently turned twenty-one – was arrested for the murder along with his friend Francis Talbot, and on 7 January the following year the two went on trial. Both men claimed that their confessions had been beaten out of them by the RUC, and the English-based republican Connolly Association paid for a London lawyer – John Hostettler – to cover the trial on their behalf. Funds for the defence were raised in Dublin, and the court room became the centre of a media circus. With doubt cast on the confessions, and little else submitted as corroborative evidence, the jury found the pair not guilty and Lord Justice Black ordered their release. Hostettler subsequently published a pamphlet entitled 'Torture Trial in Belfast', in which he stated categorically that 'Mallon and Talbot were innocent of the charges' and demanded 'an independent public enquiry into police methods in Northern Ireland'. As a PIRA volunteer, Sean O'Callaghan spent several years in Tyrone at the beginning of the Troubles and knew pretty much every activist personally. In his own book *The Informer* he wrote that 'In August 1957, RUC Sergeant Arthur Ovens … was instantly blown to bits by a mine that Mallon had planted earlier.'[11]

The killing of Arthur Ovens was a turning point. As another Tyrone republican noted, 'Kevin Mallon [was now] a local man with a reputation.' Mallon would go on to become the driving force behind the creation of the Provisionals' East Tyrone Brigade and mastermind some of the most memorable operations in the history of the Provos.

2

THE TROUBLES BEGIN

On 26 February 1962 the IRA's Army Council issued a press release under the codename of the former Tyrone Clan na Gael leader, J. McGarrity, that ended the Border Campaign: 'All arms and other matériel have been dumped and all full-time active service volunteers have been withdrawn.' The IRA blamed lack of popular support for its failure. 'Foremost among the factors motivating this course of action has been the attitude of the general public whose minds have been deliberately distracted from the supreme issue facing the Irish people – the unity and freedom of Ireland.' The Campaign was a huge defeat for the IRA and one that left it virtually moribund. It would take a global wind of change to breathe fresh life into the organisation – one that would lead to a split in republicanism, the establishment of the Provisionals and the eventual creation of the East Tyrone Brigade.

Emily Beattie was not a global wind of change but the incident she was caught up in was another part of the seismic changes happening across so many societies at the time. Emily

Beattie was just a nineteen-year-old secretary working for a County Tyrone solicitor. Like many young people her age she was desperately keen to move out of mum and dad's and get her own place, but she couldn't afford to. The answer was social housing, and in June 1968 Ms Beattie was duly awarded No. 9 Kinnard Park – one of fourteen new pebble-dashed terrace houses in the sleepy east Tyrone village of Caledon. Her brother – a local policeman – was due to move in with her; they would share the rent and hopefully start thinking about moving up the property ladder. There wasn't nearly enough social housing to go round so the Beatties could count their lucky stars – except it wasn't luck. The Beattie siblings were Protestants, and Emily's boss was solicitor to the Unionist councillor who controlled housing allocations – all fourteen properties were assigned to Protestants. As Emily's name was being pencilled in for No. 9, there were in fact 269 other names on the Caledon housing list, mostly Catholic families who had waited in vain for years for a property to come vacant. With those same Catholic families forced to resort to squatting or endure terrible overcrowding, the Beattie case made headlines, especially when the local Nationalist MP, Austin Currie, occupied No. 9 Kinnard Park to highlight the discrimination in the system and bring it to the attention of the wider public. 'Housing was the key to the vote. The vote at local government elections was restricted to property owners and their spouses, or to tenants of local authority houses and their spouses ... the purpose ... was to ensure that Unionists had continued supremacy in the areas where they were, in fact, in the minority ... the allocation of a public authority house wasn't just the allocation of a house, it was the allocation of two votes.' Currie was right, whosoever controlled housing controlled the vote. More headlines were then garnered when the crusading MP was forcibly evicted by Ms Beattie's RUC-uniformed brother – all in front of the cameras of course.

The Cameron Commission – set up in 1969 by the Stormont government to investigate why the Troubles began – reported that the Caledon controversy not only played a part in reigniting the war but was symptomatic of a system with more than a whiff of the eighteenth-century parliamentary rotten boroughs about it.

The root of the problem lay in the 1922 Local Government Act which had been passed into law after partition with the clear purpose of gerrymandering electoral boundaries and disenfranchising poorer Catholics by insisting on property qualifications in local elections. The practical impact was to build in Unionist power. Londonderry was the most blatant example of the system, but east Tyrone wasn't much better. Dungannon, for example, had a slim nationalist electoral majority at the time but they only filled one-third of the twenty-one council seats. Elsewhere across Tyrone the situation was the same, and it hadn't changed much in almost half a century, but what had changed was the world outside Tyrone, indeed the world outside Northern Ireland altogether.

In the United States the ongoing Civil Rights campaign was combining with the anti-Vietnam War movement to give voice to a new generation desperate for a radical break from the past. It wasn't just in America either, in Paris students had rioted and almost toppled the government that same summer as across the West a public mood grew that the old order was done. However, in Northern Ireland the defining issue wasn't the colour of your skin or Vietnam, it was the church you prayed in.

A British Army officer who served there in the early days of the Troubles saw it for himself: 'I'd never come across religious discrimination before, but I could see that northern Catholics were discriminated against and treated badly. That clearly needed to change.' It wasn't just outsiders looking in that believed this to be true. A former RUC Special Branch officer said that 'something was wrong, and no matter what way you look at it the bulk of that something was a privileged old Unionist elite unwilling to share power and accommodate nationalists.' A sectarian divide, which had long ago ceased to hold any real power in England, was still a dominant fact of life in Northern Ireland. A future PIRA volunteer simply said, 'I wasn't political but I knew about discrimination and a feeling of being unwelcome in the society where I'd been born.'

Nevertheless, despite the justice of the cause, the clamour for change was profoundly unsettling for Northern Ireland's Protestant majority, and tensions soon snowballed into the violence of the Troubles. The main flash points were the big cities, with Derry engulfed in the Battle of the Bogside in August 1969, and successive sectarian riots disfiguring Belfast as families – the overwhelming majority being Catholics – were burnt out of their own homes. Angered by what they viewed as the existing leadership's abandonment of Catholics to the mercy of marauding Protestant mobs, several senior IRA figures – mostly veterans of the Border Campaign – split from the organisation in late 1969 and announced the establishment of a 'new' IRA – the Provisional IRA. From the start, the Provisionals were wholly committed to an armed struggle, launching dozens of attacks on what they termed 'the Crown forces'; the RUC, the British Army and – from 1970 – the Ulster Defence Regiment.

While gun battles and explosions echoed across the housing estates of Belfast and Derry, Tyrone was relatively calm. There was some unrest in Dungannon and Coalisland, but east Tyrone was a long way from the centre of the crisis, and, unlike in the cities, there were no packs of baying Protestant unionists burning out their Catholic nationalist neighbours, so while the Catholic Defender tradition was strong in the county, there wasn't the immediate threat to life and property that required an armed response. The former soldier and historian of the Troubles, Simon Taylor, said, 'None of the Provisionals' first leaders were Tyrone men, and Belfast was seen as a world away. Local people in Tyrone didn't want what was happening there to be replicated in their own towns and villages.' That view was reinforced when an IRA landmine intended for a British Army mobile patrol instead accidentally blew up five civilians on their way to service a BBC transmitter near Trillick in February 1971. As with Arthur Ovens's murder, local people were shocked and dismayed, and subsequent attempts by the Provisionals to gain a foothold in the county met with little success, as the former republican prisoner Tommy McKearney acknowledged: 'By mid-1971, while the Provisional IRA had established a basic skeleton organisation in the county, they were still a minority in comparison to the Official IRA.' As another republican explained, 'it was the Stickies [as the Provos nicknamed their former OIRA comrades] who were strong in Tyrone, not the Provisionals.'

A young British soldier who served in the county in those

early days remembered that 'there wasn't a big Provo threat then. Most of the locals were friendly and we only had about a couple of dozen suspects we'd been told to keep a look out for, and they were all pretty low-level.' Soldiers were even allowed to go drinking in the local pubs when off-duty, something that would be unheard of just a few short years later.

As for the regular British Army in general, its initial response was often *ad hoc*, as 'Davie' – not his real name – realised after volunteering as one of the Army's new Military Intelligence Officers (MIOs) for Northern Ireland: 'I sailed from Liverpool on a normal ferry, surrounded by squaddies in uniform while there was me in civvie clothes with my long hair and beard. When I arrived I went straight to the movement's boys – they were in a portacabin on the docks at the time – and asked where I was meant to go. They just looked at me all clueless. They'd never heard of me and had no idea what an MIO was or what we did. I ended up hitching a lift on an Army wagon down to Tyrone and having to sort it all out from there.'

'Davie' wasn't the only one who recognised the rudimentary nature of the Army operation at the time. In Dungannon a jock (as Scottish soldiers are unimaginatively known in the British Army) recalled how 'the grounds of Killymeal House [old farm on Castle Hill taken over as the Army's base in the town] were used for helicopter operations ... there were no markings, no watchtowers or fencing – it was literally just the garden, and Wessex helicopters used to fly in and out of there quite happily'. As for the local UDR contingent they used an old caravan parked up in the centre of town as their base, storing ten rifles and 200 rounds of ammunition in it while something longer term was looked for.

Then, on 9 August 1971 internment [imprisonment without trial] was declared by the Northern Ireland government, supported by London. That same day the Provisionals killed their first UDR soldier in Tyrone. Twenty-two-year-old Winston Donnell – one of four brothers all serving in the regiment – was shot dead at a Vehicle Check Point (VCP) in Clady near Strabane.

Strabane is in the far west of the county, on the border with Donegal, but east Tyrone wasn't spared for long. Just over a month later John Rudman became the first regular British Army soldier to be killed in Tyrone. A member of 2nd Battalion The Light Infantry, Rudman was one of three brothers in the regiment, and at the time was in the back of an Army truck on its way to Coalisland when an IRA gun team opened fire from the grounds of St Malachy Catholic Church in Edendork. Rudman was hit in the back of the head and died in hospital hours later. Tragically, Rudman's brother Thomas would also be killed by PIRA a year later in the Ardoyne in north Belfast. Simon Taylor believes that internment was the key to the uptick in violence in the county: 'Internment was a godsend for PIRA in Tyrone … people were aghast that the country of Magna Carta was locking up its own citizens without trial, and worse, internment blatantly targeted Catholics and not loyalists.' The lack of any Protestant suspects on the Army round-up lists – despite sectarian killings by the likes of the new incarnation of the loyalist UVF – was not only a travesty but a gift for militant republicans who knew that the finer points of Northern Ireland's devolved status meant nothing to the world's media. Westminster would carry the can for blatant discrimination, not Stormont.

The policy of internment would also drive two individuals into the ranks of the Provos who would become key figures in the future East Tyrone Brigade. One was seventeen-year-old Pádraig McKearney from the village of Moy on the banks of the River Blackwater that marks the Tyrone–Armagh boundary. His sister Margaret adored the tall, rangy teenager and described him in an interview years later with the BBC journalist Peter Taylor as 'my big brother. I was so small and he was nearly six foot ... I felt so terribly close to him.' Pádraig's elder brother Tommy was already a volunteer, and young Pádraig followed the same path, even though under PIRA's own rules he wasn't officially allowed on operations until he turned eighteen.

The second would-be volunteer was Kevin McKenna. Born on the family farm in the Brantry near Aughnacloy on the Tyrone–Monaghan border, he'd briefly been involved with the IRA in his youth before emigrating to Canada. Appalled by internment, he went home and re-joined the Provisionals. An IRA source told the journalist Ed Moloney: 'His [Kevin McKenna's] rise in the IRA was accounted for by the fact that back in those days there would have been three types of IRA men; the bulk were eighteen- to nineteen-year-olds, some in their fifties and sixties who were veterans of the '56–62 campaign, and a small number like Kevin, in their mid-twenties and the right age to take the lead. He'd come back from Canada with a bit of money, enough to buy a car. He was mobile, single, and willing to work, and away he went.' Along with his best friend, Daniel McAnallen, he formed an IRA unit in the Eglish–Aughnacloy area. Sean O'Callaghan would help train McKenna and his team on PIRA's homemade mortars, regarding him as someone who 'never had a lot to say but he instilled a quiet confidence. There was no doubt that he was very much the person in charge.'[12] He also impressed the Kerry man by being 'noticeably more concerned about security than anyone I had ever met'. The only drawback to that was that he was also 'very difficult … McKenna trusted no-one and would readily believe his own mother could be an informer.'

While internment was, without question, a significant factor in the evolution of what would become PIRA's East Tyrone Brigade, another was the emergence of a leader with the ability and drive to draw the local volunteers together, Kevin Mallon. Having been acquitted of Arty Ovens's murder, Mallon had later been re-arrested and convicted on explosives charges and spent most of his twenties in prison. Now in his mid-thirties and a free man once more, he began to impose himself on the burgeoning Provisional set-up in the east of the county. The Dublin volunteer, Kieran Conway, met him for the first time during that period. 'Mallon was a hard-drinking, hard-talking, seriously hard man with buckets of charisma and an unrivalled capacity to motivate people … [he was] always armed … those who worked for him adored him.' However, Conway was perceptive enough to also see Mallon's faults as a leader: 'while he could control his people, the special forces feel he fed into them – the virtual contempt for the rest of the Army [PIRA itself] – meant that discipline fell away once he was arrested and his men pretty much did as they pleased'. Having said that, Conway felt that in Mallon, Tyrone PIRA had a leader like few others in the movement: 'he was the closest thing the modern IRA had to a Michael Collins' – within republicanism that was high praise indeed.

Nineteen-seventy-two – the year after the introduction of internment – was a watershed in the war. Violence across Northern Ireland reached a crescendo, and the death toll rocketed. In Tyrone, PIRA finally began to make its mark. That March it killed its first RUC officer: William Logan, a twenty-three-year-old from Derry, shot dead in a gun attack on the Land Rover he was driving in on the Brackaville Rd near Coalisland – Kevin Mallon's stomping ground. Then, in September, it detonated a landmine under a British Army Saracen – an 11-tonne 6-wheeled armoured personnel carrier. The bomb was the largest used by the IRA to date in what was a devastating attack. In the words of one interviewee, 'I was in Dungannon with "A" Company, 1st Battalion The Argyll and Sutherland Highlanders. My section … were due to go out in a Saracen, but it was blown up by an IRA landmine on 10 September while carrying another patrol between Dungannon and Benburb. Three other members of "A" Company were killed. I guess we had a lucky escape.'

Then, in what became a turning point for the Provisionals in the county, the Official IRA gave them a helping hand, as one senior PIRA activist remembered: 'The head of the Tyrone Officials at the time was Paddy Mullan, a very intelligent man who'd decided to split his weapons in two; half the Officials would keep and half would go to the Provisionals.' Mullan's decision was a big deal, as the UDR soldier George Boyd only too readily realised: '[before that] PIRA's entire arsenal in County Tyrone … consisted of a few old rifles and handguns stored after the Border Campaign.' Now, Tyrone's Provisionals could escalate their campaign. However, Mullan didn't live long enough to see the results of his largesse. On 16 October he and another senior Official, Hugh Herron, were shot dead by the Army while in their car at a VCP in the village of Coagh.

With Mullan gone and the Provisionals in possession of half the Officials' arsenal, it was the Provos who were in the driving seat in Tyrone as another volunteer recalled: 'roughly speaking the Officials were men of words, the Provisionals were men of action'. That 'action' was increasingly led by Kevin Mallon as one local UDR soldier remembered: 'Tommy Hamill was the big man in Dungannon PIRA, he lived on the Lisnahull estate and was thick as thieves with the likes of Brendan Hughes and Whitey Quinn. All hard, vicious men, but it was Mallon that was making the running.'

However, it was still a very different war from what it would become in the years to follow as Jay Nethercott, a young UDR soldier at the time, recalled: 'There was still some decency in the early days. A hit was due to go in against one of ours, but as they [the Provos] recce'd the house they saw lots of terry nappies hanging on the line – this was before disposables so you had to wash them – as the family had just had a wee baby, so the leader said let's leave it a wee while.' George Boyd was of the same opinion: 'east Tyrone hadn't the hardliners at that stage and they hadn't started the whole genocide thing'.[13]

As for the rest of the burgeoning security force response across Tyrone, 'Davie' was incredibly frustrated by the lack of cooperation between the RUC and the Army. 'As soon as I arrived I was told my main job was to try and get the RUC to talk to us, but when I went to their offices they pointed to a chair in the corridor and said, "That's ya chair, don't come into the office. When we've got something for ya we'll give it ya."' It was an attitude that would bedevil the security forces for years.

However, there was still no East Tyrone Brigade, but the pressure of war was bringing change – and fast. Firstly, PIRA's overall leadership was changing. While the war was mainly being fought by northerners, most of the movement's senior men were southerners, many of them a good deal older than the volunteers they were directing. Mid-Ulster Command was a case in point. Most of its rank and file were from Fermanagh and Tyrone, but it was headed up by a County Cork man, Eddie Collins. Secondly, there was a realisation at the very top of the IRA – in its seven-man Army Council – that something had to give in Tyrone. In the chaos of what was still a very new war, PIRA's organisation outside Belfast and Derry was more than a little fluid, and Tyrone had initially been part of its 'North–West Command' before its replacement with Mid-Ulster Command, both of which were far too large to be truly effective.

What was needed to make change inevitable was a catalyst, and as so often in conflict, that catalyst was money. Wars are ruinously expensive, and by 1973 the Provisionals were feeling the pinch as a prominent republican confessed: 'The IRA was almost broke and the Army Council needed money.' So desperate was the need for cash – particularly to fund the purchase of guns from the United States – that the Provisional leadership decided to break one of its golden rules. In May 1973, in direct contravention of General Army Order No. 8 which forbids armed IRA action in the Republic, the Army Council authorised the creation of a team that would use IRA weapons and logistics to carry out armed robberies of banks and post offices in the south, with all stolen monies then sent north. The volunteer chosen to head up this new team was Brendan Hughes, not Brendan 'Darkie' Hughes from Belfast, but his namesake from east Tyrone. In his own words, 'I was born in Drummurrer near Coalisland … but I always considered myself an Ardboe man.' Having left school aged fifteen, 'I literally jumped the school fence to begin working', it wasn't long before Hughes swapped his life as a husband, father and plasterer for that of a full-time Provisional volunteer, forming a strong bond with Kevin Mallon and another volunteer, Seamus 'Sig' Dillon – Brackaville-born like Mallon.

The trio had quickly become the cutting edge of Provisional activity in the east of the county, occasionally fighting running gun battles with the security forces amongst Tyrone's hedgerows and sunken lanes, and all three were high up on the security forces' wanted list. Now the order came down to Hughes from 'the Army Council to base myself in the south and raise as much money as possible'. For at least the next decade Tyrone PIRA would play a major role in funding the IRA's war.

The first target selected was a Post Office van in County Kerry used to collect cash from the surrounding sub-post offices, but when the local IRA defied the Army Council and threw Hughes and his men out of town on their arrival the scene was set for a showdown. A four-man delegation went to Kerry to clear the situation up. It was led by none other than the IRA's military supremo – its Chief of Staff, Séamus Twomey. Twomey, a former bookie's runner from Belfast known as 'Thumper' on account of his habit of banging the table during meetings to make his point, was famously short-tempered and in no mood to have his orders ignored by the old guard in Kerry. Twomey took with him his Adjutant – the veteran IRA man J.B. O'Hagan – and the highly regarded Brian Keenan from Derry. The fourth member of the delegation was Kevin Mallon, PIRA's 'Director of Operations' and 'perhaps the most important IRA figure then not in prison' according to Kieran Conway. The heavyweight foursome brooked no opposition, and on arrival sacked the existing leadership, replacing it with younger men who would do as they were told. Within days Hughes and his team robbed the van and PIRA was several thousand pounds richer.

Clearly Mallon's star was rising in PIRA, but his ascendancy – and the East Tyrone Brigade's gestation – was abruptly derailed when a few months later he was arrested in the south and convicted of IRA membership. Sent to Dublin's Mountjoy Prison – 'the Joy' as republicans nicknamed it – he was joined in the cells by both Twomey and O'Hagan, until just twenty-eight days later on Wednesday, 31 October, when, in one of the most daring PIRA operations of the war, all three jumped on board a hijacked Alouette II helicopter that had landed in the prison's exercise yard. It was Mallon's plan but Brendan Hughes's operation: '[it] was an east Tyrone job'. Flown to a disused racecourse, a gruff Mallon turned to Hughes, 'Well done, as usual ... but you were f**king late!'[14] Now officially On-The-Run (OTR), Mallon would only stay free until 10 December when he 'was recaptured [by the Gardaí] in a dance hall. He had been free for all of six weeks'.

Mallon was soon followed to prison by both Hughes and Dillon. The former had been OTR when he was 'offered just £300 [by PIRA to relocate to the USA with his family] ... I went

berserk ... I decided I would bankroll myself ... I would rob
for myself.' Caught and convicted, Hughes would serve sixteen
years, and within the Provisionals he was ghosted. The IRA's
Chief of Staff at the time 'issued a Standing Order banning
anyone from speaking to me'. The two men knew each other
well and were never friends: 'we never did get along. You could
say there was mutual disrespect.' Even Kevin Mallon 'who was
very much his own man and could have ignored the *diktat*,
made sure nobody even passed on the local Tyrone newspaper
for me to read'. Hughes was baffled by his former comrade's
behaviour: 'I don't know to this day why he took such a set
against me.' Kieran Conway may not have been as surprised
as his erstwhile comrade, describing Mallon as 'a tough and
occasionally ruthless user of people'.

As for Dillon, he was charged in the north with
involvement in the killing of John Rudman, the Light Infantry
soldier shot in Edendork. Acquitted in that case, he was finally
convicted and sentenced to life for two other murders and
two attempted murders. After being released in 1994, Dillon
severed all paramilitary ties and was working as a bouncer
at the Glengannon Hotel in Dungannon on the night of 27
December 1997 when gunmen from the Loyalist Volunteer
Force (LVF) targeted the Catholic youth disco taking place
there that night. He was shot dead confronting the attackers.

With the triumvirate of Mallon, Hughes and Dillon out of
the picture, the IRA in Tyrone increasingly followed the lead
given by Kevin McKenna and his Eglish–Aughnacloy unit – a
unit that was perfecting its use of the landmine, killing three
British Army soldiers and an RUC officer in separate attacks.
A young lance-corporal in the Royal Anglian Regiment was on

his first tour at the time: 'the main threat was from landmines and culvert bombs and we spent most of our time searching for them'. Those efforts were not a success as Jay Nethercott admitted. 'McKenna and his boys basically blew us off the roads, landmine after landmine.' As a senior Tyrone republican proudly boasted, 'Those boys were active as f**k, operation after operation. The Brits were in real trouble.'

Those landmines were made of homemade explosive – Anfo Annie as it was called. Sean O'Callaghan explained its manufacture: 'This involved first placing four bags of Net nitrate fertiliser in a 40-gallon barrel raised off the floor on concrete blocks, combining it with several gallons of water and heating it ... our aim was to produce ammonium nitrate, which, when mixed with diesel oil, was the primary ingredient of IRA bombs.'

Landmines weren't the Tyrone IRA's only method of attack. At 9 am on 10 May 1973 an Aughnacloy farmer and married father of one, Franklin Caddoo, was leaving four milk churns for collection by the creamery lorry at the lane side on his farm when he was set upon by a PIRA gun team. Pulling him out of the cab of his tractor the gunmen shot him twice at point blank range; once in the neck and once in the head. Alerted by the shooting, his father went to see what had happened and found his son dead. Caddoo was a part-time member of the UDR and was off duty at the time. McKenna was the chief suspect in the killing, but he swiftly fled south of the border to a new address in County Monaghan where he was out of reach of the British authorities. Another suspect, twenty-six-year-old Patrick Carty from Dungannon, was blown up six weeks later, along with two other volunteers – Sean Loughran also from Dungannon, and eighteen-year-old Dermot Crowley from County Cork – when the bomb they were transporting went off prematurely. Accidents like this – 'own goals' as British soldiers termed them – were all too common given the homemade nature of IRA bombs and the lack of training among many volunteers.

Three months later McKenna and his men launched an altogether more ambitious attack on the joint Army/RUC station in Pomeroy in the middle of the night. Norman Irwin was the UDR guard commander at the time: 'I was in the top sangar [small, sandbagged structure] when the first RPG-7 [Soviet-manufactured Rocket Propelled Grenade] was fired … I heard the "whuss" as it went over the top.' Irwin was clear this was a major attack. 'They were firing off a lorry and … they were firing down the town – two different angles.' He then saw a third firing point: 'They were also out at Donnelly's. There was an old shed there they were shooting from.'[15]

After about twenty minutes red flares shot up into the sky and the PIRA team abruptly stopped firing and disappeared. Norman Irwin checked his men and was relieved to find there were no casualties inside the base – outside it was a different matter. A hasty follow-up operation at first found nothing in the darkness, but a further search in the morning revealed 'two bodies lying at the side of the road. At 0625hrs the report was confirmed … they'd died as the result of an explosion.' Disaster had struck McKenna's men: 'Twenty-seven-year-old Daniel McAnallen and eighteen-year-old Patsy Quinn had been killed when the mortar bomb they were firing exploded prematurely … McKenna … had looked on helplessly as Quinn and McAnallen – who was his best friend – died.' Patsy

Quinn's younger brother, Frankie, remembered the local priest arriving at the door to give his mother the news: 'It was the squeal [his mother's screams] that people describe that comes from the pit of the stomach, that you'll never hear again and you'll never forget.'[16]

The use of mortars – albeit homemade – in the Pomeroy attack was a shock for the security forces in Tyrone. The UDR's George Boyd remembered the new weapon: 'They were all steel piping. They were well made – factory manufacturing – and then explosives were put inside the copper nose. They were drilled in the bottom and there was a .22 cartridge that went down onto a firing point that detonated the mortar. They'd have a range of about three hundred metres.'

Relatively well-made the mortars may have been, but they clearly weren't fool-proof, and Pomeroy showed PIRA were still learning. The point was painfully rammed home in December with another 'own goal'. James Lynagh – a young volunteer from Monaghan in the Republic – was badly injured near the McKearney's home in Moy when the detonator of the bomb he was holding on his lap exploded. Luckily for him it didn't ignite the main 5lb charge. In a bizarre turn of events his life was saved by a passing UDR patrol who administered first aid, something at least one of them later regretted: 'If I'd known what a b****d he'd turn out to be I'd have let him f**kin' die.' As it was, Lynagh survived and would spend the next five years in Long Kesh prison.

Kevin McKenna and his border team led the attack on Pomeroy, but credit for PIRA's new homemade mortars was attributed to somewhere altogether different – a tiny village in the east Tyrone uplands called Cappagh.

With a name meaning 'land of the tree stumps', Cappagh was – and still is – a place apart. Perched below the mountain from which it takes its name, many of its houses and farms have been home to the same families for generations. At one time on the main provincial north–south stagecoach route, it is now far off the beaten track. Its people are wary of outsiders – some might say suspicious – and have long had an arms-length relationship with any form of authority. A small place by any measure, at one end of the high street sits Boyles Bar. Often the centre of village social life it is not the loveliest of buildings, but its prominence as the locals' watering hole has seen it become the backdrop to some of east Tyrone's horror. The first chapter of that horror was enacted at around half past seven on a cold mid-January night in 1974 when two gunmen walked into Boyles and opened fire indiscriminately on the terrified occupants. As glasses shattered and tables went flying, seventy-three-year-old Daniel Hughes, a retired farmer, was hit eleven times and died on the floor; three others were injured. The attack was claimed by the 'Donaghmore–Pomeroy Battalion of the UVF' in retaliation for the murder by the IRA earlier that same day near Trillick of an off-duty UDR solider, Robert Jameson.

PIRA's targeting of members of the locally raised UDR and RUC was a result of the UK government's decision to 'Ulsterise' the conflict by forming the UDR in 1970 and giving the RUC primacy over the Army in defeating the Provisionals. In many ways this put the majority of the British Army – the stated main enemy of the Provos – into a supporting role and put local Ulstermen and women on the frontline. The unique nature of the UDR with its significant part-time element, also meant that large numbers of its members held down civilian jobs in their communities as well as donning a uniform for their hours of service. Originally, all of Tyrone was covered by the UDR's 6th Battalion, but this changed in 1971 with a new battalion: the 8th (County Tyrone) Battalion or more simply 8 UDR, raised to cover the east of the county. Recruitment into 8 UDR was brisk, with almost half its ranks filled with ex-B Specials [a controversial former auxiliary police force] – something that provided security continuity but was anathema to many members of the nationalist community who viewed the B Specials as nothing more than Protestant bully boys and bigots. One former East Tyrone volunteer described how he viewed the local units ranged against him: 'The Prods [Protestants] used to keep us down with border reivers and they're still around, in Caledon, in Coagh, villages like that. The poorer Prods would join the UDR – some of them could barely read and write – while the more middle-class ones joined the RUC Reserve [part-time members of the RUC], cleaner there you see, you wouldn't get your hands dirty.'

At first, Catholics also joined the UDR, but their numbers fell rapidly, with some becoming disillusioned by the bigotry they were sometimes subjected to, and others intimidated into leaving. One recruit – a family man – from the overwhelmingly Catholic village of Clady near Strabane woke up one morning to find his front door daubed with the words: 'Get out of the UDR or be shot – IRA.' Refusing to be intimidated he ignored the warning. A fortnight later a shotgun blast in the middle of the night blew out some of his windows. He left the regiment the next day.

Those that stayed – Protestant and Catholic – were potentially extremely dangerous for the Provisionals. Locally born and raised they knew their communities inside out; who was who, what they did, what looked out of place and what didn't. Simply put they were a unique threat to the IRA, and it was no surprise that they were targeted from the start. Tommy McKearney was clear as to the Provos reasoning: 'a county Derry accent would go unnoticed … if questioned in south Tyrone by Londoners, but would immediately draw the suspicion of a Dungannon UDR patrol … A dustman may appear to be a harmless worker until he sifts through the bin for information … Whether on or off-duty, these men acted not only as the eyes and ears of the regular Army but actively supported it logistically and militarily. That they had dual military and civilian roles added to the danger they posed to the IRA.'[17] In an interview with the journalist Peter Taylor conducted in the late 1980s, McKearney's mother Maura echoed her son's argument in far simpler terms: 'Is a UDR man … ever off duty?'

This was the crux as far as PIRA was concerned; off-duty or not, if you were a member of the Crown forces you were a legitimate target, and it was usually easier to kill you when you weren't in uniform. PIRA's logic was unanswerable, but with the vast majority of 8 UDR and the local RUC being Protestants, the campaign against them was always going to be seen as sectarian, or worse, as the prominent Belfast loyalist Clifford Peeples made clear: 'the IRA campaign in Tyrone and Fermanagh wasn't just sectarian, it was ethnic cleansing, no doubt about it'.

That accusation of ethnic cleansing was – and still is – vehemently denied by the Provisionals but it echoed all the way back to partition. In 1921 William E. Wylie, a Dublin-born jurist and Law Advisor to the Irish Government, predicted that the new border would mean 'in Tyrone there would be an unceasing and unending civil war'. Wylie's apocalyptic forecast may have been somewhat overblown, but a spate of sectarian attacks along the border between 1921 and 1923 boded ill for the future in a land where the two communities lived cheek by jowl. The prominent Tyrone Unionist and Somme veteran, Ambrose Ricardo, remarked with terrible foresight that those same killings had created 'a group of personal blood feuds which will last for generations to come'. Among a population numbering just 60,000 – roughly half Catholic, half Protestant – a war that so powerfully identified the two traditions with opposing sides had an inexorable logic of atrocity. This would be east Tyrone's real tragedy – the barbarity of sectarianism.

Typical of the type of attack Peeples and his fellow loyalists viewed as ethnic cleansing was the murder of postman Stanley Adams on 28 October 1976. Adams, a twenty-nine-year-old off-duty UDR lance-corporal, was shot dead at a remote farmhouse two miles south of Pomeroy, delivering a letter the IRA had purposefully sent to lure him there. Tommy McKearney was charged with the killing, convicted, and sentenced to life, although he denied any involvement, as did his mother: 'He wasn't there, although I'm not saying he wasn't at other things. Two thousand people didn't die in Northern Ireland without someone pulling the trigger.' Two years earlier, Tommy's youngest brother – nineteen-year-old Séan – had been killed in an own goal as he and best friend Eugene Martin attempted to plant a bomb at the Donnydeade petrol station near Dungannon. The two teenagers had driven the 20lb bomb onto the forecourt in the Martin family's Austin Maxi just before midnight on 13 May. A UDR solider who attended the scene is still haunted by it. 'We had to recover the bodies, well, what was left of them – it was awful – even now I don't want to talk about it, an explosion makes an absolute mess of a human body, it really does.' As was standard practice, two RUC officers went to deliver the terrible news to the family. 'The father [Paddy] asked the policemen in, gave them a drink and thanked them for coming in person, but from the mother there was just venom … that happened a lot, from the fathers there was some understanding – I wouldn't say they were reasonable people mind – but from a lot of the mothers there was just hatred, hatred of everything Brit.' Maura McKearney later talked to the journalist Peter Taylor about that night. 'He [Séan] joined at Easter and was killed in May. It was possibly the first thing they sent him out to do. It's hard to explain the shock. You don't expect your son to die; you expect him to live on when you're gone.'

The war would end up ravaging the McKearneys. As early as 1972 the family had become a target, with the UVF sending them a typed warning note: 'You have two sons associated with the IRA. This Command has decided that if there are any more explosions in the area or shootings at the security forces, you and your family have to get out within two days. This is final.' Those 'two sons' were now gone; Tommy was serving life and Séan was dead. Tragically, they wouldn't be the last members of the family to suffer in the war. Their two remaining brothers would both be killed, with the youngest, Kevin, murdered in 1992 by the UVF while working in the family butcher's shop. Of their two sisters, one, Margaret, would end up wanted by the British police for involvement in one of the IRA's bombing campaigns in England during the 1970s, although she has always denied membership of the Provisionals. Over a period of twenty years, only one of the six McKearney children escaped death, imprisonment or the police.

With the Troubles reigniting sectarian strife along the border, a vicious pattern of tit-for-tat killings soon became embedded in Tyrone, and at its heart would be an escalating battle between the Provisionals and the loyalist UVF.

Resurrected by the fear of an IRA resurgence, the new incarnation of the UVF in Tyrone was not the grass-roots movement of its early twentieth-century namesake, and initially it struggled to get organised. As Clifford Peeples explained, 'loyalists struggled with money – all paramilitary organisations do – so the UVF had to use the same sources of cash as the Provos; bank robberies, protection money, taxis, illegal drinking dens. But money was always tight, I knew of one volunteer who had to borrow money to put petrol in a car they'd hijacked for a job.' This lack of cash had a direct impact on the organisation's ability to wage war as the former UVF commander Billy Hutchinson acknowledged: 'the issue wasn't so much lack of people as lack of money, no doubt about it. We needed guns, and if you found someone who'd supply guns, they'd sell them to you as long as they were paid. Money was a bigger problem than guns.' However, Peeples is clear that lack of funds wasn't necessarily critical. 'The UVF at that time had some Sten guns [Second World War submachine guns], a few pistols and stuff like that, even a few homemade guns. But loyalists didn't need vast arsenals, and they always had enough guns to kill.'

Like its PIRA counterpart at the time, the newly established UVF unit covering east Tyrone was christened the 'Mid-Ulster Brigade'. Centred in Portadown in neighbouring Armagh, the Mid-Ulster UVF was initially led by Billy Hanna, a former soldier in the Royal Ulster Rifles decorated for bravery in the Korean War. However, in 1975, Hanna – suspected of being a security forces agent – was brutally murdered by his own men. He was succeeded by the main suspect in his own shooting, Robin Jackson.

Jackson worked in the Banbridge shoe factory, Down Shoes Ltd, and lived in the small village of Donaghcloney in County Down. He'd volunteered for the UDR in 1972 before being unceremoniously thrown out two years later for his paramilitary links. 'Davie' – the local MIO – met him on several occasions. 'I didn't know him well but I saw him around. He seemed a pretty personable, softly-spoken character.' In contrast to 'Davie's view, many others familiar with Jackson described him as a violent and quarrelsome man, under whose leadership Mid-Ulster UVF would commit dozens of sectarian killings, with Jackson himself becoming allegedly the most prolific murderer of the entire war.

Nicknamed The Jackal by the *Sunday World* newspaper's Northern Editor Jim Campbell – who investigated and exposed his alleged paramilitary activities and would subsequently survive an assassination attempt for his trouble – Jackson would often choose Saturday nights as his favourite time to head out and kill. Targets were often picked at random with many slaughtered on their own doorsteps or on their way home from a night out. A particularly horrific tactic Jackson employed on more than one occasion was to target a Catholic family at home, burst in during the night, and kill every adult male family member present. His preferred hunting ground – gruesomely called 'The Triangle of Death' by the two Catholic priests Raymond Murray and Denis Faul in their 1975 pamphlet of the same name – stretched from Banbridge, across Armagh to Aughnacloy on the border and back up to Pomeroy. The carnage he and his like-minded team of brutal killers inflicted was truly vile, and east Tyrone bore the brunt of it.

Unsurprisingly, the Provisionals hated Jackson and his team with a rare venom as a senior Tyrone republican source made clear: 'In the '70s the UVF in mid-Ulster was based in two places: James Mitchell's Glenanne farm near Markethill in Armagh and Ted Sinclair's farm near Moy. That b*****d Sinclair was involved in the O'Dowd atrocity [three members of the same family murdered on the night of 4 January 1976]. They were just killing Catholics for being Catholics.' Such attacks made the local Provisionals determined to hit back. 'We tried to take them out loads of times. We knew they used a work van from a construction company to meet up most Saturdays, so we were going to hit the van, but a few days before the job went down the van was sold.'

Clifford Peeples sought to explain why Mid-Ulster UVF spent the '70s simply terrorising Catholic civilians: 'When the war started the two communities didn't know each other, we didn't know who the republicans were, it was only later after the supergrass trials at the beginning of the 1980s that we began to see who was who ... so at first the loyalist campaign was brutally sectarian, people were being murdered just for walking on the wrong side of the street.'

In 1974 – a blood year in Tyrone – that meant the UDR's Robert Jameson and Boyles Bar drinker Daniel Hughes were just a foretaste of what was to come. Local people, Protestants and Catholics both, would be subjected to slaughter. In the midst of loyalist killings like those perpetrated by Jackson, the Provisionals for their part would accidentally shoot dead Mary Bingham – an innocent Protestant with no paramilitary links – in September in Dungannon after losing another two volunteers in an own goal (to make four that year in Tyrone in total), while also killing five more serving or former UDR members, including their first female victim, Eva Martin. A Greenfinch, as female UDR soldiers were known, Martin was killed on 3 May in an attack on the UDR base at the Deanery in Clogher. Sean O'Callaghan would later serve prison time for Martin's murder and recalled joining up with the attack team: 'In the house was a group of heavily armed men that included the entire east Tyrone contingent that had trained in Kerry, except Kevin McKenna.' One of the volunteers was 'Henry Louis McNally from Dungannon … a quiet, introspective and highly dangerous killer.'

McNally was suspected of being involved in a host of attacks already, including the murder of Denis Wilson on 7 December 1971. Wilson, an off-duty UDR lance-corporal from Curlagh near Caledon, had taken himself to bed with a bad cold when three gunmen knocked on his front door. When his wife opened it, one of the gunmen told her to keep quiet while his comrades ran up the stairs and shot her husband dead as he lay sleeping. Wilson was the first member of 8 UDR to be killed by the Provisionals. O'Callaghan himself described one especially callous operation McNally was in on some five weeks prior to Clogher: '... near a village called Mountfield, close to Omagh, McNally and another IRA man murdered a retired naval recruitment officer while he was walking his dog along a country road. As McNally's companion ran back to the waiting getaway car he realised McNally wasn't with him. As he turned to see what was happening another shot rang out. McNally had walked back and shot the dog. When he got back to the car his accomplice said, "What the f**k are you playing at?" and McNally calmly replied "Dead dogs tell no tales."'[18] The human victim was fifty-six-year-old Donald Farrell.

The Clogher attack itself was a major step up for Tyrone PIRA: 'Up to forty IRA men were involved ... the biggest set piece IRA operation to take place up to that time ... All roads in the area had been blocked by vehicles hijacked by local volunteers.' O'Callaghan himself would fire a homemade mortar assisted by what a regular army would term a fire controller who would 'see the shells [technically "bombs"] exploding and would then instruct me as to what adjustments needed to be made'. As well as an RPG-7 and a heavy machine gun, the rest of the team were armed with 'a selection of small arms, mainly of American origin: Armalites, Garands, M1 carbines ... The attack was to begin with the firing of an RPG-7 ... we waited expectantly but nervously for the signal.' At just after eleven that night the attack began; 'there was the sharp crackle of rifle fire and the heavier sound of the machine gun'. To his despair, O'Callaghan's wingman ran off as soon as the shooting started, but he kept on firing anyway; 'F**k it ...

some shells were exploding in the high trees surrounding the base … some detonated in the grounds, several of them failed to explode.' The UDR fought back and after about twenty-five minutes the PIRA team withdrew in the same lorry they'd arrived in. Abandoning the vehicle near the border they walked to safety and were then 'driven to an unoccupied newly built house in County Monaghan'. The atmosphere was jubilant. 'Everybody was on a high.' On hearing on the radio of Eva Martin's death, there were 'cheers and hand clapping. "Got one stiff anyway," someone said.' O'Callaghan analysed his own feelings about the Fivemiletown teacher's killing: 'I felt no remorse, but neither did I glory in Eva Martin's death … at the time I was highly motivated, I believed I was a soldier in an army fighting in a just cause.' Eva Martin's husband Richard – a full-time clerk in the UDR – was in the Deanery that same night and as he stumbled in the dark down the stairs from the mess he came across a body. 'I knew it was my wife Eva. I picked up her head and shoulders in my arms and felt her blood on my hands. I felt her pulse, and I think it stopped while I was feeling it.'

Five days after Clogher, Gertrude Devlin picked up her husband Jim, as usual, after he'd finished locking up the pub he ran in Coalisland – Jim didn't have a driving licence. They bought fish and chips and headed back to Donaghmore near Dungannon. Turning into the lane to their home, Gertrude braked as a man wearing uniform stepped into the road and waved at them to stop. The car was then sprayed with bullets. Both husband and wife were killed. Their seventeen-year-old daughter Patricia – with them in the car – miraculously survived, despite being hit five times in the arms and legs. The

Devlin family had no paramilitary links and were innocent Catholic civilians. The UVF had taken revenge for Eva Martin's death. A part-time UDR soldier and member of the notorious Glenanne gang, William Thomas Leonard would be convicted of involvement in the Devlins' murder, but not before fellow gang members blew up a car bomb in the centre of Monaghan town a fortnight after the Deanery attack, killing seven people and injuring dozens more. At Leonard's trial his defending lawyer told the judge that since the Devlins' killing his client had found God and become a committed Christian. In reply Mr Justice Kelly said, 'It is a pity he did not become a Christian before 7 May 1974 [the night of the murders].'

As it was, none of the PIRA volunteers involved in Clogher realised then that it would be eleven years before the Provisionals would launch another operation of that size and sophistication, and when it did, volunteers from Tyrone would once again be at its heart.

The IRA that would carry out that subsequent attack would be a very different organisation from the one that attacked The Deanery, and that sea change would begin three short months after Clogher when the Army Council formally established the East Tyrone Brigade as an entity in its own right, the final push in its creation coming from none other than Kevin Mallon. Languishing in Portlaoise jail after his recapture in the dance hall, he and eighteen other republican prisoners used explosives to blow their way out on 18 August and then made good their escape, despite a massive manhunt. One of the escapees – a volunteer from South Armagh – explained how a bomb blew a hole in an inner courtyard wall: 'That took us into the small courtyard where the Governor's residence was and we'd blown all the glass out of the windows. This was just before midday on a Sunday and I can remember him standing, looking out, completely mesmerised, wearing a pair of pyjamas and a jacket.'

Free once more, Mallon went straight back to the war and his new post as Officer Commanding (OC) East Tyrone. His appointment, and the creation of the Brigade itself, was part and parcel of the takeover of the Provisionals by a new generation of hard-nosed northerners – the so-called 69-ers. Having proven himself at Clogher and in subsequent operations, O'Callaghan was the only southerner given a senior role in the new Brigade: 'I was now directly in control of eight IRA units, each of which consisted of between four and eight people depending on local circumstances, and I had a hard core of four other full-time volunteers in the area. Like me, the four full-timers were all on the run.' Internally, O'Callaghan's command was titled the Brigade's 2nd Battalion, although as he himself admitted it was 'a rather grandiose title bearing little relationship to what is understood as a battalion in a regular army'. The former British Army officer Richard Kemp, who would serve a total of seven tours in Northern Ireland, was a little more forthright: 'PIRA was basically a civilian terrorist organisation and I for one resented them using military terminolgy like battalions, brigades, quartermasters etc, as it didn't reflect reality and it gave them a level of dignity and respectability they didn't deserve.'

This issue of titles, ranks and so on has raged since the IRA's creation, and is not unique to it either; the loyalists were much the same, as Billy Hutchinson described. 'Gusty Spence [a key driver behind the new UVF] had been in the

Ulster Rifles so he organised the UVF like the Army, into its sort of shadow, so it had battalions and companies; "A" Company, "B" Company and so on, and members held ranks down to Sergeant.' Call paramilitary organisations what you will – terrorists, freedom fighters, whatever – all tend to define themselves along orthodox military lines and use the nomenclature of their erstwhile foes, while in no way matching their opponents in terms of numbers or formal structure. In strict military parlance the number of men O'Callaghan led constituted a platoon, of which there are usually around fifteen in a regular British Army battalion, but that is beside the point. As the soldier turned academic Dr Dennis Vincent said of PIRA, 'Their structure was flexible and they used the names they felt comfortable with. In propaganda terms it also worked, the East Tyrone Brigade sounds a lot bigger and better than the East Tyrone platoon.' The same issue related to the use of East Tyrone as the description for the unit, as members of the Brigade sometimes operated across all Tyrone, into north Armagh and occasionally south Londonderry, with the volunteers themselves including men from both Armagh and Tyrone as well as from Monaghan across the border in the Republic. Indeed so strong was the influence of the latter in particular that the Brigade was sometimes also called the Tyrone/Monaghan Brigade. The ex-Special Branch officer John Shackles was clear, 'It's us [the security forces] that got all uppity about where they operated, where they were from and all that, not the republicans themselves. Yes, there's always been a kind of split between east and west Tyrone, with east Tyrone looking to Monaghan, whereas in the west it was Letterkenny, but it wasn't such a big deal.' Tellingly, the republican newspaper *An*

Phoblacht's (The Republic) roll of honour for PIRA brigades and their dead, lists Tyrone as a single entity.

One source who was very close to it all summed up the situation quite succinctly: 'It didn't really matter what they called themselves or where they operated; they were there, they had guns, and they used them.'

3

THE MALLON AND McKENNA YEARS

Both traditions in Northern Ireland have a soft spot for commemorations. Hardly a week in the calendar goes by that isn't marked by the remembrance of some event or other, all important to those taking part, and most springing from the island's troubled history. Republicans are wedded to them, and use them astutely both to keep the struggle alive in people's minds as well as placing their own actions in a historical context stretching back centuries. Given the 1916 Rising, Easter, naturally, is the high point for republicans, and the annual commemoration at Carrickmore in mid-Tyrone is the centre of it all. There, in the garden of remembrance on the edge of the village, republicans gather on Easter Sunday to remember their dead and hear speeches from their leaders. In 1975, when the Provisionals were engaged in a ceasefire for political talks with the British government, Sean O'Callaghan was in the crowd. He recalled, 'Kevin McKenna, recently released from jail in the Irish Republic, was in the area recuperating after a long hunger strike [McKenna would speak at the commemoration] … As the republican ceremony was taking place an IRA man approached me, pointed to someone in the crowd and said, "He's a Prod from the Bush" – a small Protestant enclave a couple of miles from Carrickmore. I approached the man but it quickly became clear that he was harmless and had the mentality of a child. I told the local IRA man to let him be.'

What happened next is disputed. O'Callaghan maintained that a few hours later he heard that 'Brendan Hughes had taken the man into a field and was beating him.' Angry, the Kerry man confronted Hughes and his compatriot. 'I told them to leave him alone. "F**k off" said Hughes's friend. I fired one shot over their heads [with a Browning pistol] and they stepped back, shocked. I walked nearer and fired again. They began to back off quickly.' A few months earlier, O'Callaghan had shot dead RUC Special Branch Detective Inspector Peter Flanagan in an Omagh pub and was clearly not a man to cross. Hughes and co. made themselves scarce. But that is not how Brendan Hughes remembers it. 'Someone told me that this young fella was being held by two volunteers who were awaiting an order to execute him. I went there and immediately realised he was being held in the wrong and ordered his release.' Hughes was so incensed by O'Callaghan's version of events that he claims it was the spur for writing his memoirs: 'O'Callaghan's twisted fiction was a pack of lies, but it prompted me to set the record straight.'[19]

Meanwhile, both men's boss – Kevin Mallon – had once again been arrested in the Republic, this time in possession of a weapon. That, and charges relating to the Mountjoy helicopter escape and the Portlaoise breakout, saw him sentenced to ten years. His imprisonment left a gap at the top of the new East Tyrone Brigade that was filled by the bulky form of Kevin McKenna, now married and still living across the border in the village of Smithborough in County Monaghan – where he would live out of reach of the British authorities for the rest of his life.

In 2019, Gerry Adams gave the eulogy at Kevin McKenna's funeral after his death from natural causes. 'When I got to know Kevin and Marcella they were living in a mobile home up behind Sheila O'Neill's. They lived a very frugal existence … Kevin fed their young family on rabbit – a big chest freezer was filled with bunny rabbits which he had lamped in his meanderings across the fields. Kevin loved the land – the sight of it, the smells, the feel of it.' This romanticised rural idyll was in complete contrast to the mayhem McKenna was presiding over in neighbouring Tyrone at the time. Hugh Gates, a UDR soldier from Cookstown, had already survived two PIRA assassination attempts and his base being mortared, when the Under Vehicle Booby Trap (UVBT) made its first appearance in the county. He remembered his friend Tommy Benson driving into the base one day in his 'green Morris Marina. He had the window down and a cigarette with a big, long end on it … he came down the yard and slid in round by the new bomb bay and I shouted: "Tommy, get out of that effin' car and don't close the door!" I was behind the MT [Motor Transport] wall! He was lucky that time. He hadn't seen it – an under-car bomb.' But luck was in short supply that year as Gates recalled with sadness: 'They [the Provisionals] put a bomb in the fireplace of their wee cottage [the Bensons] on the Dungannon road. Tommy was away ... and his sister went to light the fire and the whole thing went off. She took two weeks to die.'[20] The killing went on, 'it was one funeral after another'.

By now, individual teams in the Brigade were beginning to specialise, as Dennis Vincent explained: 'Each team had their own way of doing things, different weapons and so on. If a team became proficient at using a certain type of weapon or carrying out a certain type of attack, then they'd carry on with it until something stopped them.' Jay Nethercott underlined the same point: 'The boys from around Ardboe were gunmen, while for the lads from Dungannon and Cappagh it was landmines.' Those landmines were a case in point. Always a favoured weapon in east Tyrone, a unit from Cappagh carried out at least four such attacks in late 1975 and 1976 until they were arrested in dawn raids in November '76. Five local men, Kevin O'Brien, Dermot Boyle, Peter Kane, Pat Joe O'Neill and Martin Hurson, were convicted and jailed. At the same time at least one – probably two – other teams were focusing on shoots against RUC mobile patrols, killing Patrick Maxwell and Samuel Clarke in November 1975 and three more police officers near Ardboe eighteen months later. By now the East Tyrone Brigade was earning itself something of a reputation, as Richard Kemp knew: 'They were regarded as one of the most dangerous elements of PIRA ... They were having quite an impact and in intelligence terms were a subject of attention and focus.' Pleasing though this observation would no doubt have been to the volunteers in the Brigade, it would also bring a new player to the table, and one which would go on to ravage its ranks: Britain's SAS.

First deployed in Northern Ireland in February 1976, the use of the British Army's only special forces regiment on UK soil was controversial. Up until then the SAS had solely operated overseas, its operations shrouded by distance, yet now it would be thrust into the spotlight as never before. Its debut against the East Tyrone Brigade came on 26 February 1978. By 5 pm that Sunday it had already been dark for a while when a white Volkswagen pulled up outside a derelict farmhouse in the Killygonland area of Ardboe on the shores of Lough Neagh. The two occupants got out, walked into the yard and bent over a camouflaged weapons cache. One of them – an apprentice joiner who'd lost a kneecap in a road traffic accident three years previously – stood up from the stash holding a small homemade mortar bomb. A burst of automatic gunfire cut him down even as his accomplice ran to the car and sped off, chased by a hail of bullets. The escapee would survive – albeit having been hit three times – but Paul Duffy did not. The eldest son in a family of eleven children, Duffy had been shot dead by an SAS team that had been lying in wait for two days. Very unusually, British Army Headquarters in Lisburn confirmed to the media that it was indeed an SAS operation. The message was clear – the gloves were off against East Tyrone.

The deployment of the SAS in Tyrone marked a major shift in the British Army's strategy in Northern Ireland, one that prioritised the value of intelligence gathering and hugely increased the use of special forces and specially trained troops from the mainstream Army. Remarkably, this seismic change in approach was mirrored at almost exactly the same time by a radical new IRA strategy. Both were born out of a considered analysis of the war thus far and what was needed in the future to achieve victory.

The change in British strategy was driven by two separate reports; the Report of the Working Group to Consider Progress on Security (also called the Hannigan Report), and the subsequent 'Future Terrorist Trends' paper authored by Brigadier James 'Jimmy' Glover, while he was the senior army officer dealing with intelligence in Northern Ireland, and before he took up his appointment as Commander Land Forces Northern Ireland. The Hannigan Report focused primarily on the overall security forces response to the war and sought to encourage the evolution of the Army's approach in tackling PIRA in particular. It claimed, 'It is apparent that PIRA have problems on the manpower side. The main difficulty has been the fear of security force action and in particular worry about informers among their own ranks.' It also praised the Army for its creation of Close Observation Platoons (COPs) and the significant boost they'd given to intelligence gathering on the ground. The brainchild of Major General Dick Trant – described by a peer as 'a tall man with the genial manner of a country vicar' – COPs were specially trained soldiers whose role wouldn't be the usual round of patrolling, but rather 'intensive, static, covert surveillance'. The new platoons would be manned by volunteers subject to a tough selection and training process supervised by serving SAS instructors, before deploying to their operational areas. Once on the ground they would work in conjunction with Special Branch and Special Forces to boost the amount of intelligence being gathered and ramp up pressure on PIRA. One former Special Forces member, who spent a lot of time in Tyrone, recalled how his own unit and COP worked together: 'I'd been in Tyrone as an ordinary young solider a few years before and then went back with my new mob. I felt safer second time around, I was better trained, better equipped and we only went out on ops based on actionable intelligence. There were a lot more Provisionals by now but we had COP to help out and we worked hand in glove with them. They kept an eye on the rank-and-file Provos while we focused on the small number of senior guys.'

The COPs were a major innovation for the Army. As one former COP commander said of his own service, 'As a Second-Lieutenant [most junior officer rank in the British Army] on my first tour in Northern Ireland I commanded a multiple – 12 men split into three teams, or bricks, of four soldiers each with their own junior NCO [Non-Commissioned Officer, in this case a corporal or lance-corporal] – I knew nothing and it all felt like something of a game.' By his second tour he'd graduated to COP 'and it was a different world. We actually had intelligence and could plan operations, and we had to as the Provisionals were getting more professional.' It was that observation that Jimmy Glover – renowned for his straight-talking and no-nonsense approach – used as the starting point for his own paper, where he went into detail on the changing nature of the volunteers within PIRA's ranks. In the war's early years, Sean O'Callaghan memorably described the majority of Provisionals as 'by and large … ill-educated and ill-equipped',[21] whereas Glover now stated, 'Our evidence of the calibre of rank-and-file terrorists does not support the view that they are merely mindless hooligans drawn from the unemployed and unemployable.' Instead, he characterised the PIRA teams as being a mixture of young men 'nurtured in a climate of violence, eagerly seeking promotion to full gun-carrying status', and older 'dedicated terrorists ... tempered by up to ten-years' operational experience ... many of whom have spent time in prison'.

Many other members of the security forces disagreed with Glover's analysis, believing most volunteers were little more than criminals in balaclavas, motivated by the opportunity for financial gain and the social status within their communities that membership of PIRA brought. As one former British Army officer speculated, 'What motivated them? Kudos was important, walking into the local pub and being known as "one of the boys", that was a biggie. In Tyrone we're talking about country lads here, mainly from the middle of nowhere, and then all of a sudden older blokes are buying them drinks in the pub and slapping them on the back.' Other British veterans were offended by what they saw as the volunteers' hypocrisy: 'these so-called heroes ... would happily stand in the dole [unemployment] offices waiting for their free handouts, as far as they were concerned the British were scum, but a blind eye was turned when it came to dole day ... the more I learned about them as people the more I loathed them.'[22] Many veterans were equally clear that a heartfelt belief in republican ideology was not the main driver for much of the PIRA rank and file as far as they were concerned: 'for some, a minority I'd say, it was ideology, but not for most'. Former senior British Army officer Richard Kemp echoed that opinion: 'In most cases it wasn't ideological, it was tribalism and status.' There are, however, some former soldiers who feel differently: 'I recognised that it was a cause you gave yourself to and believed in wholeheartedly.' One former Scots Guardsman summed up the complexities expressed by many veterans: 'I had some respect for their cause, and the way they went about their business, but don't misunderstand me I'd have shot any of them dead in a heartbeat if I'd caught them red-handed.'

As for the Provisionals themselves, a year before the SAS killed Paul Duffy, a secret IRA General Headquarters (GHQ) report was discovered among the possessions of Séamus Twomey following his arrest by the Gardaí in Dublin on 3 December. The report – the brainchild of Gerry Adams – was scathing about the Provisionals' existing structure: 'we are burdened with an inefficient infrastructure of commands, brigades, battalions and companies. This old system with which the Brits and Branch [RUC Special Branch] are familiar, has to be changed.' It also acknowledged that the security forces were becoming increasingly effective. 'The three and seven-day detention orders [used in Northern Ireland] are breaking volunteers.' Those orders were controversial and abuses were committed by the RUC, but the intelligence flowing from them was hurting PIRA badly. In 1977 a record 1,308 people – mostly republicans – were charged with terrorist offences, and the ranks were thinning as the jails filled up. One republican source commented bitterly, 'we had real issues with a lack of continuity as volunteers were taken out – killed or sent to Long Kesh [gaol] – as we'd lose all their experience. It was killing us.' Tommy McKearney agreed. 'Time, and attrition inflicted by the British, sapped some of our morale and the ceasefire [1974–75] had its effect too. That left us in a situation where we found that our numbers were smaller, and a smaller number of men were carrying more and more responsibility on their shoulders. And this led directly to the reorganisation.'

The report's proposed solution was dramatic. 'We must gear ourselves towards *long-term armed struggle* [author's emphasis] ... new recruits into a new structure ... a cell system.' So were born PIRA's Active Service Units – the ASUs – as the organisation switched over to the Long War concept that would dominate the Provisionals' campaign for the next two decades. Excepting in South Armagh, the old company and battalion structure disappeared, and in its place would be ASUs, usually – but not always – part of the other four brigades: Belfast, Derry, Fermanagh and East Tyrone. These ASUs were usually around four to eight volunteers strong, and each of the volunteers would only know their fellow ASU members, so if arrested a volunteer would be able to divulge precious little under questioning. Only the ASU commander would know anyone else in the hierarchy, and only then a bare handful who were directly relevant to his role. The bulk of information that was crucial to waging the war would be concentrated in the hands of a few, senior men; the Brigade OC who would be responsible for all aspects of his brigade's involvement in the struggle, the Brigade Intelligence and Operations Officers who would originate and co-ordinate attacks, and perhaps most importantly the Brigade Quarter Master (QM) who would control the whereabouts and access to 'the stuff' as the Provisionals termed their arsenal of weapons. Even then additional security was built in with individual ASUs often having their own QM who would source weapons from a few favoured locations and people without reference to the brigade hierarchy. The same would go for target selection and intelligence gathering – security was now paramount for the Provisionals.

As well as pushing through the new cell structure, the northern 69-ers who were now running the IRA's war decided to restructure the entire command network. A secretly held mini-convention reinstituted the hitherto abandoned Northern and Southern Command framework, with Northern Command covering the six Northern Ireland counties plus Leitrim, Louth, Donegal, Cavan and Monaghan. Its primary role would be to fight the war, while the rest of Ireland became Southern Command. Sean O'Callaghan – who would eventually become its OC – described its role as 'a back-up to the war effort … supplying money – usually from armed robberies – and training sites, bomb factories, safe houses and so on.' In other words a classic insurgency support role. The reorganisation went down very well among the volunteers in the north. According to one active republican, 'There'd been an imbalance in control before, but then when Northern Command came in it got tighter, better, more focused.'

It all presaged a maturing in the war and the way it was going to be fought. A British Army veteran put it like this: 'When I was first there in the early '70s there was almost something of a Wild West feeling about it all, with shootouts going on in the middle of the street, but when the ASUs appeared it became something different, something that felt colder, and much more deadly.'

Just how cold would be experienced by Glen Espie, a twenty-one-year-old plumber from east of Cookstown, who would be one of the new East Tyrone ASU's first victims. Espie, a part-time member of 8 UDR, worked for the Northern Ireland Housing Executive in his day-job and carried out 'on average around twenty operational duties a month as a part-time soldier … it was common knowledge I was in the UDR, and we knew we were never off-duty as far as the terrorists were concerned'. By the time of Paul Duffy's shooting, Espie had gotten used to being on his guard and checking his work van for booby traps every morning. On Wednesday 22 March 1978, almost a month after Duffy's death, Espie had just finished a job in Pomeroy when his foreman 'told me he'd just received a call that there was a burst cylinder at No. 3 Lakeview Cottages, Ardboe'. Espie drove to the address, was let into the house and then – from a downstairs bathroom – 'appeared a male of stocky build … he was wearing a loose-fitting black balaclava and he had a big head. I could see his eyes and mouth perfectly. He had a pistol in a two-handed grip pointed right at me, literally only inches from my chest.' Terror gripped him. 'My first thoughts were "F**k! This is it!" Then the gunman fired, hitting me on the left side of my chest … the sheer force of it was like being kicked by a horse.' Knocked backwards, somehow Espie managed to get out of the house and across the road: 'I was shot again in the left shoulder, the impact of the bullet spun me round and I hit the ground … I saw two terrorists running from the doorway towards me to finish me off.' Pulling out his own .22 Walther pistol, he fired back only for the small calibre gun to jam. However, he'd forced his attackers to take cover and given himself time to escape across a nearby field: 'my breath was coming in large gasps, my heart was pounding and my lungs were on fire'.

Breaking into an empty bungalow, a badly bleeding Espie used the home phone to call 999 and told the operator he was wounded and desperately needed help – fearing the call was a come-on to lure the police into the area, he wasn't believed.

'What a waste of time! I slammed the phone down and saw the floor was covered in my blood.' He remembered seeing a sheepskin rug on the floor; 'all the adrenalin was draining away and all I wanted to do was lie down on that rug and sleep'. Grimly fighting the urge, and with the PIRA gun team still searching for him, he once again headed out and 'found a Mini parked in an open shed. The keys were in the ignition.' Still losing blood, he drove the five miles to Coagh where he almost crashed into a friend's house. 'I remember lying on the couch … the doctor arrived but I only really felt safe when I heard the sound of two Saracens, it was the Queen's Own Highlanders QRF [Quick Reaction Force] from Cookstown. I'd survived.' Six months later Espie was back at work and on patrol.

Jay Nethercott was clear as to why Espie had been targeted: 'It was a reprisal job. Paul Duffy had been shot dead by the SAS less than five hundred metres away. PIRA had already tried once when they'd used a Garand [American World War Two rifle] to attack another UDR man – Corporal Bert Stewart from Coagh – but they'd missed him, only by a few inches mind, so this was their second go.' Nethercott was equally clear as to who the lead gunman was. 'It was Lawrence McNally, no doubt about it. He was the main shooter around Ardboe at the time.'

One of the reasons why Nethercott could be so sure of the gunman's identity was that, at that point in time, there had been a drastic reduction in PIRA's ranks. For an organisation like PIRA it was clearly impossible to keep accurate records as to its personnel; however, it was clear that the 1,000 or so active volunteers of the mid-1970s had been whittled down to about one third that figure a decade later, with perhaps double that number acting in an unarmed support role providing logistics, safe houses and so on. This huge drop in front-line strength was most keenly felt in the big cities, where, for Dennis Vincent, the shift to ASUs and the Long War strategy made eminent sense: 'For them [PIRA] it was about survival. So, they moved away from a large, popularly based movement with a big groundswell of local support, to something far smaller and more precise.' Vincent also saw the advent of the ASUs partly as a reaction to the security forces: 'As we [the security forces] got more sophisticated so did they. They had to get better because we got better.'

However, in east Tyrone the move to smaller ASUs rather than the old companies and battalions had relatively little impact. There, the IRA had never been a mass participation movement; rather, they were – as they always had been – a tight-knit organisation drawing its members from a relatively small pool of republican sympathising strongholds and families, many with militant traditions going back decades.

The McKearneys were one such family of course, with a republican pedigree stretching back to their maternal grandfather Tom Murray who was adjutant of the IRA's North Roscommon Brigade in the 1920s. Of Maura McKearney's four sons, Tommy was serving life for murder, while Seán had been killed by his own bomb. Young Pádraig had joined PIRA in 1971, been arrested in 1973 for destroying a post office, released after six weeks, and then arrested and convicted the following year for blowing up a factory. His imprisonment was a terrible blow to his sister Margaret: 'in every family you love everybody but there's always one to whom you feel terribly close … Pádraig was that person for me.' To Margaret's relief by 1980 he was out and free, but was then arrested once more in possession of a Sten submachine gun. This time he was sentenced to fourteen years.

Arrested with him, and sentenced to one year for PIRA membership, was his friend Gerard O'Callaghan from Milltown near the village of Benburb, a bare three miles from the McKearney home in Moy. O'Callaghan was also a close friend of Patrick Kelly, the same Patrick Kelly whose uncle Liam had emigrated to the United States after forming Saor Uladh in the 1950s. By the mid-1970s the remaining Kellys had left mainly Protestant Carrickfergus and moved to the Lisnahull estate in Dungannon – Tommy Hamill's old PIRA stomping ground. Patrick's sister, Mairéad, claimed one of her earliest memories after the move was of neighbours running to tell her that her brother was being brutalised by soldiers. 'They were beating him black and blue. He was only a teenager at the time, but like a lot of young Catholics, that was his experience of the British Army.' Patrick got a job working in a Dungannon fireplace shop, married, and had three children. After work he'd sit at the kitchen table doing the books for the shop. He also joined the Provisionals. Arrested in February 1982 on the evidence of PIRA supergrass Patrick McGurk, he was released twenty months later when McGurk refused to give evidence in court, causing the collapse of a trial that lasted barely fifteen minutes.

The man who would link all three of these characters together – Pádraig McKearney, Gerard O'Callaghan and Patrick Kelly – and in so doing become pretty much the totem for the rise and fall of the East Tyrone/Monaghan Brigade, was also one of the most controversial figures of the entire war. Once described by Joseph Duffy, the Catholic Bishop of Clogher, as 'a madman', and thought to have been personally responsible for at least twenty killings, Jim Lynagh polarises opinion like few others. Mythologised by republicans, loathed by unionists, and detested by the security forces – the RUC nicknamed him 'the Executioner' – it is impossible to understand the East Tyrone Brigade without at least trying to understand him and his exploits.

Much of what has been written about Lynagh is apocryphal and paints a picture of a charismatic Che Guevara-type figure, an image which Lynagh himself was keen to cultivate. As one British Army intelligence officer opined, '[he] saw himself as the leader of a guerrilla band, not a member of a terrorist cell'. Even the well-respected Irish nationalist author Tim Pat Coogan retold a story whereupon Lynagh supposedly visited a volunteer in hospital – presumably in the Republic – who'd been shot and was worried the bullet may have 'damaged his tackle'. 'Right,' said Lynagh, 'there's only one way to find out.' He left and later reappeared with one of his own girlfriends in tow. 'OK now, hop into bed there and test out your man's tackle.' Then in the final twist a nurse came in during the middle of the tryst and on seeing what was going on remarked, 'Not too much wrong with your man.' Amusing as this story undoubtedly is, it could be judged as having the main aim of buttressing Lynagh's devil-may-care reputation, rather than being objective truth. The security forces unsurprisingly tell different tales of Lynagh, including when 'he had an argument with another man at a Monaghan cattle market over money for a cow. Next thing you know Lynagh got a gun and shot the cow dead in the middle of the market.'

As for Lynagh himself, his background and upbringing gave little hint as to his future almost mythical status; one of twelve children born into a family living on the Tully estate in the south of Monaghan Town, he had no republican back story and his parents – Seamus and Carmel – weren't political. Brought up as he was in the Irish Republic he had no personal contact with life north of the border, and having been born in 1956 he had no memory of the Border Campaign either. Nevertheless, he became a convinced republican and avowed believer in the armed struggle. First arrested – but not charged – in spring 1972 for throwing a petrol bomb at the Gardaí during a riot outside the local police station, he spent his five years in Long Kesh prison – after nearly dying in an own goal in 1973 – studying Maoist insurgency theory and finding a kindred spirit in Pádraig McKearney. Some commentators suggest he had little time for politics and was only interested in the military side of the war – a view not shared by family friend, Owen Smith: 'Jim didn't see the war as a means to an end … but as part of the overall struggle' – and indeed he stood on behalf of Sinn Féin for Monaghan Urban District Council in 1979 and was duly elected, although Ed Moloney quotes a former colleague of Lynagh's saying of him, 'He was outside the charmed circle. He was regarded [by Sinn Féin leaders] as not quite respectable enough, a bit too wild for them. He was no saint. He'd been involved in the odd punch-up … He was also a hard-line republican. I remember when the word came [from Sinn Féin HQ] not to mention the North or the war on the doorsteps while canvassing and to concentrate instead on social and economic issues, Lynagh objected and then just ignored it.'

Regardless, being an elected Sinn Féin representative didn't stop Lynagh from making his paramilitary affiliations crystal clear. In fact he seemed to enjoy his own notoriety, acting as a sort of nexus for both home-grown Monaghan republicans and Provisionals living in the town who were OTR from the North. Among his associates at the time were a number of suspected IRA volunteers including his brother-in-law Séamus Shannon, Lawrence McNally – allegedly involved in Glen Espie's attempted murder – and his own younger brother, Colm Lynagh. Colm would later be imprisoned for involvement in the murder of Gabriel Murphy, a nightclub bouncer at the Hillgrove Hotel allegedly involved in a fracas with Jim and marked for a punishment kneecapping that went wrong. But Jim Lynagh was the key, the lynchpin for all that went on around him. The former RUC Special Branch officer, Dr William Matchett, unflinchingly described him as a 'psychopath'[23] but acknowledged the ambivalence which was central to his reputation: 'probably [one of] the most prolific serial killers from these shores – yet ... regarded as a mythical figure by some'.

Jim Lynagh, Pádraig McKearney, Patrick Kelly, Gerry O'Callaghan – these were the type of experienced volunteers Brigadier Jimmy Glover alluded to in his report as being at the very heart of the Provisionals' war, and who would soon be led once more by the forceful figure of Kevin Mallon. In the meantime Tyrone suffered a wave of shootings in 1979, a few short months after Lynagh's release from Long Kesh in October the previous year. Most were of off-duty UDR or RUC men like Thomas Armstrong, killed near his farm in Tynan on Good Friday, or John 'Jack' Scott, a sixty-three-year-old milk tanker driver shot dead on his round in Ardboe on 22 June. There was something of a hiatus in the summer with the world's attention fixed on the Warrenpoint bombing on 27 August that left eighteen soldiers – mainly paratroopers – dead, and the assassination the same day in County Sligo of the Queen's cousin, Lord Louis Mountbatten, with normal service only resuming in October with the killings of James Robinson and Fred Irwin – both off-duty UDR soldiers, the latter shot dead while at work in a Dungannon council yard. As Tommy McKearney pointed out: 'In 1979, the IRA had, by its own standards, a successful year militarily.'

Under pressure to try and halt the killings, the security forces stepped up observation on known terrorist suspects in the hope of catching them red handed. One such suspect ran an electrical shop in Dungannon where he was watched every evening by plain-clothed, undercover soldiers from what became 14 Intelligence Company – the Det, as it was colloquially termed. 'The suspect was one of the two **** [author: name withheld] brothers. One of them ended up losing a hand in an own goal. He was putting a bomb together and it went off early.' A single Operator – as a Det member was called – sat over the road in a small car park on observation, with two others satelliting around in other cars and one ready to go as top-cover in a helicopter if needed: 'Jock was top cover in the heli that night, I was first on task and had been parked up for about fifteen minutes when I saw them out of the corner of my eye; two men, one with a .38 pistol and the other with a submachine gun. I think they'd come from this van parked up in the corner, anyway, they just leaned over the bonnet of the car next to me and opened fire through my window. I lunged to the left – towards the passenger seat – and tried to draw my pistol with my right hand but I was hit in the right arm and hand. With my left hand I grabbed the M-10 submachine gun [the Ingram MAC-10], that was hidden under a newspaper on the passenger seat, but was hit in that arm too so couldn't lift it to fire. The car was fitted with a concealed radio [the set was in the boot with the aerial in a loop around the roof] and I had two send buttons, one by the handbrake and the other under the clutch and I used the clutch one and shouted "Contact, contact!" into my radio as soon as I saw the gunmen, and then I heard the other cars screeching into the car park as I watched the two gunmen run off into the next-door housing estate.' 'Noddy' (not his real name) had been hit eight times and was losing a lot of blood: 'One of the other guys jumped into the car and drove as fast as he could to the local A&E but the door was locked so we had to scramble around to find a way in. Eventually we went round to the main entrance which was open – and we walked in past all these people leaving as it was the end of visiting hours. I was bleeding heavily by then and a nurse just stared at me as I stood there dripping blood all over the floor.' Put in a wheelchair, 'Noddy' was taken in and operated on. A bullet lodged in his wrist was left in at first as it was deemed non-life threatening. His right arm was broken and so was set and plastered, and the hole in his face – a bullet had gone in one cheek, knocked out several teeth and cut his tongue in two before exiting the other cheek with yet more teeth – was sewn up. The next thing 'Noddy' remembers was waking up in a hospital bed with an armed guard on the door.

The attack on 'Noddy' was a relative success for East Tyrone PIRA, but by now a steady stream of intelligence was reaching the security forces from a dizzying array of sources. The most basic kind came from soldiers on the ground reporting who they'd seen, with whom and where. Part of every battalion's Northern Ireland Training and Advisory Team (NITAT) training package carried out in Kent – or Sennelager if they were based in Germany – was using photo montages to learn the names and faces of known volunteers in the areas they were being sent to. Those montages were highly confidential, jealously guarded by intelligence staff and never taken on patrol. On patrol if a soldier saw a suspect – a 'player' as they were called – he would question them; what their name was, where they'd been, where they were going, and so on. They didn't have to answer of course but almost all did, knowing that to do otherwise would just lead to a search, an ID check, and any other number of time-wasting tactics to keep them standing there in the rain and cold. Most stops were done on vehicles at so-called snap VCPs, with a soldier standing in the middle of the road waving down cars – a red torchlight in a circular motion was used at night – and asking the occupants for ID. Whilst that was being done another soldier would be calling in the registration plate to an IT system called Vengeful – the forerunner of modern number plate recognition systems – that would flag up if the vehicle was owned by someone who was traced – a player. That could lead to a search of the vehicle and its occupants. During a patrol the commander would also pick several locations to carry out a rummage – a search of the immediate area using the Winthrop theory.

Named after Richard Winthrop, a Fusilier lieutenant who'd come up with the idea in the early '70s, it used a set of analytical features to help find PIRA weapons caches. These caches were usually buried where they could be watched by friendly eyes, often in sight of a volunteer's home, with their location marked by an easily recognised feature such as a lone tree or derelict building, and then by some small sign on that feature such as a scratch or particular mark. This description could then be given to any volunteer sent to pick up a weapon when needed. Often the cache itself was a metal milk can or plastic barrel, sealed to keep the weapons dry, although taped plastic bags were also used. If a weapon was found by a soldier during a rummage, the procedure – called Op Clean – was not to draw attention to it and simply patrol away as if nothing had happened. Then, with the cache still in sight, a report was sent into the battalion intelligence cell where a judgement was made as to what to do next. Ideally, a specialist team would be sent out to set up an Observation Point (OP) on the cache in the hope of catching whoever appeared to collect the weapon. 'Noddy' remembered this as the mainstay of the Det's job: 'I'd say more than half of the ops we did was watching weapons that'd been found out on the ground. We'd move in, find a bush or hedge where we could hide and lie there and wait.' 'Noddy' also remembered the growing professionalism of the East Tyrone Brigade: 'They weren't "dumb Paddies" like some made out. They were switched on … they'd do anti-surveillance routines if out in a car, so when they came to a roundabout they wouldn't take the first exit but would go round it once, twice, maybe more, to see if they were being followed.' At home they were just as careful. 'I remember one of their guys lived in a bungalow out in the country and he cut down every tree and bush within two hundred metres of his house so there was nowhere for us to hide. Lots of them bought dogs and let them out to roam around the fields to sniff us out, and as so many had farms they'd use cows too – cows are very inquisitive and would wander over and give you away double quick.'

Another valuable source of information was – somewhat surprisingly – local people in self-proclaimed republican areas. Richard Kemp explained: 'I met many Catholics – I'm Catholic myself of course – who, when they couldn't be overheard or seen, said "We're f**king glad you're here." They might also drop a titbit of information, like "I wouldn't be letting my kids go down that road for a while if you know what I mean," and you'd know they knew something. Then next minute they were shouting "Brits Out", but it was common in the Catholic community to have that almost double life.' Not that all members of the nationalist community were willing to provide morsels of intelligence to the security forces, or even be civil to them, as Ed Denmark, a young artilleryman who served in Tyrone in the '80s, sheepishly recalled from his first patrol: 'I decided it was time to carry out a P check [personnel check on an individual], so I moved across the road to the library and stopped a woman who was about to go in. She was so small and quiet looking and I thought she was the ideal candidate to try my first P check on. "Excuse me, can you tell me your name?" Her face creased up and she turned red, "F**k off you Brit b****d!"' Dumbfounded, Denmark persisted, only to be told 'You ain't getting my name, you b****d. The only thing you'll get is a bullet in the head, so why don't you f**k off.' An embarrassed Denmark eventually got her name.

Despite more and more weapons finds and the growing flow of intelligence to the security forces, the East Tyrone Brigade still managed to carry out an increasing number of attacks, as was lethally demonstrated in early March 1980. Henry

Livingstone was a thirty-eight-year-old Protestant whose farm near Tynan bordered that of Thomas Armstrong, the UDR soldier killed on Good Friday the previous year. Livingstone had himself been in the UDR but had left three months earlier hoping that decision would keep him and his family safe. It wouldn't. That evening – a Thursday – Livingstone went out, as usual, to check on his cattle in the hay shed. Waiting hidden behind the bales were three PIRA gunmen. They opened fire as soon as Livingstone entered the shed, hitting him twice. Still alive, he lay on the ground as two of the shooters – reportedly Jim Lynagh and Lawrence McNally – walked up to him and shot him a further six times at point-blank range. The gun team then stole Livingstone's car and drove the short distance to the border, abandoning it there before being picked up and driven to Monaghan Town. Livingstone's elderly widowed mother found her son's body and raised the alarm, and within a couple of hours the Gardaí picked up all three alleged attackers. Despite there being some forensic evidence linking them to the Livingstone hay shed, a Dublin court found there was insufficient evidence to convict and they were all released. The softest of soft targets, Henry Livingstone was the twenty-first ex-UDR member to be killed in the war – leaving the regiment was no guarantee of safety.

By 1980, after more than a decade of violence, it was increasingly difficult to shock public opinion in Northern Ireland, but Henry Livingstone's murder touched a nerve. Once again the Provisionals – and the wider republican movement – were accused of the most vicious sectarianism. It was no surprise to Sean O'Callaghan: 'The conversations I had with local IRA men and sympathisers centred around "the Prods" or "the Orangies" [disparaging nickname for Protestants] and it was becoming clear to me that PIRA were in reality representative of the Catholic "Defender" [militant eighteenth-century Catholic secret society] tradition. In rural areas of Tyrone, Fermanagh and Armagh the relationship between militant Irish nationalism and Irish Catholicism was deep and complex. There was a deep and ugly hatred – centuries old – behind it all.' O'Callaghan's views were – and still are – hugely controversial, and potentially extremely damaging for PIRA: 'the reality stared me in the face: this was a war between Catholics and Protestants, not against the British. I might want to attack a British Army patrol or barracks, but the local IRA man would rather shoot a Protestant neighbour who was in the UDR or police reserve.' Tommy McKearney doesn't agree with his former comrade-in-arms, but was forced to concede that 'Many Protestant people viewed this campaign as a sectarian assault on their community.'

The poison in the blood that was sectarianism hit the headlines again in a major way on 22 January 1981 following an attack the previous night on Tynan Abbey in County Armagh. The Abbey was the eighteenth-century ancestral stately home of the Stronge family, a pillar of the Unionist establishment. In residence on the night of 21 January 1981 were Sir Norman Stronge, the 8th baronet, and his forty-eight-year-old son James, a former Grenadier Guards officer who was now an RUC reserve constable. Sir Norman – now eighty-six-years-old – was a former Speaker of the Northern Ireland House of Commons and had won the Military Cross in the First World War for bravery on the battlefield. The *Irish Times* reported that the Stronges were 'still living in an enormous mansion though everyone knew the father and son used only a few rooms of it, with a housekeeper and a land steward who lived out'. That night, as father and son sat in the Abbey's library watching television, an eight-man team from the East Tyrone Brigade set explosive charges on the heavily ornate, oak front doors. Blowing them in, the gunmen burst into the house, found the Stronges, and shot them dead, but not before one of them – almost certainly James – managed to fire a flare out of the window and up into the night sky to alert the RUC. The killings done, the team set two incendiary bombs and then looked to escape in the two cars they'd arrived in. A UDR officer – privy to details after the attack – described how 'The RUC arrived at the gate lodge in one vehicle – an armoured Ford Cortina – and were confused when the two cars heading their way from the Abbey stopped and out got men wearing military-style uniforms and combat gear.' Thinking they might be undercover soldiers the RUC hesitated for a moment, but were quickly disabused when the 'soldiers' opened fire on them: 'There was nothing they could do but just sit there and take it. The IRA team were all over the Cortina. They tried to get a gun between the door and the door jamb to shoot in but couldn't. The windows were bullet-proof glass but the roof wasn't armoured. The Provos didn't realise about the roof. It was pure luck they survived.' Years later, an RUC officer would tell a young British Army lieutenant that on the night in question 'Lynagh jumped on the bonnet of the RUC car and just stood there firing his machine gun down into the front windscreen. The fellas in the car were terrified, but the bullet-proof glass held out, thank God.'

As automatic fire split the night the two incendiary bombs detonated, and as the Abbey went up in flames the gunmen disappeared in the confusion. The burnt bodies of the two Stronges were found in the ashes the next day; father and son had been shot executioner-style. Jay Nethercott thought this the first 'big operation by a new generation of IRA'. He was clear about who was involved: 'Pete Ryan was there, as was Lawrence McNally, Peter Sherry was OC East Tyrone at the time, but wasn't on the job. It was all Lynagh.'[24] Three years after the attack, Jim Lynagh's brother-in-law, Séamus Shannon, would be extradited from the Republic to Northern Ireland charged with being one of the PIRA hit team that night. He was later acquitted.

Once more unionist public opinion was outraged, with PIRA's statement that the Stronges had been targeted as 'symbols of hated unionism' and 'as a direct reprisal for a whole series of loyalist assassinations and murder attacks', cutting little ice. The Tyrone republican firebrand and elected Westminster MP, Bernadette McAliskey – she and her husband having barely survived an assassination attempt by a loyalist hit squad some five days earlier at their home near Coalisland – didn't condemn the attack but was far from supportive: '... it is politically counter-productive and confuses the situation, and that is totally non-progressive'. Gerry Adams meanwhile – usually very aware of the audience beyond those he was directly addressing – said of the attack, 'The only complaint I have heard from Nationalists or anti-Unionists is that he [Sir Norman Stronge] was not shot forty years ago.' In a pointed rebuke, the Catholic Social Democratic and Labour Party (SDLP) politician Austin Currie, Coalisland-born and hero of the Caledon squat protest, said that 'even at eighty-six years of age [Stronge] was still incomparably more of a man than the cowardly dregs of humanity who ended his life in this barbaric way'.

Elsewhere, East Tyrone PIRA was playing another role in the war, only this time it involved the ancient Irish tradition of the hunger strike. After several years of ineffectual dirty protest where prisoners refused to wash or wear clothes and would cover their cells in their own urine and faeces – going 'on the blanket' as it was called – late October 1980 saw the first in what would become a number of hunger strikes by republican prisoners. With volunteers chosen to represent their home areas, it was Tommy McKearney who put his hand up for Tyrone. Fifty-three days later – and close to an agonising death – he came off the strike and lived. Unfortunately it would only be a reprieve in the horror.

Having failed to achieve their desired status as 'political prisoners', republicans tried again in the new year, and in a carefully timed sequence a number of volunteers began once more to refuse food. Cappagh-born Martin Hurson was the East Tyrone Brigade's representative hunger striker this time, after his predecessor, Brendan McLaughlin, was forced to withdraw due to a perforated stomach ulcer. After forty days Hurson couldn't keep down water. He died six days later. He was twenty-four.

Belfast's Bobby Sands might have been the face of the 1981 hunger strike as far as the rest of the world was concerned, but in east Tyrone it was Martin Hurson's photo that adorned every nationalist's front window. His funeral drew huge crowds and a monument was erected to him in Cappagh. His death encouraged a new generation of recruits to join the East Tyrone Brigade. Francie Molloy, a local Sinn Féin activist at the time, attended the funeral and described the aftermath to the journalist Peter Taylor: 'I think the young people of Cappagh and the surrounding area decided then that they were going to replace them [the dead hunger strikers] tenfold. And that is what they did. The number of young people who joined up in response was massive.' Whether the actual number of recruits was indeed 'massive' is a moot point, and there were rumours Hurson was put under pressure to go on hunger strike, but what cannot be denied is that a new generation of republicans was radicalised by his death and took up arms. These young men would fuse with the likes of Jim Lynagh, Patrick Kelly and Pádraig McKearney to make the Brigade one of the most dangerous in the war; celebrated, feared and loathed in equal measure.

In the meantime, the Brigade would suffer a series of setbacks that would lead to a sea change in both its leadership and strategy. Firstly, a number of experienced volunteers were taken off the rolls, including James McGinley and Aidan McGurk – the latter previously acquitted along with Lynagh and McNally for the murder of Henry Livingstone. Having planted a 500lb landmine packed into four beer kegs and a butter churn to target an expected British Army mobile patrol, the two men walked across the border into the Republic and lay in wait on a nearby hilltop. But they'd been seen. A call went into the RUC who then informed the Gardaí. The Irish police found McGurk and McGinley asleep at their firing point. Charged in a special non-jury Dublin court with possession of explosives and IRA membership, the two men – inevitably dubbed the 'Sleeping Bombers' – were duly convicted. A British Army spokesman said at the time, 'It is very gratifying to see cooperation between them [the RUC and the Irish police] working so well. It was smart work by the Irish police.'

Then Pat McGurk – no relation to Aidan – turned IRA supergrass and whole cadres of volunteers were taken out of circulation, including Dungannon's Patrick Kelly. Not for the first time, suspicion gripped East Tyrone PIRA. Informers – touts as they are disparagingly called by paramilitaries – are despised and detested by republicans to a level far deeper even than policemen and soldiers. Anyone suspected of informing can expect to be subjected to extreme interrogation – torture in other words. Confessions were almost invariably forthcoming, often simply out of abject terror or in an attempt to stop the pain – and were swiftly followed by the condemned man (or woman) being stripped to their underwear, hooded, hands bound behind their back, their shoes removed as a special mark of disgrace, then frogmarched to a suitably remote location and shot in the back of the head.

At first, internal security, as it was dubbed, was a wholly local responsibility, with perhaps the most controversial case in Tyrone being that of Columba McVeigh back in October 1975. A nineteen-year-old Catholic from Donaghmore, McVeigh simply disappeared one day and was never seen alive again. An IRA statement released sometime later claimed he was an informer who'd been executed after confessing his guilt. His family denied the accusation, with his elder brother Eugene saying that Columba was 'a young guy who lived in a small village and was easily influenced'. Eugene acknowledged that Columba sometimes spoke to RUC officers and may have passed on titbits of information to the security forces, but in no way deserved to die for it. 'I spoke to Martin McGuinness about it years later and told him that Columba was killed by the IRA but had been put in jeopardy by British intelligence.' The waters surrounding Columba's death were further muddied by Eugene being an ex-UDR soldier: 'I joined up in 1970 and served until around 1972. At the time there were moderate Catholic leaders who called on young men like me to volunteer and show we were part of the wider community.' A former UDR colleague of Eugene's claimed his service – short as it was – contributed to Columba's fate. 'The likes of Kevin Mallon and Brendan Hughes couldn't afford to not have the community under their thumb. They needed them to be scared to death. That was why Columba was targeted. His brother was in the UDR in Dungannon, the family were Catholics and they needed to be scared off.' Eugene disagrees: 'I knew Kevin Mallon personally and I was never threatened. I left because I was trying to build a career and couldn't do that and at the same time keep on putting in the hours needed with the UDR.' Whatever the truth, the fact remains that Columba McVeigh's body has never been recovered despite almost half a dozen separate searches over the years, the latest being in October 2022.

By 1980 East Tyrone's own internal security team were supplemented by a new, centrally organised PIRA unit: the Civil Administration Team. Nicknamed the 'Nutting Squad', it would become one of the most feared and controversial elements of the republican movement. 'Martin' – a former British Army intelligence officer – described how the new set-up worked with the brigades on the ground: 'Central internal security [the Nutting Squad] was augmented at local level by volunteers responsible for day-to-day security, normally working to the OC of the local units.' In the aftermath of the supergrass malaise, the Squad had its first run out in Tyrone when suspicion fell on twenty-four-year-old volunteer and father of four Séamus Morgan. A former election worker for the hunger striker Bobby Sands, Morgan had moved his family to County Monaghan citing a threat to his life from British security forces. Abducted, tortured and murdered by his own side, his mutilated body was found dumped on the Carrickasticken Road near Forkhill in south Armagh.

With suspicion rife within its own ranks, East Tyrone needed a steadying hand, and into this febrile atmosphere stepped Kevin Mallon. Having spent the last seven years in the high security wing of Portlaoise gaol he was now free again. His third stint behind bars hadn't had the reformative effect his jailers had hoped and he went straight back to the war. Dealing with the threat of informers may have been the Brigade's main priority as far as the volunteers were concerned, but Mallon had other ideas. For him, the biggest issue was that the organisation he'd returned to was dying on its feet from a lack of cash.

At the beginning of the 1980s PIRA's revenue was about £700,000 a year, which simply wasn't enough to fund a campaign of any scale. The IRA needed more money, and Mallon thought he had the answer: kidnapping and extortion. His first target was ostensibly an easy job – the racehorse Shergar. At the time, Shergar was arguably the most famous horse on the planet. A Derby winner, he'd been retired to stud at Ballymany in Kildare. As Sean O'Callaghan pointed out: 'Mallon's thinking was … quite clever. Kidnapping a horse would never be viewed by the general public in Ireland as equivalent to kidnapping a person.

There would be no father, mother, husband or wife tearfully begging for a loved one's release ... Mallon successfully sold his idea to McKenna. Ivor Bell [reportedly PIRA Chief of Staff at the time] was also keen.' Given the green light, Mallon didn't use his loyal East Tyrone men, instead recruiting a team from Southern Command.

On the night of 8 February 1983 the operation went ahead. It was a disaster from the start. Mallon's team broke into the stud, loaded Shergar into a horsebox and headed off towards County Leitrim. But thoroughbred horses are very highly strung and the team had never handled one before. When Shergar went into a near frenzy in the horsebox he damaged a leg and became uncontrollable. A republican source claims, 'He was killed within days, even though the IRA kept up the pretence that he was alive and demanded a £5million ransom.' The second big mistake Mallon made was to completely underestimate who he was dealing with. Shergar was owned by a forty-odd strong syndicate, but real power sat with the majority shareholder, the Aga Khan. On being told of Shergar's abduction, the Shia Moslem religious leader announced he wouldn't pay a penny for his return and refused the other syndicate holders' demands to even discuss the matter.

Worse was to come for Mallon's strategy. On the morning of 24 November that same year, Don Tidey – an English-born supermarket executive – was driving his thirteen-year-old daughter Susan to school as normal when he saw what appeared to be a Gardaí checkpoint near his Dublin home. Flagged down, suddenly, armed men were everywhere. A gun was thrust into Tidey's face as his daughter was dragged from the car and dumped at the side of the road. The terrified executive was then bundled into another car and driven off. Following the kidnapping a ransom demand was made and the media went into a frenzy. Acting on information given, a massive Irish Army/Gardaí manhunt was launched, focusing on the area around Ballinamore in County Leitrim. On 16 December one of the search teams saw a man running into woodland and clearly trying to avoid them. Following up, they discovered a well-camouflaged bunker and a shoot-out began with a four-man IRA team. Trainee Garda Gary Sheehan and Irish Army private Patrick Kelly were killed before Tidey was rescued after twenty-three days in captivity.

The deaths of Sheehan and Kelly were a PR disaster for the Provisionals; killing members of the security forces in Northern Ireland was one thing but this was beyond the pale. Dublin went berserk. Someone had to take the fall and Kevin Mallon was in the frame. From being a 'big man' in republican parlance, Mallon was cast aside and, embittered and disgruntled, more or less abandoned the Provos. A former volunteer who knew Mallon well shed few tears at his side-lining. 'Kevin Mallon wasn't a leader, he needed leadership. He was too erratic; he would've shot up everything. He was brave but crazy, definitely not a cool head. He had no fear and lots of country cunning but that's not enough to lead a big unit like East Tyrone.'

The Army Council now had a problem. Regardless of the failures of the kidnapping campaign, Mallon was adored by his East Tyrone Brigade, and even the Belfast men dominating the organisation couldn't afford to blithely ignore the views of one of their largest and most effective units. Their answer was Kevin McKenna. Safely ensconced in Smithborough, McKenna had been elevated to Chief of Staff in September when the incumbent – Ivor Bell – had been arrested. The Provos rules about such matters were clear; when an Army Council member was arrested he automatically resigned his post and was replaced so the organisation could carry on. Bell's departure opened the door for McKenna. As a former Provisional made clear to Ed Moloney, 'McKenna would have been seen as keeping Tyrone out of politicking and troublemaking … he'd be there to keep Tyrone happy, so they could say their man was Chief of Staff.' Moloney's interviewee gave his opinions anonymously but it isn't hard to discern more than a whiff of metropolitan bias in some of his comments: 'He [McKenna] knew the price of cows and was happy wearing wellies … but the macro stuff left him trailing.' Damned with such faint praise, McKenna would nevertheless go on to became the longest serving Chief of Staff in PIRA's history.

His appointment may have pleased East Tyrone, but it wasn't universally welcomed, with Sean O'Callaghan for one not a big fan. While O'Callaghan respected McKenna's near obsession with security and his quiet, determined manner, he considered him sectarian to his bones. The Kerry man recalled an incident when 'I was making tea when a television news report announced that a policewoman had been killed in a bomb explosion in Bangor. McKenna turned his head … and said, "Maybe she was pregnant and we got two for the price of one." It was an off-the-cuff remark that said it all.' For O'Callaghan this callous sectarian comment typified the dark side of the Provisionals; however, it must be said that the same remark was attributed to another senior republican – Dáithí Ó Conaill – by the writer Christopher Hitchens, and that Kieran

Conway disputes it was ever said at all. To be fair, having passed away in 2017 Sean O'Callaghan is unable to confirm its veracity.[25]

Regardless, with McKenna as Chief of Staff and Mallon cut adrift, the East Tyrone Brigade was in a state of flux, a situation which was dramatically worsened by the return to the county of Britain's special forces.

When the SAS first appeared in Northern Ireland back in 1976, they were not a household name, but all that changed on 5 May 1980 when the Regiment was thrust into the world's spotlight on the balconies of the Iranian Embassy in London's Prince's Gate. Now it was back in Northern Ireland and ready to strike once more.

The SAS's re-engagement with Northern Ireland was the result of nothing less than a revolution in the intelligence war instigated by the British Prime Minister Margaret Thatcher herself. 'When the Troubles first started the RUC was totally unprepared and it was only when Thatcher came in with Maurice Oldfield [former head of MI6] and reworked the whole thing that finally the intelligence side started to get up to scratch,' said John Shackles who was part of that whole 're-working', transferring over from the UDR to the RUC and joining Special Branch, where 'sources', as they were termed, were the service's lifeblood. 'Mostly these people [IRA members] only realised they were involved when it was too late, when they couldn't get out ... so what I was looking for in a possible source was someone young enough to have a future in the organisation, someone who could move up the ranks.' Shackles was clear that it was a process where SB had time on its side: 'I'd know everything about them before I'd make an approach: family, friends, finances, you name it. I could have their home phone bugged, I could have them shadowed, I could play good cop bad cop, I could see who they confided in after I approached them, and if I didn't succeed at first then try, try again, so you can be f***ed off once, twice, three times and you just keep on going, then the penny drops and they realise this f***er's not going away. If we wanted you then most times that's it, we'd get you.' Shackles described a range of incentives used to recruit and motivate sources. 'One source I had liked golf and because of his job had good reason to travel, so we'd arrange for him to play at all the big-name courses on the mainland; St Andrews and all that, he loved it.' Others had different drivers: 'I had one source in East Tyrone, a very good one, both politically and operationally, he appreciated direct talking, and if I explained what the problem was he'd say, "Leave it with me" and he was an expert at getting the finger pointed at someone else. He had weaknesses, he was quite a bit older, never married, lived at home with his mother, hadn't had a great deal of success with women, so we treated him to weekends in London or Glasgow or wherever, and he was looked after – if you know what I mean – and would have the best weekend ever.' Overall though Shackles says it boils down to one thing above all: 'It's a total falsehood that when you join a terrorist organisation it's some sort of fellowship; that's bo***cks. Eyes are on you all the time and once you're in you are f***ed. I was offering them a way out. So you show them you're not James Bond, you're their caretaker, and your primary concern is their welfare, you're there to look after them and theirs.'

Uniformed police were making a difference too, as the RUC's Alan Douglas explained: 'I think it was Pomeroy station that got mortared again and Margaret Thatcher heard that the Provies had paraded the van with the mortars all loaded on the back through Cappagh and Carrickmore for everyone to see. Anyway she went nuts and ordered security be upped so I was part of the team that opened Carrickmore RUC station for the first time in a long time. It was an old rectory. There was me and around eight or nine constables, we were well armed and I preferred we patrolled without the Army. I knew the locals wouldn't like us but I hoped they'd tolerate us.' Douglas had his own way of working: 'I never got physical with suspects. There were no fisticuffs or anything like that, but we'd be in their face, you know what I mean; so I'd be at the end of their drive when they were putting their bins out at night, and there again the next morning as they set off for work, then we'd dash off to get to wherever they were working that day and stop them again as they arrived. The whole idea was to disrupt their rhythm, to dominate them without threatening them.' Douglas was proud of what he and his team were achieving. 'We heard that the senior boys in Dungannon wanted Cappagh to do a landmine job but the Cappagh lads told them "No way, we can't p**s over here without them being all over us."'

The efforts of Shackles, Douglas and co. were now bearing fruit, as Tyrone PIRA would learn to its cost. It was the beginning of December 1983, and as was now becoming almost routine, a Special Branch handler received a tipoff from an informer about a temporary weapons cache hidden in a hedgerow off the Cloghog Road near Coalisland. A covert search uncovered an Armalite assault rifle, a shotgun, balaclavas and gloves. Briefing his team, 'Soldier A' – a senior NCO in the SAS – subsequently stated, 'It was my intention …

to apprehend any terrorist attempting to take any weapons or clothing from the cache and the team was briefed accordingly.' Soldier A and five other SAS troopers then set up observation around the hide from three separate points. Each point was manned by two troopers with one watching while the other slept, ate or attended to nature. After two nights, and getting on for three days, a brown Talbot car with three men inside pulled up near the cache. It was 3 pm on Sunday, 4 December and it was still light.

Two men in civilian clothes got out of the Talbot, went through a gap in the hedge and walked straight to the hide. Neither man was armed. On reaching the cache the first man knelt and pulled out the Armalite, handing it to his comrade. At that point Soldier A later stated he shouted a warning as required by the Army's rules of engagement: 'Halt, security forces!' The kneeling man 'pivoted round, pointing the shotgun in my direction', at which point, 'I then thought my life was in immediate danger, and fearing for my life, and that of my comrades, I opened fire.' The shotgun-wielding volunteer was hit thirteen times. His compatriot with the Armalite also turned round and was shot – twice. The driver jumped back into the car and sped off, only to be fired at by Soldiers E and F, shattering the windscreen. He escaped, the car was found two miles away, abandoned and covered in blood. Believed to have been spirited across the border for medical treatment, the third man reportedly survived but was 'a cabbage'. Colm McGirr – twenty-two years old – was the dead volunteer with the shotgun. The youngest of eleven children, he had been arrested and held for questioning only the week before. His comrade with the Armalite – nineteen-year-old Brian

Campbell – was still alive, as an SAS trooper recounted: 'he was losing a lot of blood, I put a field dressing on it [an exit wound in his shoulder] ... he was going into deep shock and having difficulty breathing. I immediately inserted a plastic breathing tube in his throat to assist his breathing and placed him in the recovery position. I stayed with him ... for about five minutes until he died.'[26]

Shocked at the loss of the two volunteers, the Provisionals' excellent media machine went into action, insisting that no warnings were given, that the men were unarmed when shot and were then finished off execution-style. This mantra would become the standard PIRA response to all SAS operations that resulted in the death of a volunteer. Both Campbell and McGirr were given full paramilitary funerals. While McGirr's shotgun had been reported stolen from a local farm, forensic tests on Campbell's Armalite linked it to at least a dozen shootings including four murders – all of off-duty members of the security forces – including that of the milk tanker driver, and father of nine, Jack Scott back in 1979. His son, David, said: 'My father was murdered with the very weapon these men were found in possession of ... He [his father] was a hard-working, decent, ordinary man ... He wasn't sectarian, he wasn't involved in terrorism, he was known by many and liked by everyone he met. They came and got me in school to give me the news [that his father was dead] ... I was only fifteen.'

A former COP commander described the chilling effect the SAS had on PIRA in Tyrone: 'Their very presence made a difference as without doubt the IRA was afraid of them and thought they were everywhere. There were never very many of them and they carried out relatively few operations, but as far as the IRA was concerned they were in every hedgerow, waiting.'

Within the SAS itself there was intense debate, and not a little disquiet, about their involvement in Northern Ireland. Used to operating in warfighting scenarios governed by the international rules of the Geneva Convention and not the homegrown edicts of Westminster, the Regiment recognised the need for the rules of engagement they had to function under, but unsurprisingly found those same rules restrictive. A former SAS officer told the author John Parker that even as far back as 1976, 'A lot of the boys coming in from Dhofar [the campaign in Oman in the Middle East] left the Regiment and the Army. They said if this [Northern Ireland] was the future, forget it!' The same officer went further and said, 'We'd had one or two incidents which had come under close scrutiny and some criticism because the correct procedures hadn't been strictly followed.' His own summation of the SAS's time in Northern Ireland was dramatic: 'It [Northern Ireland] was never a happy hunting ground for the Regiment as such. It wasn't our scene.' That would've been news to East Tyrone PIRA.

Bad as Cloghog Road was for the Brigade, it was more than balanced out by one of those spectacular incidents that occurred intermittently during the war – the Maze break-out. The largest prison escape in UK history – inevitably immortalised by republicans as 'the Great Escape'; on 25 September 1983 some thirty-eight PIRA prisoners managed to flee from Block 7 using guns smuggled in beforehand. Sixteen were recaptured fairly quickly, but twenty-two got away. As was customary, on reporting back to the IRA the escapees were offered the choice of staying and continuing the war or taking the boat to the United States and the possibility of a new life. Much would hinge on their decisions. With years of experience between them, if they opted to stay then the Provisionals' war effort would receive a major boost. Among them was Tommy McKearney's brother, Pádraig. Three years into his sentence for weapons possession he didn't hesitate and chose to return to the war. As Lenin famously asserted 'insurrection is not a game to be played by amateurs', and McKearney's return would help usher in the most dramatic period in the life of the East Tyrone Brigade, filled with blood and death.

4

COMRADE MAO'S LIBERATED ZONES AND NORTHERN IRELAND

So far the war in Northern Ireland had been roughly one of two phases; first, there had been the initial surge of mass riots, shootings and bombings in the early 1970s which had failed to drive the British out in one massive push. The result was that PIRA had adopted Gerry Adams's Long War strategy, only to see it settle at a level that caused carnage but was ultimately containable by the security forces. Realising this, Adams and his long-time confidant, Martin McGuinness, had begun to explore the possibility of political options – albeit tentatively and extremely discreetly. Sinn Féin, the political wing of the republican movement and hitherto PIRA's junior partner in the struggle, would increasingly move centre stage, and – to the horror of many hard-liners – begin to gobble up more and more of what was still a limited pot of republican cash.

Pádraig McKearney was one of those hard-liners, and now he was out of the Maze he knew exactly what he wanted to do – defeat the Brits once and for all and win the war. The question was, how? He'd had plenty of time to think about the answer, not only during his incarceration but following the breakout when – according to the Dublin journalist Derek Dunne in his book *Out of the Maze* – he and seven other escapees stayed hidden under the living room floorboards of a safe house in the North for two weeks, even as the manhunt for them went on around them. Apparently the smell from their cramped living conditions grew so strong they were forced to pass out their socks to be washed to put any passing sniffer dogs off the scent, as it were. Once the initial search was called off, Pádraig went south to recuperate, before heading back north to the war and the East Tyrone Brigade, where he was welcomed with open arms by his old comrades. Prison hadn't mellowed McKearney. He still believed in a military solution to partition and he was still willing to pull a trigger. In his view there should be 'total war or no war at all'.

What prison had done was provide McKearney with the time and opportunity to broaden his education. The Maze was sometimes seen as something of a university for the prisoners incarcerated there, with many republicans spending their days learning the Irish language or taking courses in history, politics or even philosophy. McKearney – like his friend Jim Lynagh – had discovered a fascination with the writings of Mao Zedong. In particular he'd devoured the dead Chinese Communist leader's thinking on how to win a revolutionary war. When reunited with Lynagh, after the latter's release from Portlaoise gaol in April 1986, the two men would fuse much of

Mao's playbook with twentieth-century republican tactics and come up with the Liberated Zones strategy.

In the 1966 film *The Battle of Algiers*, about the war against the colonial authorities, a semi-fictional French para colonel, when asked by journalists, said that at some point the early terrorism phase of any insurgency leads to an armed insurrection and that was what he and his men had to stop at all costs. In Lynagh and McKearney's thinking, the time for armed insurrection in Northern Ireland was nigh. This was their 'third phase of the struggle' – what McKearney termed the 'strategic defensive'.

The strategy itself was relatively simple, as a senior IRA source told Ed Moloney: 'The idea was to take and hold areas in Armagh, Tyrone and Fermanagh, and to force the British either to use maximum force or to hold off.' This wasn't something new for republicanism. The IRA had done much the same back in the Anglo-Irish War, and the Border Campaign had been similar, as Francie Molloy told Peter Taylor: 'The Tyrone IRA would have been trying to do what Tom Barry's flying columns did [in Cork] in 1920–21.'

If the IRA could physically expunge the security presence from border areas it could become the *de facto* authority in those same areas. The only way this could be countered would be via a massive military reaction which would inevitably lead to civilian casualties, global media condemnation and a total transformation of the war in the Provisionals' favour. However, at that point in time McKearney wasn't in a position to turn his thinking into action – not yet.

In the meantime an old enemy of the East Tyrone Brigade stepped into the fray once more. It had been almost eight months since the deaths of Colm McGirr and Brian Campbell beside a Cloghog Road hedgerow, and now a nine-member SAS team from D Squadron was once again lying in wait for an ASU out on a job, this time the attempted fire-bombing of the Forbes kitchen factory in Ardboe. A tenth trooper – Soldier J – was with a waiting QRF from 1st Battalion The Queen's Regiment.

First to move up were Soldiers D and E who took up position as a cut-off on the Mullanhoe Road opposite the factory itself. It was 10.35 pm on 12 July 1984.

Half an hour later the rest of the SAS team moved into the area after being dropped off by van. Splitting into two groups, the troopers hunkered down and waited.

At just past one in the morning four armed men approached the factory. When they were thirty metres away Soldier A shouted a challenge. 'The man raised his hands up very fast. I believed he was going to shoot me so I fired one aimed shot at the centre of his body. I heard him scream.' The remaining three turned and fled. Two ran straight out onto Mullanhoe Road where the cut-off group was waiting. Soldier D shouted a warning: 'Stop or I'll fire!' One stopped and raised his hands, the other ran on and Soldier D opened fire. 'I thought he was going to escape so I took two quick aimed shots.' Terrified, the would-be escaper flung himself to the ground where he was arrested by Soldier E. Back in the field the other troopers were searching the area for the remaining two ASU members when Soldier A came across the man he had shot minutes earlier: '[he] made a sudden movement of his hands towards me.'[27] Soldier A fired and killed him. The fourth man had made good his escape.

The failed bombing was a major blow for the East Tyrone Brigade. Timed to coincide with the third anniversary of Martin Hurson's death on hunger strike, it left one volunteer – twenty-eight-year-old William Price – dead, and two others: Raymond Francis O'Neill and Thomas Quillan, in custody and facing nine years in jail. Two pistols were found near Price's body, one an old fashioned .455 Smith & Wesson revolver, along with more than one incendiary device. Price's sister later claimed that her brother's head had been blown apart like an eggshell, and republicans also claimed that O'Neill and Quillan were about to be executed by the SAS men when a local woman – Mrs Mary Forbes – leaned out of her window and shouted at them to stop. An IRA statement released at the time described how: 'When they [the ASU] got within twenty yards or so of the bushes, three to four figures rose in front of them, and suddenly the whole place lit up with gunfire. William Price fell moaning. The other volunteer crawled back through the long grass to make his escape. From the time William Price was shot and wounded to the time the other volunteer got out of the firing line, the shooting never stopped. Sometime after that shooting the other volunteers heard the SAS whooping hysterically like Indians in a Wild West film. A good three minutes after the firing, there seemed to be one shot and then a burst of shots.'

Price – the son of a former British Army soldier and five years a volunteer – was buried in his home village of Brockagh, his funeral becoming notorious as the first where the security forces tried to stop the IRA's usual military-style honours being paid.

That wasn't the last controversy to surround the whole drama. Some sixteen years later when the journalist Peter Taylor was interviewing people for his BBC 2 series on the Troubles, one interviewee – 'Anna', a member of the Det – described the immediate aftermath of the ambush: 'We celebrated, if you like, as the IRA would if they'd shot somebody. They made no secret of the fact that they celebrated the death of a soldier or a policeman, and they can be highly public about their celebrations. We celebrated in the same way. We went to the bar. We drank quite a lot. The cooks made us a cake … a cake with his [William Price's] name on it.' The BBC released a photograph of Price's cake which was in the form of a cross with RIP written in icing. When Taylor asked 'Anna' if she thought the celebration was macabre, she replied, 'Possibly, but the saying is "Live by the sword, die by the sword."'

For the security forces the operation was a great success. Soldier A was awarded the Military Medal, and it was clear the intelligence used to mount the ambush was first rate, with Soldier F at the subsequent inquest confirming that he and the team were briefed to expect a four-man ASU, that they would be armed and that the target was the Forbes factory. The fear of informers – ever present among PIRA ranks – reared its head again.

Not that all SAS operations were successful – far from it. Some three months later in mid-October, Special Branch received a tip-off that a three-man team from East Tyrone PIRA was going to kill an off-duty member of the UDR on the outskirts of Tamnamore village near Dungannon. The team would be led by Peter Sherry, aged twenty-six at the time, a renowned gunman nicknamed 'the Armalite Kid' and believed to be behind dozens of earlier attacks. Armed with good intelligence, an SAS team, which included the now-famous author and former special forces soldier Andy McNab, deployed early on the morning of 19 October to ambush the volunteers. It was a disaster. When the stolen yellow Ford van containing the PIRA men arrived, the SAS tried to block it in only for it to barge its way through in a hail of gunfire. At that moment forty-eight-year-old Frederick Jackson, a local businessman and married father of four, was just driving out of the Capper & Lamb Haulage Yard opposite the ambush site. He was hit in the crossfire. In great pain and losing a lot of blood, Jackson staggered out of his car and back into the yard where he collapsed. He later died in hospital. It was an SAS bullet which killed him. As for the ASU, despite being chased at breakneck speed they managed to evade their pursuers, ditch the van and escape on foot. The abandoned vehicle was found by the UDR in the follow-up operation: 'The Troop [nickname for the SAS contingent in Northern Ireland] told us they'd riddled it with bullets during the pursuit, but all we found was a couple of bullet holes through the passenger wing mirror – riddled my a**e!' It was not the Regiment's finest hour.

Having said that, Sherry may have been quite relieved when the Army Council ordered him over the water to England to carry out a major series of assassinations planned for 1985 – a campaign shelved after Sherry's arrest that June. In his absence the senior men in East Tyrone put their heads together and Patrick Kelly got the nod. A republican source described the process. 'Northern Command would have a say in who took over, you know, but it would've still been a local matter really. The boys knew and trusted Kelly, and so he got the job.'

Even though he was the Brigade commander during the most critical time in East Tyrone's war, Kelly has long been overshadowed, especially by Jim Lynagh. Not possessing the kind of charisma that was Lynagh's trademark, he wasn't idolised by the rank and file, neither was he regarded as a strategist like Pádraig McKearney, but a senior Tyrone republican is clear about him. 'Paddy Kelly knew what he was about. He was tough, and while he didn't have the same amount of military experience as Jim and Pádraig, those three were peas in a pod.' Indeed, Kelly and McKearney in particular formed a close bond, with the two men carrying out a host of gun attacks together from then on. As for the security forces, the former UDR officer Jay Nethercott thought Kelly was 'an evil b****d, downright evil' but conceded he was also 'an underestimated character, he was experienced, very determined and knew what he was doing'.

It would be Patrick Kelly – along with Pádraig McKearney – who would form a unit from amongst the ranks of the Brigade which would gain notoriety as the 'A Team' – named after the eponymous American TV action show.

At the team's core was a younger generation of volunteers drawn almost exclusively from the townlands of Cappagh and Galbally. Eugene Kelly was the oldest having been born in Galbally in July 1962. One of seven children, with two brothers and four sisters, Kelly had known Martin Hurson and was inspired to join the Provisionals after his friend's death on hunger strike. Wavy-haired and with something of a crooked smile, Kelly was suspected of involvement in the killing of a UDR solider and his workmate in Dungannon in 1984. A now-retired RUC officer serving in the Cappagh area at the time remembered Kelly: 'I stopped his father Mickey at a checkpoint and said, "Look, he's mixing with the wrong people, he's actively involved and I don't want to have to be the one to come tell you he's been arrested or worse, that you won't be seeing him again on this earth.'" It did little good. 'A few months later I stopped Mickey again and he told me he'd tried to speak to Eugene and had even offered to buy him a ticket to America, but he just wouldn't go.'

Just three months younger than Kelly, and from the same school year, was his best friend Tony Gormley. Known as 'Big Tony', Gormley was the second eldest of six children and lived on the same lane as the Hurson family, behind the Galbally Pearses Gaelic Athletic Association (GAA) Club. 'Big Tony was away in Australia earning a lot of money and doing well for himself, but with it all kicking off over here he came back and joined back up, he was mad for it,' according to a leading Tyrone republican. Gormley was also a childhood friend of Séamus Donnelly and Declan Arthurs. While Donnelly was born and raised in the hamlet of Aughnaskea, Galbally, the Arthurs' family farm was just outside Cappagh. There they raised cattle, pigs and chickens, and Declan, the third youngest of six and mad keen on anything with an engine, helped out on the farm, as did all his siblings, including his elder brother Brian who was already suspected of PIRA involvement. Their mother Amelia – when interviewed by Peter Taylor – told how she implored Declan not to join the IRA: 'What was his future? Life imprisonment? On the run? Or was he going to be killed? I knew his future wasn't going to be any good … I begged him, often I begged him, but to no avail.'

As for Séamus Donnelly, 'he was already considered a potential future leader in East Tyrone. He was always thinking, you know, always looking at jobs. He was young, but a serious volunteer'. He was also a regular at the GAA, and remembered as a good Gaelic footballer, although not as good as his friend Martin McCaughey. Indeed, McCaughey not only played for the Pearses but had been selected for the Tyrone Minor team, becoming something of a local sporting celebrity into the bargain. All of them, Kelly, Gormley, Arthurs, McCaughey and Donnelly – the youngest of the group having only been born in 1968 – knew each other, watched and played football together and travelled to the same local discos. As one British Army intelligence officer described, 'East Tyrone PIRA wasn't really a pyramid structure by that stage, it was dominated by individual ASUs which more and more resembled extended family circles.'

Not that everyone who hailed from Cappagh or Galbally was a diehard republican, as the 8 UDR soldier Dean McGucken remembered: 'initially we just saw the whole community as terrorists, but very soon our commanders taught us who the real threat was from, who the terrorists were, and out of the whole community probably only ten people were our real targets of interest. The rest of the community had to suffer them too … Cappagh was a PIRA stronghold … but we had more friends than enemies, although they could never be seen talking to us of course.'

McKearney and Lynagh weren't from Cappagh, of course, and neither was another member of the team who, age-wise, was more their contemporary – Gerard O'Callaghan. Only a couple of years younger than Lynagh, O'Callaghan had a partner and young child, had been arrested with McKearney back in 1980, was sent to prison and joined the blanket protest. On release he'd re-joined the war and reportedly became the A

Team's quartermaster, controlling the weapons and equipment they used.

Other volunteers were involved in their operations, of course – the A Team never acted alone – but what set these men apart was their willingness to carry a weapon, pull the trigger and kill. This was by no means a universal trait among PIRA volunteers, even in the East Tyrone Brigade. To fire a gun at another human being with the intention of killing them, often at close quarters, is a traumatic, life-changing experience, and the vast majority of people instinctively shy away from it. So, most volunteers would carry out non-lethal tasks such as being look-outs – 'dicking' as it was known – or acting as drivers or scouts. If they proved themselves capable and reliable, they might be asked to transport a weapon to or from a hide, or take part in the manufacture of homemade explosives, but relatively few were either asked – or were willing – to kill someone. Studies from a host of twentieth-century wars consistently report that as few as 10 per cent of combatants actively engage the enemy, with the rest opting to keep their heads down and just try and stay alive. The A Team were the 10 per cent, and in 1985 they would demonstrate exactly what they were capable of.

5

THE A TEAM

On 23 February 1985 a five-man PIRA ASU was waiting to ambush a British Army mobile patrol in west Tyrone, but when the patrol failed to materialise the operation was called off. Two of the volunteers headed home while the other three returned the weapons to a hide off the Plumbridge Road near Strabane. All three were then shot dead by the SAS. Two were brothers, Michael and David Devine, while the third was the local PIRA commander, Charles Breslin. Michael was an amateur snooker champion known locally as Bunty; his brother David was just seventeen years old. The police recovered an arsenal of weapons at the scene including three FN assault rifles and two grenade launchers.

Was an informer involved in the Strabane ambush? PIRA thought so, and in the autumn they dumped the lifeless body of twenty-year-old Damien McCrory at the side of the Drumrallagh Road outside the town. McCrory had been shot twice in the head. An IRA statement claimed the young Catholic had admitted he was the informer, something his family vehemently denied, saying it was well known that Damien was 'educationally subnormal' and had a learning disability.

The death of Charlie Breslin crippled West Tyrone PIRA, and while it didn't stop the Strabane–Castlederg area from remaining a hot bed of republican militancy – Strabane was still called 'the most bombed city in Europe' – it did see the local volunteers increasingly taking their lead from the East Tyrone Brigade. The ambush was also another reminder that as 1985 dawned, Britain's Special Forces were now very much a fact of life – and death – in Northern Ireland.

The response from the East Tyrone Brigade, and their allies in South Armagh, was an upsurge in violence. Just five days after the Strabane killings, on a wet Monday night, the Provisionals launched a devastating mortar attack on the Edward Street RUC station in Newry, County Armagh. The canteen – full of officers on a tea-break – received a direct hit. A survivor said, 'Nothing that I had ever been trained for or experienced could describe the scene I saw there. There were people dead and people in the process of dying. We tried to help one young woman who was lapsing in and out of consciousness. She lay there crying and saying nothing … She died soon afterwards.' She was one of two female officers who were killed alongside another seven of their male counterparts. In the aftermath of the attack most fingers were pointed at East Tyrone, whereas in truth it was 'a South Armagh job, along with Len "Hardbap" Hardy's Newry ASU', albeit all three PIRA units were coordinating their attacks to some extent.

In fact, at the time of the Newry attack, East Tyrone were busy using a fifty-yard-long command wire to detonate a bomb attached to a telegraph pole on the Cavanskeeran Road in Pomeroy. Intended for a passing 8 UDR foot patrol, Private Gary Patterson was wounded and thirty-six-year-old Private Trevor Harkness was killed in the blast. Brian Hamilton was the patrol commander: 'it was a night patrol ... the same night that the policemen were murdered in that mortar attack in Newry'. Plagued by bad communications Hamilton planned to patrol to Pomeroy's RUC station and try and sort the radios out: 'We were well spaced out; two men at the front, Melvin and myself in the middle and then Trevor and Gary bringing up the rear.' Melvin Marks then recalled, 'All I heard was "Bang!" and when I looked round all I could see was dust and smoke and bits of trees. Then it sort of cleared a bit and I could see Trevor lying on the ground. I tried to get a pulse but I got nothing.' Gary Patterson, dazed and in shock, was bleeding: 'the gas plug of Trevor's SLR [Army issue Self-Loading Rifle] sheared off, went up and cut the spinal cord at the back of his neck, then came straight across the road, went in through my left elbow, out again and into my ribcage'. The bombers quickly made good their escape: 'We heard and then saw a car speed off ... it went away so fast we could only see the taillights and in the dark we couldn't recognise the make and model. You couldn't risk firing a shot either just in case you hit somebody else.'[28] Newry grabbed the headlines: 'Trevor didn't even get a mention on the TV that night, not a word.'

Having made such an impact in Newry, South Armagh tried to replicate their success in June by launching a mortar attack on the hated Army/RUC base in the centre of Crossmaglen. Four mortars were fired but no-one was injured.

As for East Tyrone, Patrick Kelly and Pádraig McKearney

were keen to carry out the latter's liberated zones strategy, even if only a scaled-down version. Relatively quiet that summer, the volunteers were far from idle as they prepared for a winter campaign like no other. Their targets would be the network of small, isolated RUC stations scattered across rural Tyrone and Armagh, usually manned by between four to five officers and only open during the day.

There would be an element of co-ordination with the likes of South Armagh and West Tyrone, but it would be East Tyrone that would do the heavy lifting as they attempted to replicate the success the same strategy had achieved in the early days of the Anglo-Irish War.

However, almost as if by coincidence, starting in August 1985 the British Army began Operation Nicola. Under control of 20 and 33 Field Squadrons of the Royal Engineers, an upgrading of some thirty-five rural RUC stations was launched. The programme included strengthening defences with anti-rocket barriers and the hardening of roofs and blast walls. You could be forgiven for thinking the timing fortuitous for the security forces.

Nevertheless, Op Nicola was far from completed when the A Team began their offensive on Saturday, 7 December 1985 in the sleepy south Tyrone village of Ballygawley. Home to around 500 people – mostly Catholics – and close to the border, Kelly and McKearney selected the local RUC station as the perfect start point for their campaign. The plan was simple: a gun team would force their way into the station, killing any RUC officers they met, and then a second team would enter the building, scooping up any documents they could find for intelligence purposes, before planting a bomb. Once all the volunteers had gotten out, the bomb would be detonated and the station destroyed.

The attack began just before 7 pm that night and was described by the republican *IRIS Magazine*: 'One volunteer took up a position close to the front gate. Two RUC men opened the gate and the volunteer calmly stepped forward, shooting them both dead at point-blank range. Volunteers firing AK-47 and Armalite rifles moved into the barracks, raking it with gunfire. Having secured the building, they planted a 100lb bomb inside. The bomb exploded, totally destroying the building after the volunteers had withdrawn to safety.'

Timing was key. Seven pm was knock-off time for the five RUC officers on duty, and one of them – interviewed years later – remembered how he was in the locker room at the back of the station getting changed into his civilian clothes when he heard gunfire from the front of the building. Running out into the yard he saw a beer keg on the ground right in front of him and knew exactly what it was. Screaming at his colleagues to 'Run for it!', he then recalled, 'the whole place just erupted. The blast lifted me and threw me into a wall about fifteen feet away. I had great difficulty trying to breathe because all the air had been sucked out of me.' Everywhere was dark, the explosion having knocked out electricity to the whole village. Deafened and in shock he scrambled out of the rubble and saw 'Billy Clements. I lifted his head up to see if I could feel a pulse in his neck, but he was dead. Then we found George, covered in rubble. He was dead too.' The dead men were thirty-four-year-old Constable George Gilliland – Sammy Brush's saviour back in 1981 – and fifty-two-year-old reserve Constable William Clements. The remaining three

RUC officers were all wounded but survived. Clements's Ruger Security-Six revolver was nowhere to be found. A senior Tyrone republican later admitted that 'Pádraig [McKearney] took the short [nickname for a pistol, a 'long' was a rifle] off the dead copper and used it from then on.'

Tyrone PIRA were elated. The operation had been a huge success as one republican proudly recalled: 'Ballygawley was probably the best job the Brigade ever did. Everything went right, it was perfect.' The only failure in republican eyes was that three RUC officers had survived – they would need to rectify that in future attacks, and future attacks there would be, lots of them.

Just four days later, South Armagh mortared Tynan RUC station, wounding four officers. Nine days after that it was West Tyrone's turn to hit Castlederg. This time seven people were injured and 250 local families had to be evacuated as three of the six mortars failed to explode and had to be rendered safe. An RUC spokesman at the scene announced, 'We are awaiting reports from the ATOs [Army Technical Officers – bomb disposal] at the scene … It may be daylight before we know the full extent of the damage … In a situation like that you don't go around with a notebook making detailed damage assessments.' The Provos had once again attacked at 7 pm, hitting power lines and plunging the village into darkness. With typical gallows humour, soldiers in Castlederg joked that the base was in such a poor state of repair you couldn't tell if it had been mortared or not. 'The whole place was a mess. Our team were bunked together in an old Portacabin which had a hole down one end with a bucket below to catch the rain. There was muck and mould everywhere and it stank.' The month ended with one further mortar attack, this time on Carrickmore, as an RUC officer described to Colin Breen: 'it was all Portacabins at the time; there were no mortar proof bunkers in those days ... I was in the toilet ... then there was like a thump and a blinding flash and all the air was taken out of the room and I'm blown forward. This Mark-10 mortar had landed about five or six yards away ... the lights went out, I got up, p**s and s**t all over the place. I literally thought this was it, but luckily I wasn't badly hurt.'[29]

As presents were placed under trees and turkeys put into ovens, the East Tyrone Brigade could look back on the preceding year with a sense of satisfaction. They had launched their long-awaited liberated zones strategy – albeit watered down – and in just one month had destroyed or badly damaged three RUC stations, killing two policemen and wounding many more, while not losing a single volunteer. Surely 1986 would bring more good fortune and start turning the war decisively in the Provos' favour.

As for the security forces, the end of 1985 brought cold comfort. The RUC in particular had taken a beating, losing twenty-four of its officers across Northern Ireland, including one who was only an applicant at the time he was killed. They would have been even more downcast had they known that on top of everything else, the first of Gaddafi's promised arms shipments had been landed on the Clogga Strand in County Wicklow back in the autumn. Ten tonnes of arms, including crates of AK-47 assault rifles, pistols, hand grenades and ammunition, came ashore along with RPG-7 rocket launchers. The following month another shipment arrived, this time including a cache of Soviet-made DShK heavy machine guns capable of bringing down helicopters. By the following September there would be a total of five successful shipments, bringing in dozens of RPGs and DShKs, 2,000 AK-47s, hundreds of thousands of rounds of ammunition, and ten tons of the incredibly powerful Czech-made Semtex plastic explosive. From then on Semtex – impossible to detect – would form the basis of almost every bomb the IRA planted. But the icing on the cake was surface to air missiles – SAM-7s to be exact, helicopter killers. Gaddafi even threw in £2million in cash to help bankroll the organisation.

For the security forces January 1986 kicked off in the same depressing way that December 1985 had ended, with a rash of attacks across Tyrone; mortars were fired at the UDR base in Dungannon, and Coalisland RUC station was badly damaged by a large van bomb, but far worse was the death of off-duty UDR member Victor Foster on 15 January in Castlederg when he didn't check his car well enough and an Under Vehicle Booby Trap exploded, killing him. The following month it was Foster's UDR comrade Thomas Irwin's turn to be assassinated. Jay Nethercott recalled Irwin's death with bitter frustration: 'There was intelligence, good intelligence, that he was in danger, but he refused to wear body armour and refused the offer of a PPW [Personal Protection Weapon – a pistol]. For f***'s sake, he even gave us the wrong location of where he'd be working the next day.' As it was, Irwin – aged fifty-two, married with four children and a Department of the Environment employee at the Mountfield sewage works – was digging in a ditch with two other workmates a mere thirty yards from the main Omagh–Cookstown road, when a lone gunman calmly walked up and, at point-blank range, shot him dead. He then got into a getaway car and was driven off. Irwin's colleagues were left in shock, remembering afterwards that the gunman wasn't even wearing a mask.

By now the East Tyrone Brigade was recognised by the security forces as an extremely dangerous opponent: 'East Tyrone's reputation was growing and they were dangerous, no doubt about it.' Sir John Hermon, Chief Constable of the RUC at the time, said of the Brigade, '[they were] highly regarded in terms of their proficiency, capacity, [and] confidence'. Hermon was in a unique position to know, given he had been promoted back in 1957 to fill the vacancy left by the murder of Arty Ovens in Brackaville by Kevin Mallon.

However, fate was about to take a hand and radically alter the future of the Brigade. Since the split in republicanism back in 1969 that had created the Provisional IRA, primacy in the movement had always gone to the armed struggle, with politics a very distant second. But now that position had changed, as Tommy McKearney understood: 'By 1986 the IRA was firmly in the hands of former internees from Belfast who had been advocating entry into parliament since the late 1970s.' The roadblock these 'former internees' needed to remove so the IRA could progress politically, was called abstentionism. In essence abstentionism was Sinn Féin's policy not to take up seats the party might win in any parliament. It was a cornerstone of republican ideology and its importance could not be overstated. Now though, the Provisional leadership, dominated by Gerry Adams and Martin McGuinness, had decided to discard it and move politics onto at least an equal footing with the war. The formal decision was due to be taken at Sinn Féin's Ard Fheis (annual conference) in Dublin that

November, but first a secret General Army Convention (GAC – the IRA's supreme internal authority) was called in the spring to bring the volunteers on side before the leadership went public with the move.

Delegates from across PIRA made their way to the tiny village of Clontibret in County Monaghan, where the fateful discussions were due to take place. Among the audience were Patrick Kelly, Pádraig McKearney and Jim Lynagh – Lynagh having just been released from Portlaoise in April. Along with other hard-liners all three opposed the abandonment of abstentionism. Tommy McKearney described how they felt: 'they feared that the movement would, in time, fall into the hands of career-minded individuals ... they argued that once ambitious politicians gained the upper hand they would do any deal and accept any compromise in order to gain and retain office'. In particular, they dreaded the movement becoming totally dominated by those they disparagingly nicknamed 'long rifles' who were focused on 'politics rather than operations'. This was dangerous ground, but in the end the Tyrone men were outmanoeuvred. Kelly reportedly told Lynagh, 'We've been shafted.' As McKearney astutely recognised, 'they [Kelly, Lynagh, and Pádraig] realised with alarm that their own influence in the organisation ... was limited. Too late they had come to recognise that front-line fighting men may achieve a certain status, but those who remain safely back at base ... have an enormous advantage in a debate about tactics and strategy.' Abstentionism was duly dropped.

Having lost the political battle, East Tyrone PIRA went back to what they did best – the war. Lynagh was impressed by what Patrick Kelly and his old friend Pádraig McKearney had achieved whilst he was locked up in the Republic, but he was convinced they could do more, and – together with McKearney – approached Kevin McKenna as Chief of Staff with a proposal to create a 'flying column' very much in the mould of Tom Barry's campaign in the Tan War. What Lynagh and McKearney asked for was the men, weaponry and logistics to make it happen – which was tricky. First, on the manpower side they wanted between twenty and thirty handpicked volunteers who would live as full-time armed guerrillas. They would have their own weapons – the best PIRA had available – and permanent training bases deep in the Republic. They would also be independent from Northern Command to minimise the potential for leaks. Constantly on the move, the column would be PIRA's élite, and would have the authority to call on all other ASUs for support when required. Those same ASUs would carry out reconnaissance and prepare lists of possible targets for the column to attack. Lynagh and McKearney would then select three to five targets to hit in a year, with the emphasis being on so-called 'spectaculars' that would cause mass security force casualties.

The request gave McKenna a dilemma. On the one hand 'he felt a great deal of loyalty to his top men in Tyrone; Lynagh, McKearney and Kelly, they were his top boys, and they were loyal to him', but at the same time he thought the idea 'too impractical, too ambitious, and unsustainable'.

In the end McKenna said no. How much this refusal rankled with his top boys has been a source of controversy ever since, with several sources quoted as saying it caused serious friction between the IRA Chief of Staff and his home Brigade. 'McKenna tried to put Lynagh in one zone and McKearney in the other', said an associate; 'it was possibly an attempt to divide and conquer, to cause rivalry ... and the like'. Another source muddied the waters further, telling Ed Moloney that 'Pádraig and McKenna had never really got on ... Pádraig got the feeling McKenna would have liked to see him take the boat [head to the United States after the Maze escape]'.

The two ringleaders had no more luck over their request for more and better weaponry. Once again they were turned down flat.

What Lynagh and McKearney didn't know at the time was that an operation was underway which was intended to totally transform the IRA's war by providing a huge new arsenal of modern weapons, and significant funds to boot. While most of PIRA's early armoury was bought in the USA and then smuggled across the Atlantic, there had been some guns gifted to the Provisionals by the revolutionary Libyan Arab dictator, Muammar Gaddafi. But by late 1984 – impressed by the dedication of the hunger strikers and always keen to foment discord in the democracies of the West – Gaddafi had agreed to provide PIRA with a treasure trove the like of which it had only dreamed, including tonnes of high explosives, heavy machine guns and surface-to-air missiles. Shrouded in secrecy, Kevin McKenna was privy to the plan along with a handful of others. The question was what to do with this bounty from the desert. The answer was the so-called 'Tet Offensive'.

Back in 1968 at the height of the Vietnam War, the communist regime of North Vietnam had launched a massive all-out campaign across the South during the annual Tet festivities, which – although it failed to achieve military victory over the Americans and their South Vietnamese allies

– succeeded in persuading the American public that the war couldn't be won. It was the turning point in the conflict and paved the way for the North's future triumph and reunification of the peninsula. Little wonder then that it held such fascination for the Provisionals. This was what those in the know at the top of the IRA wanted to emulate, but the key was surprise. If the IRA could use the new weapons to shoot down a host of helicopters and cause mass casualties among the security forces then the British would be paralysed and the initiative would shift in favour of the Provisionals. With such a prize in mind there was no chance the powers-that-be were going to agree to switch the new weaponry to Lynagh and McKearney's flying column concept instead.

Their big idea rebuffed, Lynagh and McKearney reconciled themselves to continuing their campaign in Tyrone. Having destroyed or damaged several RUC stations, the next phase of the plan was to stop them being repaired or rebuilt. Those sorts of jobs were usually done by local civilian building firms who tendered for the work like any other government contract, and the biggest of the lot was Henry Brothers. Only set up in 1985, the firm had drawn on the huge experience in the building trade of its co-founders, the brothers Jim and Harold Henry, to specialise in work for the security forces. Getting paid two to three times the going rate, the firm had grown quickly, relying on labour from outside republican areas with workers bussed to and from jobs. As far as East Tyrone were concerned that made them targets, and the Army Council agreed, declaring, 'we are of the opinion that the contractors involved are assisting the British in reinforcing their illegal and immoral presence'. The softest of soft targets, the first contractor to be killed had been forty-six-year-old Seamus McAvoy from Coalisland. A supplier of mobile offices to the RUC, McAvoy was a Catholic and was shot dead at his second home in Dublin. Two days later on 22 August 1985 it was the turn of Daniel Mallon. Mistaken for a well-known local contractor, the sixty-five-year-old Catholic was gunned down in The Railway Bar in Strabane while enjoying a drink. Now, a year later, another pub became a murder scene, this time McCullagh's Bar in Greencastle, where forty-year-old John Kyle was shot dead on 30 July. The publican remembered the attack: 'You wouldn't believe how quickly it happened; the customers were watching the racing on TV and some stranger just walked in, opened fire and then disappeared.'

But it was the Henry brothers that East Tyrone really wanted, and they weren't alone. With the firm based just over the border in neighbouring County Londonderry, the Derry Brigade were keen to get in on the act and were happy to work with their southern neighbours in carrying out attacks. Three months after John Kyle's murder, PIRA made their move as Jim Henry's car sat on the roadside in Magherafelt. Two men on a motorcycle pulled up next to the parked car and the pillion passenger opened fired. There were actually two men in the car – neither was Jim Henry: 'I heard a shot and looked over and saw that the driver's window had been smashed and that Ken had been shot. I then heard, I think, three more shots and I knew I'd been hit as well. When I looked at Ken I knew he was dead.' The dead man was Jim Henry's shop manager, Kenneth Johnston. Johnston had borrowed his boss's car to take a sales rep to lunch. The rep, hit in the nose and right side, managed to sound the horn to summon help as the gunman sped off on the back of the motorcycle. Forensics proved that Thomas Irwin, John Kyle and Ken Johnston were all killed by Billy Clements's Ruger revolver.

In between these killings, the A Team would repeat their Ballygawley operation, only this time with a few upgrades.

Their target was the RUC station at the Birches, a small village about six miles northwest of Portadown in County Armagh. The operation itself was a complex one involving several teams. One team hijacked a number of cars in the Washing Bay area, east of Dungannon, to act as scout vehicles and transport the shooters to and from the job. In a significant change from Ballygawley the hijack team also stole a JCB digger. This time the bomb wouldn't be in a beer keg but would instead be loaded into the digger's bucket and driven through the security fence and right up to the very doors of the station. Declan Arthurs – having used a digger on his family's farm – would drive the JCB and then light the bomb fuse. The shooters would rake the station with gunfire before the bomb exploded, although as the attack was going to be mounted when the station was unmanned they didn't anticipate killing anyone. Last, but not least, another team were tasked with staging a bomb attack in Pomeroy as a diversion to draw away the security forces. A senior republican source confirmed that 'Yes, Declan Arthurs was at the Birches, and Gormley, Donnelly and O'Callaghan were all on the Pomeroy diversion attack.'

All in all around thirty-five volunteers were involved in the operation, the majority of the Brigade in fact. One volunteer who apparently wasn't involved was Pádraig McKearney. On McKenna's orders McKearney was stood down: '[Pádraig was] excluded from the attack on the Birches ... it was like McKenna was trying to tell the others they didn't need Pádraig.' Without him, it was Patrick Kelly who planned and led the operation in partnership with Jim Lynagh.

On Monday, 11 August the op was a go and the individual teams went about their tasks. Arriving on the scene the gun team debussed from their vehicles and raked the empty station with automatic fire. Declan Arthurs then crashed the digger through the high-wire perimeter fence and drove it up to the station wall. Lighting the fuse, Arthurs then ran back through the newly made gap in the fence and he and all the other volunteers made good their escape in the getaway cars. When the 200lb bomb exploded the blast destroyed most of the station, damaged some nearby buildings and even blew the roof off a bar across the road. Six locals and a disabled American tourist visiting at the time were injured – none seriously.

Once again, the A Team's plan had worked like clockwork. The digger idea had been a success, everyone had gotten away, and another RUC station lay in ruins.

The second year of East Tyrone's liberated zones campaign had seen the Brigade continue its attacks on vulnerable RUC stations, and then broaden out into targeting the civilian contractors the State needed to rebuild them. *An Phoblacht* attributed nearly a quarter of all IRA operations in 1986 to Kelly and his men.

As one security force source acknowledged, 'South Armagh was still the most dangerous lot the Provisionals had, but East Tyrone weren't far behind.'

6

LOUGHGALL

He looked around at the cold bare walls, the faded paint only
just covering the brickwork underneath. Lying on the hard
bunk he tried to doze off, hoping the Peelers would see him
asleep and think how unconcerned he was with their bully
boy tactics. But he couldn't sleep, despite being exhausted by
the endless rounds of questions they hammered at him again
and again. Like all volunteers he'd read the *Green Book* (the
IRA's internal manual) and knew the drill: 'remain COOL,
COLLECTED, CALM, and SAY NOTHING'. After all this
wasn't his first time in Gough Barracks, and it probably
wouldn't be his last either. He almost smiled to himself – soon
enough he'd be out, back on the farm and behind the wheel
of his beloved digger, and then another op. It'd be good to see
the boys again. It was January 1987 and Declan Arthurs was
twenty-one years old.

He'd end up spending almost the entire month in a cell
in Gough Barracks, being held for seven days' questioning,
released without charge, detained again a couple of days later,

held for seven days' questioning, released without charge and so on. It was the kind of conveyor-belt approach the RUC had perfected in Castlereagh interrogation centre back in the 1970s, the seven-day detentions in particular breaking volunteer after volunteer and peppering the IRA with informers. Back then, it had almost destroyed the organisation, its ranks so riddled with touts that Gerry Adams's ASU-cell strategy was seized on in desperation. Better recruit selection and training had turned the tide, aided by the ruthlessness of the newly created Nutting Squad, whose gruesome methods were only whispered about in hushed tones and put the fear of God into anyone tempted to talk to Special Branch. But talk they still did, and the IRA was paranoid about them. But East Tyrone – just like their next-door neighbours in South Armagh – were proving tough to crack, as the RUC Chief Constable opined: 'the East Tyrone Brigade was renowned for its difficulty to penetrate'. A security review at the time echoed RUC Chief Constable Hermon's opinion: 'East Tyrone PIRA is … particularly secure [from penetration].' Dramatic events in 1987 would, however, test that premise to breaking point.

Monday, 26 January 1987 was bin day on Coalisland Road, Dungannon. The weather was mild but grey, an overcast sky glowering down on wet fields and damp streets. George Shaw was taking his bins to the bottom of the drive to leave them for collection. It was around 8.30 in the morning. As he reached the pavement, two gunmen hidden in a hedge opposite opened fire. Shaw was hit in the head and body. Hearing the shots his wife went outside and saw her husband lying on the ground. Along with a female neighbour she ran to help him. 'He was still conscious and trying to speak [to his wife] but he couldn't talk as he was choking on his own blood.' Shaw was fifty-seven years old, a father of two and a major in the UDR. The East Tyrone Brigade had claimed its first victim of the year.

Their second was another off-duty UDR soldier, Corporal Jimmy Oldman – this time in a joint attack with members of the neighbouring Fermanagh Brigade. Oldman was the manager of Jones's Hardware Shop in Ederney, County Fermanagh, and had given a lift into town to his twelve-year-old niece, Caroline Bratton, so she could catch the bus to school. After pulling up outside Jones's on Market Street, at around 8 am, at least two gunmen came up behind his car and opened fire through the rear windscreen. Hitting Oldman, the gunmen then ordered a terrified Caroline out of the car before finishing off their target with another burst of fire as he sat bleeding in the driver's seat. Having held hostage the family who owned and ran the fish and chip shop across the road all the previous night, the gun team made their escape in the family's Vauxhall Cavalier.

The killing marked a change in the Brigade's behaviour. Previously, its volunteers had been happy to co-operate with their neighbours on one-off operations depending on what was needed and when, but on an invitation-only basis. Fermanagh, however, was another brigade's area, and its leader, Séamus McElwaine, was ferociously independent. Having become OC Fermanagh Brigade at just nineteen, McElwaine had turned it into a lethal unit, more often than not leading operations himself. A friend of Lynagh, McKearney and Patrick Kelly, he was eventually shot dead in an SAS ambush near Rosslea on 26 April 1986. His death shattered the Brigade, leaving a gap into which the A Team moved, the county becoming part of their growing empire.

The A Team didn't stop in Fermanagh either. Eighteen days after killing Corporal Oldman, its members were in the small village of the Loup, near Moneymore in County Londonderry – they were after one of the Henry brothers again. At 11 pm on 21 April, fifty-two-year-old Harold Henry was at home watching TV when the doorbell rang. Opening the door Harold was confronted by five balaclava-clad gunmen. After demanding the keys to his car the gunmen smashed the house phone and ordered their captive outside into the backyard. There he was told to stand up against the wall and killed in a hail of gunfire. Just as with John Kyle and Ken Johnston the previous year, the A Team's strategy of targeting those who would rebuild the likes of Ballygawley and the Birches had claimed another victim. Harold's brother Jim raged, 'the IRA are murderers. You couldn't call them anything else. It took five of them to take my brother Harry out and blow the head off him.' East Tyrone would shrug off Jim Henry's anger but what they couldn't shrug off was that killing his brother didn't have the desired effect: 'We've worked for the security forces and kept working for them and we intend to go on working for them.' A fortnight before Christmas 1988 PIRA would try again, this time hitting Jim Henry in his fortress-like compound with mortars – they missed and Henry Brothers continued to work for the security forces.

In between killing Oldman and Harry Henry, the A Team were busy on their home patch too. Glen Espie – having recovered from the wounds he suffered in Ardboe in 1978 – was back with 8 UDR and now lived with his family east of

Cookstown on the family farm. He was still a plumber with the Housing Executive and every morning he would get into his car, head down the drive and turn west into town. He'd practised anti-ambush drills and kept his hedges short so he could see if anyone was waiting for him, and 'I'd changed and upgraded my protection weapon to a semi-automatic pistol with a magazine able to hold more ammunition than the revolver.' On the morning of 19 March he went through his usual routine, checking his car for a UVBT before heading to work. He'd barely left his driveway when a car appeared in front of him and screeched to a halt, blocking the road. 'There were three people in the car, all wearing balaclavas, and I thought … not again … Two gunmen got out of the car armed with G3 7.62mm assault rifles and opened fire, just two or three lengths away from me. My car vibrated from the bursts of automatic fire hitting it.'

Remembering his drills Espie dived out of his car and into the drainage ditch next to the road, firing at his attackers as he went: 'Linford Christie [British Olympic medal-winning sprinter] couldn't have done it any faster.' One of the gunmen seemed to disappear when Espie fired back and 'took no further part in the attack', and the driver stayed glued to his seat, but as for the other man, 'he was wearing a German Army-style parka – it was cold that morning – I could see his trousers tucked into the top of his boots and it was obvious he'd done this before and wasn't going to stop.' The two men were only about ten to fifteen metres apart and automatic fire was 'tearing up the ground around me, lifting sods of grass and throwing dirt in my face'. Espie remembered looking into his assailant's eyes and 'seeing nothing, no sign of any feelings, any humanity' and he also remembered thinking that 'never in my life before or after have I ever wanted to kill another person so much'. Then, 'the gunman yelled into the car, fired one more burst at me and slid into the front passenger seat as they drove off'. Espie fired one more round at the now speeding car before getting back into his own vehicle and heading into town to alert the security forces. He'd been shot in the left arm and his wrist was shattered. 'I was in pain, terrible pain from the gunshot wounds. By God it hurt.'

Just as with the attack on Jimmy Oldman and so many others, the PIRA team had taken over a nearby house the previous night – this time Espie's neighbours the Croziers – and held the family hostage until they were ready to go. Espie was later told by Fred Crozier, 'at daybreak on the morning of the attack they overheard the gun team leader discussing my routine: "the curtains will be opened and Glen will scan the area from his house. Then he'll go outside, check the car and go back inside."' It was clearly a carefully planned operation, even down to the fact that the car the gun team had hijacked from a family in Ardboe to use on the job was the same colour Ford Orion as another one of Espie's neighbours, so as not to arouse suspicion. But even with all that planning it hadn't worked. Marion Espie – Glen's wife – breathed a huge sigh of relief when her husband agreed they should move house and he was later medically discharged from the UDR. What she was less pleased about was the police follow-up to the attack. 'It was a year before they interviewed me – a year! The gun that was used … had been used previously to shoot Harry Henry. I think it was Lynagh's.' For once though, it seems Lynagh wasn't involved, as a security force source made clear: 'the main gunman that day was Patrick Kelly, and the other was almost certainly Pádraig McKearney'.

However, Marion Espie had inadvertently stumbled onto an increasing feature of East Tyrone's operations – their members' preference for the same weapons. In the British Army it's standard procedure that each soldier has their own personal weapon. It is registered in the armoury as theirs and they are responsible for its use and maintenance. The same was increasingly the case for PIRA ASUs. Individual gunmen would want to use the same weapon again and again as they knew how it worked, what its characteristics were and whether it could be relied on. More and more, individual guns were becoming the personal firearms of the men who used them. Loughgall would prove just how true this now was.

Undismayed by the failure of their attack on Glen Espie, the A Team sought another target and happened on William Graham. A forty-four-year-old member of the UDR, Graham was working in the yard of his farm off the Gortscraheen Road near Pomeroy when two masked men armed with assault rifles – probably the same two volunteers from the Espie attack – walked up behind him. His wife – looking out of the kitchen window at the time – screamed a warning to her husband, but it was too late. The gunmen opened fire, shooting him in the back. The two of them then finished him off as he lay on the ground. They fired at least nineteen times.

That same day – 25 April 1987 – the South Armagh Brigade were even busier. Maurice and Cecily Gibson were returning home from holiday when they were blown up by a bomb hidden in a parked car as they crossed from the Republic into

Northern Ireland. Maurice Gibson was the Chief Justice and second most senior judge in the North. Coming hard on the heels of the firing squad-type murder of Harold Henry, the killings shocked the British government and increased their determination to hit back at the Provisionals. They wouldn't have long to wait.

Understanding Loughgall does not automatically mean you understand East Tyrone PIRA and what happened to it, but it's impossible to understand without it. By 1987 the armed struggle was at something of a stalemate. The initially chaotic nature of the security forces' approach had become far more streamlined and professional as Special Branch's star rose, and innovations such as the creation of the Tasking and Co-ordinating Groups (known as TCGs) began to come into their own. The IRA's Army Council had also come to realise that large-scale attacks weren't a viable option in the cities, partly due to the possibility of accidental civilian deaths that would harden their own community against them, with the likes of Adams and McGuinness knowing only too well Mao's maxim that 'the guerrilla must move amongst the people as a fish swims in the sea'. The best place, therefore, where PIRA could cause the security forces mass casualties without jeopardising their own supporters, was out in the countryside. McKearney and Lynagh instinctively understood that and were determined to break the deadlock with their liberated zones strategy. A senior Tyrone republican recalled how 'the word from Belfast was push, push, push for military targets'. That meant either South Armagh or East Tyrone. The Gibson killings had shown just how deadly the former was, but East Tyrone had the A Team as the Belfast leadership appreciated: 'They knew we had the boys to do it so it naturally fell to us.' They'd demonstrated what they could do at Ballygawley and the Birches, and now it was the turn of a sleepy little village in the heart of north Armagh's orchard country, Loughgall.

Back in February 1921, at the height of the Anglo-Irish War, the twenty men who comprised Diarmuid O'Hurley's 4th Battalion, 1st Cork Brigade of the IRA, were holed up in a disused farmhouse next to the village of Clonmult in County Cork. Taken by surprise, and surrounded by troops from the Hampshire Regiment and the RIC, twelve IRA men were killed, four were wounded and four captured. The unit was wiped out in what was the largest single loss of life in the IRA's history. So traumatic was the incident for republicans that a memorial now stands on the site to commemorate the event. Loughgall was to become the second largest loss of life the IRA ever suffered, and its impact was to be far greater.

Loughgall is a pretty village; it takes its name from a small nearby loch and its houses and their well-ordered gardens are surrounded by the orchards celebrating its heritage as an area settled in the Plantation by fruit farmers from Worcestershire's Vale of Evesham. Its population in 1987 of around 350 were mostly Protestants, and it holds a treasured place in the unionist lexicon as the site of the founding of the Orange Society – soon renamed the Orange Order – back in 1795 after a vicious little fight nearby between Catholic Defenders and Protestant Peep-o'-Day Boys which left some thirty people dead at the so-called Battle of the Diamond. It had so far been left unscathed by the war, its small two-storey RUC station only manned part-time for a few hours a day by three officers and left empty at night. It was a perfect target for the A Team.

This time round the plan was subtlety different from both Ballygawley and the Birches. The digger idea, having worked well at the latter, was going to be employed once more, and there'd be a split between the gun and bomb teams, but this time there'd be no diversionary attack to draw away the security forces. This would mean far fewer volunteers would be involved, down from thirty-five to around fifteen, which would improve security – or so it was thought. Last, but definitely not least, the team intended to kill the officers manning the station – this would be no bloodless Birches. This last point is one of a host of controversies about Loughgall, with the likes of Tim Pat Coogan insisting that the timing of the attack – at around its 7 pm closing time – clearly indicated the objective was to destroy the base without causing loss of life. However, the *Irish News* reporter Connla Young interviewed a source on the thirtieth anniversary in May 2017 who admitted he'd been involved in the attack as a scout and was thereafter referred to in the piece as Scout One: 'The point of the operation was to get in before they [the RUC officers] left, to take them out.' This flatly contradicts the assertion that the building itself was the only target, and chimes with the fact that the Ballygawley attack was planned for the same witching hour – knocking-off time – when the station's crew would be at their most vulnerable.

As East Tyrone PIRA made its preparations, intelligence for the attack was key, and as Lynagh thought Northern Command leaked like a sieve, he insisted the Brigade do its own information gathering. This was a big breach of IRA rules. Only the previous year the Army Council had stipulated that all operations of any significance had to be cleared by Northern

Command to avoid the sort of PR disasters the movement had recently suffered. Lynagh got his way. 'Liam Ryan did the intelligence work for Loughgall,' stated Connla Young's source. Born in Ardboe in 1950, Liam Ryan had emigrated to the USA in his youth, settling amongst the large Irish American community in the Bronx in New York. There, he got a good job with a power company – Con Edison – and rented an apartment near Gaelic Park, from where he applied for, and was granted, dual US citizenship. He also became involved in supporting the IRA back home through the Irish Northern Aid Committee (NORAID) and the Tyrone-dominated Clan na Gael, both of which raised funds to send to republicans in Northern Ireland. More involved than most, Ryan was arrested in 1985 by the American authorities for using forged documents to buy three Armalite rifles to smuggle to the IRA. He received a suspended sentence. He'd moved back to the North a short while later, buying the Battery Bar in his native Ardboe, a functional rather than pretty watering hole, yards from the shore of Lough Neagh. Related to several East Tyrone PIRA members – Michael 'Pete' Ryan was a cousin – he fitted seamlessly into the Brigade and by 1987 was the unit's Intelligence Officer (IO). He confirmed to the A Team that Loughgall station was open for four hours a day, from 9 am to 11 am and then again from 5 pm to 7 pm. There was one police car at the station and at closing time the three officers took turns changing into civilian clothes before locking up and heading home. As was usual, the station was surrounded by a high-wire fence intended to protect it from rocks, petrol bombs and RPGs, but that would be no barrier to the weight and heft of a JCB digger.

Kevin Mallon – East Tyrone PIRA's Brigade Commander for much of the 1970s and a man revered by most of his men.

Kevin McKenna (standing) gives a speech at the annual republican gathering in Carrickmore, Easter 1975. (Courtesy of *An Phoblacht*)

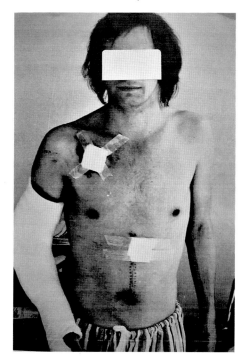

Noddie, an Operator in 14 Intelligence Company, in Dungannon hospital after being shot eight times by East Tyrone PIRA during a stakeout in 1979.

The funeral of the hunger striker Martin Hurson in Cappagh, 1981.

Left: The first two East Tyrone Brigade volunteers to be killed by the SAS; on the left Colm McGirr and on the right Brian Campbell, both shot dead near Coalisland in December 1983.

Below: Close-up of the 'A Team's' HiAce van with metal rods pushed through the bullet holes in its riddled side. The windscreen also shows multiple bullet holes.

Aerial view of the aftermath of the Loughgall attack. The RUC station is partially demolished and the JCB digger has been almost vaporised.

The A Team, clockwise from top left: Padraig McKearney, Tony Gormley, Jim Lynagh, Patrick Kelly (East Tyrone Brigade OC), Eugene Kelly, Seamus Donnelly, Gerard O'Callaghan and Declan Arthurs.

Loughgall today; the RUC station was on the left and has now been demolished and replaced by mews houses.

Sinn Féin President Gerry Adams helps carry the coffin of Patrick Kelly at his funeral, 1987.

Aftermath of the Ballygawley bus bombing in 1988 that killed eight soldiers from the Light Infantry. (Courtesy of *News Letter* archive)

Cordon around the site of the Drumnakilly ambush.

The Mid-Tyrone ASU wiped out at Drumnakilly. From left: Brian Mullin, Gerard Harte (OC), and his younger brother Martin Harte.

Dessie Grew (left), one of East Tyrone PIRA's most experienced volunteers, and Martin McCaughey from Cappagh.

The four men shot dead by Mid-Ulster UVF during the attack on Boyles Bar in Cappagh. From left: PIRA volunteers Dwayne O'Donnell, John Quinn and Malcolm Nugent, and innocent bystander Thomas Armstrong.

British soldiers cordon off the car park of Boyles Bar in Cappagh in 1991 following the UVF gun attack. The ASU's car can be seen with its shot-in back window.

Billy 'King Rat' Wright was OC of the UVF's Mid-Ulster Brigade and led a sustained campaign against the East Tyrone PIRA. (Courtesy of PA Images/ Alamy Stock Photo)

Above: The funeral of the East Tyrone volunteer Lawrence McNally in 1991 following his death in an SAS ambush in the village of Coagh.

Right: One of the East Tyrone Brigade's most experienced volunteers, Michael 'Pete' Ryan.

The car park of St Patrick's RC church in Clonoe the morning after the SAS ambush that killed four East Tyrone volunteers in 1992. The truck they used in their unsuccessful attack on Coalisland RUC station can be seen on the far right.

Above: The Coalisland ASU killed at Clonoe. From left: Peter Clancy, Kevin Barry O'Donnell, Sean O'Farrell and Patrick Vincent.

Left: Mark 15 PIRA homemade mortar on the back of a tractor used by East Tyrone Brigade to attack Aughnacloy Permanent Vehicle Check Point in 1994.

Below: The vz.58 assault rifle used by Mid-Ulster UVF to murder Roseanne Mallon – among several others – after its discovery by 1 Royal Anglian on the Mullycar road, Greystone, in May 1994.

The digger, however, was something of a double-edged sword. It would necessarily have to be stolen locally, and once reported as such there could be only two reasonable conclusions for the RUC to draw; it was either being driven south across the border to be sold, or it was going to be used in an attack like the Birches. If a digger was stolen in north Armagh the distance to the border was too great for simple theft to be likely; therefore, it would raise a red flag that an attack somewhere nearby was imminent. Reportedly, a PIRA reconnaissance team doing a scout of the area – and specifically looking for possible diggers – used a traced vehicle and then broke down. As something of an unusual event, a note of the registration plate was made and fed into the Vengeful system, immediately flagging the car as owned by a suspect living in Monaghan. To those involved on the intelligence-gathering side of the security forces this was of great interest. As one Army intelligence officer who served in Tyrone explained: 'There were Army LOs [Liaison Officers] based in the bigger RUC stations but we got next to nothing from them, but in my Int Cell [Intelligence Cell typically manned by one officer, two to three senior NCOs and a platoon of junior NCOs and soldiers] I had an RUC LO who was very knowledgable and who would really provide the bulk of intelligence. His local knowledge was such that when we'd get maybe a couple of hundred plate checks a day he'd skim through them in two minutes and be able to pick out which few were useful: "Oh, so he was there was he, interesting."'Most of the time titbits such as this led to nothing, but a picture was beginning to build up.

Back with the A Team, Friday, 8 May was set as the target day. Just which team members knew what beforehand is open to conjecture. Patrick Kelly as the Brigade OC was the man who would ultimately give the go-ahead or not, and it is inconceivable that Jim Lynagh and Pádraig McKearney wouldn't have been in on the plan – McKearney not having been excluded this time as he supposedly was at the Birches. If Gerry O'Callaghan was acting as the team's Quartermaster, he would have been let in on it all as well, as he would need to arrange for the team's usual weapons to be collected from their hides and brought to the embussing point, preferably not too far from the target to minimise the chances of running into a random vehicle check point on the way. Whosoever was slated to drive the digger would almost certainly need advance warning so they could familiarise themselves with the route they'd have to drive, and on that point several sources agree that Declan Arthurs was a late addition to the roster, as the preferred driver was unavailable. Declan had been On-The-Run in Monaghan Town since late January, early February, after narrowly escaping being caught on an operation, and so was ready to go. The SB's John Shackles had no problem with that decision: 'It suited us that Declan was brought in … it meant that after the operation that [decision] just pointed the finger at the man who was supposed to be there.' How much Eugene Kelly, Seamus Donnelly and Tony Gormley knew and when is debatable, with some PIRA sources allegedly stating they were only told of the impending operation the morning of the attack, although this would seem improbable. Most of these men had grown up together, and by now all of them had been on multiple operations as a team and never once been compromised, so it was reasonable for them to assume there'd be no leaks, and therefore everyone could be thoroughly briefed in good time.

On the other side, Operation Judy – as it was codenamed – was in full swing. For obvious reasons the full intelligence picture the security forces had at the time has never been revealed, but it appears that there were a number of sources coming together to create an actionable picture, this included SIGINT (signals intelligence) such as information from the bugging of suspects' homes, as well as HUMINT (human intelligence) i.e. from informers, and the 'jarking' of IRA 'gear' – weapons and explosives, 'jarking' being the placing of tiny tracking devices onto PIRA armaments enabling the security forces to see a weapon move from hide to hide, giving away locations, personnel and methods of transportation until the time was considered right to intervene. 'Noddy' from 14 Company explained how it was done: 'A green army patrol, or whatever, would find a hide and not give the game away to the Provos. Then it would radio it in and if it seemed suitable we'd be tasked with going in and setting up a covert OP to watch it. Next thing a guy – someone specially trained – would be sent over from London, you know, and they'd tip up and jark whatever was in the hide while we covered them. Then, when the job was done, we'd all move out and that was our bit finished.' For Op Judy it's been reported that the digger bomb – manufactured in the Ardboe area from Semtex previously stored near Coalisland – was jarked and under surveillance by the likes of 14 Company and the RUC's covert E4A squad, although other reports say it was the team's guns which were being watched. Whatever the truth, as a former SB officer intimately involved with the operation said, 'we knew lots, most of it really, but we didn't know it all'.

It was clear that Judy had been in play for quite some

time, although reports that it had been up and running for five weeks or more beforehand seem far-fetched. However, the biggest issue the security forces faced was confirmation of exactly which RUC station was the intended target, and when it was going to be hit. Despite republican fears to the contrary, there simply weren't enough SAS troopers to cover a plethora of possible objectives, nor could a sizeable operation be kept in place for any length of time without risking compromise. 'James Rennie' – the pseudonym of a former 14 Company member – wrote, 'we'd become aware of a terrorist plan to attack a police station ... although we understood the outline plan, we lacked the fine detail.' So, did an informer provide those key pieces of information? Tommy McKearney believed it likely: 'by the mid-1980s the British government's intelligence agencies had heavily penetrated the IRA.' A retired SB officer was more prosaic: 'When we saw Ballygawley, then the Birches and the pattern from then on, we could narrow it down; we could even sow the seed, you know, push them towards Loughgall, and we did.'

Whatever the truth, at least two days before the attack the security forces knew the target was Loughgall, they knew who was going to be involved and they knew roughly when it was going to be hit. Interviewed by Peter Taylor, 'Matt', another SB officer, was himself part of the security force plan: 'We were briefed on personalities ... We knew they were a lethal unit and a ruthless outfit of PIRA.' Dropped off during the hours of darkness on the night of Thursday, 7 May, 'Matt' and two other SB volunteers silently made their way into the station along with six SAS troopers 'led by one of the Regiment's most experienced senior NCOs'. Once in, they made themselves as comfortable as possible; they'd brought sandwiches and sleeping bags and there was tea and coffee in the station kitchen. A sentry roster had been agreed – 'stag' as the military terms it – and those off duty got their heads down to grab some shut eye. 'Matt' and his comrades would play a vital part in making Judy a success; they would take the place of the usual RUC staff, so protecting them from possible harm, while acting like normal policemen during the day and allaying any suspicions PIRA might have when they made their inevitable pre-attack reconnaissance. They would be bait of course, but 'Matt' was remarkably sanguine about it. 'I knew there was danger. Every tasking we were on was a danger. But I took it in my stride, followed my orders, and was quite happy to do so.'

With the main team safely ensconced in the RUC station, a cordon composed of Det operators, deployed in vehicles covering all the approach roads, was set some three to four miles out. 'Anna' – also at the Willie Price ambush – was one of the operators involved. All she knew beforehand was that the RUC station was probably going to be attacked at some point by a heavily armed PIRA unit travelling by vehicle and they had to give as much warning as possible. Apart from that she could only guess.

The exact whereabouts of all members of the PIRA team in the run up to the operation is disputed. The majority just went about their everyday lives, but things were different for Jim Lynagh, Pádraig McKearney and Declan Arthurs. Both the former were Charlie 1 in British Army parlance: 'Arrest on sight. If you got one of those guys who was Charlie 1 you didn't mess about or try anything clever, you just arrested them and that was that.' Lynagh had already been served with a lifetime exclusion order from Great Britain and Northern Ireland so if picked up could be held before being deported to the Republic, while for Arthurs as he was On-The-Run he'd be arrested if stopped and taken for questioning. For McKearney it was far more serious. He still had eleven years of his previous sentence to serve, and his breakout from the Maze would only add to that, so if he was arrested, he'd be looking at spending twenty years inside, not an outcome a republican associate said he was prepared to accept: 'There was no way McKearney was going back inside. He never even wore gloves for f**k's sake! He always carried a short – his was the Ruger he took from Billy Clements at Ballygawley – if he was stopped he'd shoot his way out or die trying.' It made sense therefore for all three men to stay in the Republic until the last minute, so reducing their exposure in the North as much as possible – even though Lynagh had been stopped and searched by the Gardaí in the week before the attack – though a senior republican source was adamant that wasn't what happened: 'McKearney and Lynagh were already in the North days before Loughgall. On the Tuesday night [5 May] they were up on a job on the lough shore warning off a guy who was originally going to be shot dead but at the last minute the word came down it was only going to be a warning – that was up at Gaugers Inn in Ballyronan.' Did either man then head back south? It seems not, and Lynagh's flat at the bottom of Dublin Street in Monaghan Town stayed empty.

On the Thursday night both McKearney and Lynagh reportedly stayed in a safe house in Coalisland making final preparations for the following day's operation. Where Arthurs was is unknown. This was going to be a spectacular, bigger even than Ballygawley or the Birches, an attack aimed at the heart of the detested Crown forces, carried out by the top gun team in all PIRA and led by some of their most experienced commanders. This would show the faint hearts on the Army Council that the only way the Brits were going to leave the island of Ireland was by force.

The following morning the operation began to accelerate as the moving parts fell into place one by one. Firstly the digger bomb – all 200lb of it – was packed into an oil drum and, according to sources, transported south across Lough Neagh by boat from Ardboe down to Maghery to avoid any checkpoints. Next, a blue Toyota HiAce van, earmarked for the job, was stolen by two members of the support crew from some business premises in Dungannon. The van was then driven to a rendezvous point where it was stashed ready for the arrival of the gun team. In the meantime five volunteers turned up at Peter Mackle's farm, just off the Lislasly Road, about halfway between Moy and Loughgall. When Peter Mackle's wife and daughters pulled into the driveway in the family car a few minutes later, they were met by masked IRA gunmen. Understandably terrified they were reassured that nothing would happen to them if they didn't make any trouble. Their captors also told them they were taking their car, the farm's digger, and some diesel oil. Two of the hostage takers drove off in the Mackles' car, while two more stayed to keep the family quiet and stop them from warning the authorities. The fifth volunteer drove the digger away.

Where the bomb was loaded onto the JCB is a mystery. A digger is a slow-moving beast and it's a good twenty-five-minute drive from the Mackles' farm to Maghery, from where it would be another half hour to Loughgall, all the time risking detection in a vehicle that was easy to spot. 'The digger they were going to use at Loughgall wasn't the Mackles', it was going to be one that was a lot closer to Loughgall, but for some reason someone – f**k knows who – decided to go for the Mackles' one instead.' As the exasperated republican source exclaimed, the choice of the Mackles' JCB as the bomb vehicle was just one of a number of puzzling choices made by the A Team that day.

Whatever the reason, the safest option now was for the bomb to be transported to a location out of sight – a disused barn or farm building relatively close to Loughgall – where it would marry up with the digger, which almost certainly was now being driven by Declan Arthurs. Whatever the mechanics of the loading operation, the oil drum bomb was now in the digger's bucket and partially screened by some bricks and rubble to disguise it to any casual observer. Two forty-second fuses were connected up and readied, one as main, the other as back-up. Detonation was easy – light the fuses with a lighter, just like in the movies, and run like hell.

It was now past 6 pm and, with everything in place, the attack team assembled at the chosen rendezvous. There were four vehicles, including the digger, and at least eleven volunteers. Liam Ryan, and another two volunteers who would act as scouts, were dressed in their normal clothes and unarmed. The eight members of the A Team changed into boiler suits and pumps, putting their civilian clothes and shoes in bags into the two cars which would first act as recce vehicles and then as getaway cars. They grabbed their balaclavas and helped themselves to weapons. They had a formidable selection to choose from. There were six modern assault rifles: three former Norwegian Army Heckler & Koch G3s, two FN FNCs and one FN FAL; a Franchi SPAS-12T pump action combat shotgun and, of course, Billy Clements's Ruger pistol. Everyone had their favourite. The team loaded up. The youngest volunteer, Seamus Donnelly, would drive the HiAce van, with his Brigade OC, Patrick Kelly, in the passenger seat and in command. Jim Lynagh, Pádraig McKearney, Eugene Kelly, Gerry O'Callaghan and Tony Gormley all got into the back. Declan Arthurs climbed into the digger cab and fired up the ignition. With one scout car leading and another bringing up the rear, the convoy headed off towards the target on what was a fine, bright, spring evening.

In Loughgall itself all was peaceful. St Luke's church hall was filled with parents and youngsters for the annual gala of the Girls' Friendly Society, and those townsfolk not in attendance were mostly sitting at home about to tune into the latest instalment of the *Wogan* chat show – guests that night included the famous opera singer Kiri Te Kanawa, and the actress Joanna Lumley. With the working week done there was no traffic to speak of, and nothing to show that beneath the surface lay one of the most carefully crafted ambushes of the entire war.

The ambush was laid out in a flattened D-shape with as many as twenty-four SAS troopers in three main firing positions. This in itself was extraordinary, given the Regiment usually deployed in teams of six maximum – Operation Judy was a very big deal for Britain and her special forces. The idea was to completely cover the area selected as the 'kill zone' while minimising the chances of accidentally shooting one another – a 'blue on blue' as it's termed. It was a classic formation, closely resembling the famous Second World War Soviet sniper Vasily Zaitsev's renowned Sixes tactic. 'The main gun team was in the station itself, another was in the church graveyard up on the hill, and a third was at the other end, up by the T-junction in the small wood there.' One of the teams outside the station had been discovered hours earlier by a local out walking his dog, but having been visited by Special Branch had agreed to tell no-one – local RUC vouched for his discretion.

All the SAS troopers were armed with assault rifles, but by far the greatest weight of firepower would be delivered by two 7.62mm General Purpose Machine Guns (GPMGs). Belt-fed and with a bipod at the front, the GPMG has a rate of fire of anywhere between 650 to 1,000 rounds a minute. It is an excellent weapon and in the hands of a professional, truly deadly.

Back on the outer perimeter, 'Anna' saw a van approach her position seemingly stuck behind a slow-moving digger, but then clocked the digger driver was wearing blue overalls, and the pieces fell into place: 'You suddenly realise that it's a previous MO [*Modus Operandi* – method of operation] used by the East Tyrone Brigade … it was like a replay. But this time we were on top of it and knew what was happening. So we passed on the info and pulled off.' According to 'James Rennie', one of the covert cordon team, 'the first indication on the ground of terrorist activity was unmissable, a convoy of … vehicles – a car scouting the route for police or Army patrols, followed by the JCB, and behind it a Nissan van [author: it was actually a Toyota] – passed through the covert outer cordon encircling the village'.

According to Scout One the IRA convoy drove into Loughgall from the direction of Portadown on the Red Lion Road, and as instructed he drove his recce car down past the RUC station to the T-junction, turning into a disused farm track. 'We were to sit there until the boys came back around again, until the bomb went off and they had shot it [the RUC station] up.' The plan was that after the attack the A Team would get back into the blue HiAce, re-join the two recce cars and make their getaway over the border.

The trap was set and all it needed now was for the A Team to walk into it. As John Shackles confirmed, 'The recce went through and everything was teed up and ready to go.'

But something was wrong. The digger and the HiAce van drove by the target, turned into the farm track and parked up. Apparently, Declan Arthurs was spooked. It seemed to Scout One that the young digger driver thought the whole village too quiet and that perhaps they were late and the RUC officers had already left for the night. 'He said at the start, "There's no point in doing the operation, the target is away."' The whole team conferred. A republican source, in a position to know, insisted: 'Declan wanted to call the job off, so did Big Tony [Gormley] and Eugene Kelly. But they weren't calling the shots, neither was Paddy Kelly – even though he was OC. Pádraig and Jim wanted to carry on, but it was Seamus Donnelly and Gerry O'Callaghan who really pushed for it to go ahead. Those two were peas in a pod and they both said "Come on, let's get on and do the f***ing job!" ... Half the team wanted to call the job off, half didn't.'

For the SAS if the operation was cancelled it would spell failure. If the volunteers didn't attack there was no justification to open fire, and to spring the ambush regardless and attempt a mass arrest was not what they were either positioned or prepared for. Equally, as several of the post-operation investigations pointed out, an arrest attempt would have certainly led to a gunfight and the very real possibility of having one or more of their own men killed – it had happened before in 1978 when SAS Lance Corporal David Jones had been shot dead by Francie Hughes. But as one former COP commander explained: 'That was the way it was. I know the other side don't think it's true and [think] that we always opened fire regardless, but that wasn't the case. My own team spent an entire six-month tour in South Armagh trying to get a multi-gun team we knew were operating, and we got close twice; the first time the fog came in and we couldn't see ten feet so had to call it off, and the next time for some reason they didn't attack and cancelled the op. We had them bang in our sights but that was that for us; we couldn't do a thing.'

By now it was just after 7 pm and, according to Scout One, Kelly decided the op was to go ahead regardless. 'Paddy Kelly said we are going to go in and blow the barracks up and fire a few rounds ... Declan went into the digger and the boys followed him.' Everyone put on balaclavas, and Tony Gormley and Gerry O'Callaghan joined Arthurs on the digger, literally riding shotgun as it seems the latter was armed with the Franchi SPAS-12T. With the digger in front and the van behind, both vehicles did one more drive-by, turned round and then the attack began.

On board the digger, the bomb fuses were lit – probably one by Gormley and the other by Arthurs – and then Arthurs accelerated, swinging the JCB hard right into and through the security gates which burst open with a wrench. Driving up to the eastern end of the station building, Arthurs, Gormley and O'Callaghan jumped off just as the HiAce van – which had driven fifty or so yards further on – came to a stop. Inside the station 'Matt' saw the digger crash through the gates: 'Bomb! I just thought of the Birches and Ballygawley.' Quick as a flash he turned and ran towards the back of the station.

On the road Patrick Kelly had gotten out of the van's passenger seat, leaving Seamus Donnelly at the wheel. From the rear of the van he was joined by Eugene Kelly. Then 'the terrorist leader raised his rifle and opened fire on the police station'. Scout One heard 'a rattle of stuff' as the two Kellys opened fire. There was now a clear threat to life and the ambush was sprung. John Shackles described what happened: 'Opposite the station is a playing field [Loughgall FC's ground] and beyond it was a line of conifers – fir trees. Anyway, the Troop [the SAS] had strung detcord [thin flexible plastic tube filled with high explosives] along the trees and they fired it … it was a loud bang so all the Provos swung round to see what the f**k was going on. They were then facing the wrong way you know.'

The British Army teach that the key to a successful ambush is to bring down as much fire as possible onto the enemy before they can react, and that is exactly what now happened. As 'James Rennie' pointed out, 'he [Patrick Kelly] must have been surprised by the answering volley from the score of SAS weapons that were pointing at him'. Scout One heard 'a rattle of heavy stuff [the SAS GPMGs]. I turned to [Scout Two – an unidentified volunteer] and said: "They're giving her some throttle there."'

A former SB officer 'John Clarke' – not his real name –

said, 'Paddy Kelly was standing a few feet away from the van and was killed right away. The driver – Seamus Donnelly – was still sitting in the driver's seat and didn't know what hit him.'

'Rennie' related how the A Team reacted: 'some terrorists tried to get back in the van as others tried to get out, but it was impossible to escape the hail of bullets that were scything through the thin sheet metal'.[30] The van was indeed riddled with automatic fire, pictures taken afterwards show the bodywork completely peppered with bullet holes. Lynagh and McKearney were killed in the back. Reportedly both were wearing flak vests, but if so it did them no good. At the subsequent inquest in June 1995 a statement from one of the SAS GPMG gunners was read out stating that he fired at the van 'until there was no more movement from that target'. Eugene Kelly was killed where he stood. Tony Gormley fired a burst, and O'Callaghan got off one shotgun shell, before both died in a torrent of fire. Declan Arthurs tried to make a run for it but he too was shot dead in what Scout One described as 'fierce firing' that 'went on and on and on, for what seemed like three or four minutes'. In reality 'the gunfire only lasted a few seconds and then there were a few odd shots but it was over very quickly'.

Then the digger exploded. 'We were at the pick-up point and then there was a rip as the bomb went up.'

For 'Matt' it was a whole lot closer: 'The next minute there was an almighty bang. I was hit in the face, knocked to the ground and buried. I thought, "I'm dead", simple as that. But the fact I was still thinking made me realise I was alive. I found myself buried at the corner of the station in rubble, inhaling dust and in darkness. A colleague grabbed my belt and we pushed our way through to the rear of the station, covered in dust and rubble. Our green [RUC] uniforms were now grey. I saw the light of a window at the back and just went for it. I don't know where I got the strength from, but I just pushed myself through it. Colleagues helped us out and gave us first aid.'

At the same time the SAS team in the graveyard saw a white Citroen GS Special desperately trying to reverse out of the area. Two men were inside the car, both in overalls. The SAS made a decision and opened fire. The two men were brothers, Anthony and Oliver Hughes, and both were wholly innocent. Forty rounds hit the car. Oliver told Peter Taylor what he remembered: 'He [his brother Anthony] gave a bit of a shout, "Oliver, Oliver, help me!" Those were the last words he said.' Anthony died. Oliver, hit in the body and head and lucky to be alive, was given first aid and taken to Craigavon Hospital for treatment. He survived but suffered life-changing injuries. Anthony's widow received substantial compensation from the British government but obviously it couldn't make up for the loss – the couple had three children. The Hughes brothers were wearing overalls for work and were driving home at the time. Oliver Hughes thought the security forces should have stopped civilians driving unawares into the area. 'I think it was very unjust ... they could have had a checkpoint and stopped us from going in there and told us about the danger, but they didn't.'

As suddenly as it began, it was over.

Scout One 'saw out in the distance a helicopter and I turned to [Scout Two] and said "there's something badly wrong here". At this stage we were waiting on them [the A Team] to come down and get away.' Fearing the worst, they drove back into

Loughgall and then, 'Another couple of cars with civilians came behind us and two SAS men jumped out and they turned their weapons on us ... I didn't know what was going to happen.' Scout One also told the reporter that at this point another soldier, whom he assumed to be an SAS trooper, stood a few feet in front of the car aiming an Armalite assault rifle directly at him. 'I know for a fact to this day, when you look in someone's eyes, they knew we were involved ...' Sitting frozen in his seat he could see the HiAce van and bodies lying around it. 'I knew they were wiped out at the time. I could see the carnage down at the van ... it was a shock to know everybody was away [dead].'

Tim Pat Coogan wrote that according to a highly placed republican contact he'd known and trusted for over twenty years, while five of the volunteers were indeed killed immediately, the other three – two from the digger and one from the van – were captured alive, ordered to lie down on the road and then executed. This could, potentially, be corroborated by Scout One but given he and Scout Two were in line of sight of the van and the road at the time it seems extremely unlikely, especially as the two men were then allowed to leave unmolested. 'I swore I was going to be dragged out.' If cold-blooded execution was the goal of the SAS team then there was no way Liam Ryan and the scouts would have been allowed to leave alive as John Shackles reiterated. 'No-one got out of Loughgall who wasn't allowed. Only the three-man recce party got out. Two of them had false ID and the third was so well known that false ID would've been useless, but they were all made and let go to protect a source. That was why.' As for Scouts One and Two a soldier told them to drive away. 'I turned the vehicle thinking we were going to get emptied [shot].'

As was standard procedure, the helicopter Scout One saw landed on the playing field and took away some of the SAS team, leaving an 8 UDR QRF to take over the scene. The remainder of the SAS were flown out minutes later as soldiers from the Queen's Lancashire Regiment arrived to support the UDR.

The silence after the helicopters departed was deafening, even as the cordite from the gunfire lay thick in the air, mixed with dust from the bomb blast that had partially demolished the RUC station and the telephone exchange next door. The rest of the scene was carnage. The digger had been almost vaporised in the explosion, and the HiAce van and the Hughes' Citroen were wrecks. A report in the British *Guardian* newspaper written in 2002 on the fifteenth anniversary of the incident described how, 'When the shooting stopped, police, troops and civilian witnesses reported that the spent bullet cartridges were scattered across the killing ground like confetti at a wedding.' It was an apt description. As a report by the European Court of Human Rights (EHCR) detailed some years later, over six hundred rounds had been fired by the SAS and seventy-eight by the A Team, and the casings littered the ground.

A few miles away in the Operations Room of the Tasking and Co-ordinating Group South in Gough Barracks in Armagh, representatives of half a dozen agencies and units were waiting to hear what had happened when an SAS officer got a message on the radio. As he listened, he turned to the room and said clearly, 'Eight.' Someone shot back, 'Eight arrested?' The officer shook his head, put his hand out and gave a thumbs down. The entire A Team was dead.

For the security force members involved, it was a moment of celebration. At 8 UDR's Operations Room at Killymeal House in Dungannon, where Op Judy had been run from, there was an overwhelming feeling of relief and vindication. 'Those b***ds had murdered a lot of good people. Patrick Kelly alone was credited with five kills, and now they were dead themselves, thank God.'

'Anna' – based at Aldergrove – said, 'There was a huge party and it probably went on for over twenty-four hours … A lot of beer was drunk. We were jubilant, there's no two ways about it. We thought it was a job well done.' She was clear as to what they'd achieved: 'It sent shock waves through the terrorist world that we were back on top. It was a huge blow for the IRA.' Did she regret the deaths: 'They're all volunteers and actively engaged against the British Army. They're at war, as they would describe it, so no.' An SAS soldier was slightly wounded by flying glass in the attack, and two of the three RUC stand-ins in the station were injured. 'Matt' ended up in hospital: 'I hate to see anybody being killed, but they were there to kill us. If we hadn't been there the police officers in the station would have been annihilated. These guys were responsible for lots and lots of deaths in that area and other parts of the province. Dead terrorists are better than dead policemen.'

Without the internet and social media, news of the ambush travelled fairly slowly. When an initial news report broadcast that there had been a big attack on an RUC station with a number of fatalities the republican prisoners inside Crumlin Road gaol in Belfast cheered and jeered their loyalist fellow prisoners. When confirmation came through that the fatalities were PIRA men, the boot was on the other foot.

Within republicanism the shock at what had happened was palpable. Professional as ever, the Provisionals' media machine went into action, releasing a statement that 'Volunteers who shot their way out of the ambush and escaped, saw other volunteers being shot on the ground after being captured.' This, of course, was the line taken by Coogan among others, and played to the ongoing IRA theme of a British government 'shoot to kill' policy. However, not all republicans parroted the party line on 'shoot to kill', as one volunteer told Tim Pat Coogan, 'It was war. They'd have done the same.' Frankie Quinn, the Dungannon volunteer related to the Arthurs, was similarly hard faced about it: 'We were out with guns and if we met British soldiers or UDR or RUC they were dead, so if they killed me, so be it, that's life.' Quinn knew what he was talking about. Released along with thirteen others around the same time, only two were still alive when he gave an interview about his time in PIRA to Freya Clements of the *Irish Times* in August 2019. 'The rest were killed, in Loughgall and places like that.'

Among republicans at large there were some sporadic outbursts of street violence in Coalisland, Newry and Strabane as well as elsewhere, but it was pretty muted. Not since Clonmult some sixty-six years before had the IRA lost so many men in a single action, and not just any men, this was the A Team, the cutting edge of the deadly East Tyrone Brigade. This was Jim Lynagh, Pádraig McKearney, Patrick Kelly – all dead. Something had gone terribly wrong for the Provos. The question was what?

The British government media response – not always the

most effective – for once made a concerted effort to present a positive picture of a successful security force action that had thwarted a dangerous IRA unit. Front and centre in the story were the eight weapons recovered at the scene, which were forensically tested and then presented to the world's press by RUC Chief Superintendent Harry Breen, who linked them to at least a dozen attempted murders as well as seven confirmed killings. To hammer the point home the RUC even made the unusual gesture of releasing details of the dates, places and names of those killed by the weapons, including the off-duty UDR members George Shaw and William Graham, as well as the building contractors John Kyle, Ken Johnston and Harold Henry. In fact, as Brett Campbell from the *Belfast Telegraph* reported in December 2017, on the release of a number of previously classified documents from the National Archives in Dublin, the British government had ballistic tests that showed that the weapons recovered from the A Team members had actually been used in as many as forty to fifty killings in total, including every PIRA murder in the counties of Fermanagh and Tyrone in 1987 up to the day of the ambush. This was a hugely significant finding, linking individual volunteers to the attacks they'd almost certainly taken part in and the men they'd killed. It also painted in big letters in the sky just how important to the armed struggle in Tyrone – and indeed Fermanagh – the A Team had been.

Away from the glare of the cameras a chill now ran down the spine of the IRA – the bogeyman was back – the tout. As far as the Army Council was concerned there had to have been a leak, someone was informing. With the Brigade OC dead there was no-one on the ground to head up an internal investigation, so Belfast purportedly sent a key member of the Nutting Squad to take over the inquest. According to an *Irish News* report from 2019, that man was Freddie Scappaticci. Given the revelations of recent years about Scappaticci's probable but unconfirmed role as a British agent, the irony of sending him to try and unearth the truth about what went wrong at Loughgall is farcical. However, what couldn't be disputed was that the British had known the attack was going to take place and had been waiting. The answer as to how, has been – and still is – a conspirator's paradise.

The most easily discounted theory is that the British got lucky, that they had some fairly general intelligence that an isolated rural RUC station was going to be attacked and so had laid ambushes in multiple locations, and it just so happened Loughgall was one such location. Put simply, the SAS wasn't nearly big enough for a plan like that.

The most persistent claim is that of the informer, and more specifically an informer on the A Team itself. Peter Taylor stated in his book *Provos* that a high-level security source told him the informer was on the Loughgall operation and had been killed, while another source at an equally senior level told him it was possible that AN informer had indeed been killed at Loughgall, but it wasn't THE informer. By the time Taylor brought out his next book *Brits* four years later, he confirmed that THE informer had actually been killed on the operation in what had been a security force mess-up.

Tony Geraghty – author, journalist, former British Army paratrooper and dual Irish/British citizen – claimed that an SAS trooper present at Loughgall told him, 'the fact of the matter is that the informer was one of the eight people attacking us that day … He shouldn't have been slotted. We were supposed to identify him quite easily because he would be wearing a red woolly hat or a scarf. He wasn't wearing either.' The reason for the omission was because 'the Loughgall team leader, Jim Lynagh, was a sharp operator. When he called a volunteer in, that man never knew whether it was to be court-martialled, congratulated, or told, "Get the overalls on, we're going to war." The informer was probably caught on the hop and wasn't carrying his little red marker.'

On the face of it the use of a visible marker like a red scarf or hat seems plausible, until you consider the situation at the time and the characters of the other team members. Firstly, the weather. It was a warm, bright, spring evening; why would anyone wear a woolly hat or scarf, particularly over the team 'uniform' of overalls and balaclava? Secondly, if one of the team had suddenly donned such a distinctive piece of clothing it would have immediately aroused suspicions. The likes of Lynagh, McKearney and Kelly were very experienced operators, ever on the look-out for anything that smacked of betrayal, and something like said clothing item would have set alarm bells ringing.

The possible identity of any informer on the team is another controversy. At least two well-informed writers – including the former Queen's University Belfast professor, Richard English – name Tony Gormley as a Special Branch source, and English even said his nickname was 'the Banker' due to the large amounts of money he was paid, although he doesn't go so far as point the finger at him for Loughgall. Other rumours swirled around hinting that Gormley was sacrificed to protect an even more important informer, although who that could be is anyone's guess. Tony Gormley's family have always vigorously denied any suggestion that he was an informer.

Gormley, of course, was dead, and so unable to be questioned by Freddie Scappaticci, or anyone else for that matter. One person who was still alive and whom the Provisionals did show more than a passing interest in was a certain Colette O'Neill. On 21 May – a fortnight after Loughgall – the RUC stopped a car near the republican stronghold of Ardboe. The driver and front-seat passenger were both well-known PIRA suspects, and in the back under some coats was a near-hysterical Colette O'Neill. Ms O'Neill – in her thirties and a resident of Ardboe – admitted that a phone call made from her house on 8 May had set the PIRA attack on Loughgall in motion in the first place, and, in a move seemed designed to paint her as the missing piece of the jigsaw, she and her two children were then taken into protective custody and spirited away to a safe house in Nottingham in the English Midlands. Geraghty didn't name her as an informer but did say that she was saved by a tiny transmitter on her person from which she sent an SOS to Special Branch who arranged the subsequent traffic stop. Perhaps while in England she may have bumped into the mysterious ASU member that Ed Moloney suggests was a no-show the night of Loughgall, who, after protesting his innocence to his PIRA comrades, skipped out and disappeared to England never to be seen again.

A criminal case was prepared against the two men caught with Ms O'Neill, but in the meantime, like so many others in her situation over the years, Colette O'Neill grew homesick and brokered a deal with the Provisionals – through her mother – to be allowed to go home in safety on the proviso she withdrew her evidence against both men. The case collapsed and they were released. A Tyrone republican explained, 'Colette O'Neill was definitely involved, and a message was sent from her house, but she wasn't the big source.'

Then there was Liam Ryan. The source who firmly stated that the Brigade IO was responsible personally for all the intelligence related to Loughgall, also said that 'he [Ryan] insisted that he had compartmentalised everything, that no single participant would have known all the details ...' This would mitigate against the single informer theory, which suited neither side. For the Provisionals, being able to lay the blame for the Loughgall disaster on a lone tout who had then been killed by Crown forces was uncomfortable but far and away the best option. Meanwhile for the security forces, a belief within PIRA that the informer had been killed, while secretly still having him or her in place, was a boon. In other words both sides wanted to let sleeping dogs lie. Neither – though for very different reasons – wanted to highlight Tommy McKearney's belief that 'The greatest threat to a cell system ... is when someone from HQ is working for the opposition', or, as Liam Ryan's confidant explained, 'the leak had to be at a centralised level; he [Ryan] would have concluded that it had to be higher up than Tyrone.'

However, in a sign of just how powerful the spectre of the Loughgall informer still is, even decades on, in late December 2017 the *Irish Times* published a report that the mysterious tout was none other than Gerry Adams. The story was based on a rumour passed to the Republic's Department of Foreign

Affairs by the highly influential Northern Irish Catholic priest, Fr [Father] Denis Faul, a few months after Loughgall. Faul – a man with a long history in the Troubles – said he had been told that 'the IRA team were set up by Gerry Adams himself'. He had also been told that Jim Lynagh and Pádraig McKearney 'had threatened to execute Adams shortly before the Loughgall event' because they 'disliked Adams's political policy'. A Sinn Féin spokesman at the time dismissed the claim as 'utter nonsense'. When approached for comment Tommy McKearney said, 'It's no secret that I have long-held political differences with Gerry, but I don't give these claims any credence whatsoever and I certainly don't point the finger at Mr Adams … Setting aside his denials that he was ever even in the IRA, I don't think he would have any hands-on knowledge of this particular operation.' McKearney was clear who he thought was behind the reports: 'This is evidence of a classic dirty trick by the British intelligence services designed to exacerbate divisions within republicanism at that time … I'm not saying my brother didn't have differences with the movement, many did in 1987 due to a split the previous year, but to suggest that anyone was contemplating the execution of Gerry Adams is a bizarre piece of misinformation.' However, the rumours linger on, partly fed by McKearney himself when he went on to say: 'I think it is fair to assume that the British would have had an idea of what was going on internally within the republican movement at that time. By killing the IRA unit at Loughgall, and particularly people like my brother and Jim Lynagh, they had taken away people who would have potentially been critical of subsequent strategic developments within the movement.' By 'strategic developments' McKearney meant the eventual abandonment of the armed struggle in favour of politics – the very issue his brother Pádraig, Jim Lynagh and Patrick Kelly had been so worried about.

Other commentators have waded into the debate, with one claiming he was told during a drunken conversation with a British MI5 officer that 'Adams was one of ours', while Ed Moloney suggested that any internal move against the A Team could have been triggered by a secret meeting held in an isolated house on the Fermanagh/Monaghan border in the spring of 1987 not long before Loughgall. The house was the family home of Séamus McElwaine, the former commander of PIRA's Fermanagh Brigade killed by the SAS a year earlier. The location was symbolic given McElwaine's own strong opposition to the Adams/McGuinness policy line. Reportedly both Jim Lynagh and Pádraig McKearney were there and the talk was about leaving the Provisionals and forming a breakaway movement steadfastly committed to the war. Moloney also says McKearney had been trying to source non-Provo weapons in the Republic for any breakaway as far back as 1986. The theory then goes that news of the meeting got back to Belfast and – given Tyrone's history with Liam Kelly's defection to set up Saor Uladh in the early 1950s – the leadership decided to act.

All of this is highly circumstantial, and in an organisation where most attacks were planned and run at a local level it is difficult – though not impossible – to see how someone in the republican movement as senior as Gerry Adams would be told the kind of details which would allow the security forces to mount a response like Operation Judy.

A more prosaic answer as to what went wrong for the East Tyrone Brigade at Loughgall is that the crucial intelligence required by the security forces was pieced together from a wide range of sources, some human, others technological. Indeed, the former undercover security force officer Martin Ingram was clear with the journalist Greg Harkin that 'the entire SAS operation was planned as a result of electronic devices planted in the home of an IRA member, and not one of those volunteers who died'. The former SB officer Dr William Matchett said, 'the truth is the intelligence machinery was so sophisticated that they [the security forces] didn't need anyone from the top of the tree'. This machinery included the use of telephone taps, electronic bugging of homes, the jarking of weapons, physical suspect surveillance and so on. He also pointed the finger firmly at mistakes made by the A Team themselves, with the neglect for reconnaissance and a thorough sweep of the area beforehand being glaring errors. 'McKearney and Lynagh got carried away with themselves and didn't need anyone to trip them up – it was always inevitable they would do that.' John Shackles agrees: 'If it had been my call I wouldn't have taken McKearney or Lynagh on the job because their motivation was personal. You've got to be cool and emotionless about these things, but those two just wanted to see dead bodies.'

Away from the recriminations, the human cost of Loughgall was keenly felt. Every death in Northern Ireland during the war was a personal tragedy for the family involved. According to the Dublin-based *Magill* magazine Declan Arthurs's older brother Brian had been living in San Francisco for over six months when he heard about Loughgall: 'When I knew that

Declan was involved, I obviously hoped he'd gotten away. He nearly did – he was a fast runner and made it to the edge of where the ambush was, but unfortunately he didn't escape ... I was devastated by the news. When I flew back home, the cops at the airport started questioning me [author: including the then-head of RUC Special Branch according to Arthurs himself], and within a few weeks I had been arrested by the RUC in Tyrone. They showed me photographs of Declan after the attack, it was par for the course for them.' Brian's mother Amelia, 'who was really the driving force behind the family's republicanism' according to a Branch source, couldn't hide her bitterness at her son's death: 'He was mowed down ... the SAS never gave him a chance.' Scout One was of the same opinion: 'They [the security forces] could have rammed the van; the boys were sitting in a vulnerable situation ... There was a ten-minute window from the lads going through the village the first time to when they went back in again ... There was ample time for arrests to be made.'

As was customary the funerals were opportunities for republican leaders to address both the local audience, as well as wider public opinion. They were some of the biggest seen since those of the hunger strikers back in 1981, as the A Team were laid to rest as the Loughgall Martyrs. Colm Lynagh – five years into his sentence for the murder of the nightclub bouncer Gabriel Murphy – was released on parole for the day to act as a pall bearer for his brother's coffin. One of the other pall bearers was Gerry Adams. Adams gave the graveside oration, roundly criticising Fr Sean Nolan who conducted the requiem mass without mentioning the circumstances of Lynagh's death: 'Jim Lynagh died of an injustice. At Mass this morning I thought he may have died of pneumonia.' He went on to say that 'it [the British government] does not understand the Jim Lynaghs, the Pádraig McKearneys or the Séamus McElwaines. It thinks it can defeat them. It never will.'

Declan Arthurs's brother Brian was of the same opinion, and claimed that, far from being a success, Loughgall was actually a grave error by the British government. 'When the volunteers were killed at Loughgall it didn't put people off joining the IRA. Far from it. There was a huge influx of new people who wanted to join the movement after Loughgall. The message from the republican community was that British oppression wouldn't be tolerated.' This was always the fear among some members of the security forces as one former soldier made clear: 'We knew what had happened after the hunger strikes and what we didn't want were loads more young lads putting their hands up to join [the Provisionals].' An ex-COP commander had much the same view but with a different emphasis: 'It was in our interests not to … kill these people because then we'd get new people in PIRA whom maybe we didn't know and we'd have to start all over again.' 'Anna' thought very differently: 'I don't think volunteers were particularly willing to go on missions after that because obviously they didn't want to die or be captured.'

The question in everyone's mind was what would happen now?

One senior Tyrone republican was clear as to what wouldn't now happen. 'The Tet offensive was geared up to start in July '87, and probably would've only lasted three months as everyone would've gotten killed, but they would've done it anyway, but Loughgall stopped it dead – no more Tet.'

Shackles was just as clear: 'The cross-border team were

waiting for the boys [the A Team] at a rendezvous point so they could take the weapons and clothes and so on, and then it was down south and a f**king good weekend in Monaghan … But as it turned out Loughgall was the end of big shooting operations for East Tyrone, and it was back to murdering some poor wee f**ker at their work.'

7

THE WAR GOES ON

It was cold. Cold and dark. He dropped the cigarette butt on the dirty concrete floor of the yard and ground it out with his boot, exhaling the last of the smoke at the same time. Turning, he thrust his hands deep into his coat pockets and walked to the side door of the barn. Opening the door he was struck by the light of the overhead lamps and the smell of hay. Being careful to close the door behind him he strode over to the gaggle of men standing around the crates stacked on the floor near the far wall. He knew everyone there, some by reputation only, but most personally. Nodding his greetings, he stared down. This was what they'd all been waiting for – longing for – those crates were the future of loyalist violence.

Gathered in that barn at a farm on the outskirts of Portadown were senior figures from the main two loyalist paramilitary organisations in Northern Ireland and a relative newcomer. The biggest group in the North was the Ulster Defence Association (UDA) which usually carried out its attacks under the cover name of the Ulster Freedom Fighters

(UFF). Mainly Belfast based, the UDA/UFF also had units in Antrim and Londonderry, but tonight it was in the heartland of its sister – and occasionally rival – organisation: the Ulster Volunteer Force. The UVF was also strong in Belfast, as well as in mid-Ulster and Armagh – Portadown in particular. Relations between the UVF and the UDA/UFF could be difficult, but as the UFF commander Johnny Adair made clear, 'if there were problems it was usually down to personality clashes; mostly we got along just fine'. And tonight was just too important for any such problems. The Provos might be able to use Irish American dollars to buy Armalite assault rifles or rely on Gaddafi for AK-47s, but with no sympathetic diaspora or anti-imperialist revolutionary benefactor, loyalist paramilitaries had always struggled to source modern weapons and the money needed to buy them; as Adair conceded, 'we never had the sophisticated arsenal the IRA had'.

Now all that had changed. As far as the hard-line loyalists gathered in the barn were concerned, the contents of the crates on the concrete floor in front of them were a gift from God – or rather a gift purchased via the good offices of South Africa's apartheid regime; some fifty Czech-made vz.58 assault rifles, thirty Browning 9mm pistols, thousands of rounds of ammunition for both and around 150 Soviet-made RGD-5 grenades. The loyalists had never seen anything like it, and this was only a fraction of what they'd bought from the Lebanese gunrunner Joe Fawzi with £300,000 stolen from the Northern Bank a few miles away in the city itself. Introduced to Fawzi by Douglas Bernhardt, an American-born agent in Pretoria's much-feared Bureau of State Security, the weapons were part of a haul captured by Lebanese Christian militias from Yasser Arafat's Palestine Liberation Organisation (PLO) back in 1982. Routed through Armscor – the South African armaments corporation – in return for loyalist help in obtaining embargoed anti-aircraft missile components from Belfast's Short Brothers factory, the huge cache was smuggled into Northern Ireland – one third each for the UDA/UFF, the UVF and Ulster Resistance (UR), the johnny-cum-lately of the trio and only established the year before. A UFF brigade commander confirmed the plan: 'The robbery was done for the weapons, with the UVF storing the cash before it was handed over, and then the weapons were split three ways. Then the eagle has landed, the weapons arrived and went into Armagh and kept on a farm outside Portadown.' Jubilation was soon replaced by anger as 'most of them were seized because we were riddled with government agents. The biggest threat we had was from within ... So the UDA share was taken, and so was over half the UVF share. But Ulster Resistance were very friendly and agreed to share some of their cut with the rest of us. We got vz.58s – lovely weapons – and grenades. They were a godsend, and I knew just how precious those weapons were.'

Many of the guns would be recovered by the RUC over the next few years, but those that weren't formed the mainstay of the loyalist arsenal for the rest of the war and wreaked havoc across Northern Ireland. In the following four years loyalists would kill 138 people, almost all Catholics, many of them innocent civilians. East Tyrone would suffer particularly badly.

As for the other side, the A Team were gone. The liberated zones strategy, so long cherished by Jim Lynagh and Pádraig

McKearney, died with them in the gun smoke at Loughgall. Lynagh's loss was particularly hard felt among republicans. All wars need charismatic figures, individuals who – for good or ill – come to embody the struggle for whoever's side they are fighting on, and the republican movement was, perhaps, prone to such sentiment more than most. Lynagh was one such figure. Stories about him had swirled around for years, and whether true or not it didn't really matter. Put on a pedestal, he'd ranked alongside the likes of Derry's Francie Hughes and Fermanagh's Séamus McElwaine, and outlived both – for a while.

It wasn't just senior men who'd been lost either, almost an entire generation of younger volunteers had died with them. The likes of Eugene Kelly, Seamus Donnelly and Declan Arthurs were all being prepared to take their places as the future leaders and 'hard men' of the East Tyrone Brigade, and their loss was a body blow, as one Tyrone republican source reluctantly admitted: 'In the short term it wasn't too bad, but in the long term it became clear it was irreparable, it was a disaster. The new recruits were just as brave but they lacked experience and there was no-one to teach them, and they didn't know what they were going up against … look at the footage of Jim Lynagh's funeral in Monaghan. There's boys there with brand new G3s [assault rifles], some of the ones we got from Norway, and when they go to fire over the grave two of them jam and they don't even know how to clear it for f**k's sake!'

Unsurprisingly in the aftermath of Loughgall, East Tyrone PIRA were visibly subdued. With Scappaticci and his ilk looking for informers round every corner, the remaining volunteers and activists felt under almost unbearable scrutiny and endeavoured to keep their heads down. The shadow of relative calm that fell over the county in the latter half of the year was borne out by the numbers. In 1986 the East Tyrone Brigade had accounted for almost one in four attacks across Northern Ireland; in 1987 it was less than one in ten. Not that everyone felt a new dawn might be at hand. A member of a new British Army unit flying into the west of the county that September remembered how 'even before we'd cleared the helicopter the soldiers from the King's Regiment [the battalion they were replacing] were trying to get up the rear ramp ... one of their officers had to shout at them to let us off first. I looked at my mate John and said "F**k me! Is it that bad?"'

Many hoped the peace would last. They'd be disappointed. On 24 September 1987, pretty much five months to the day since the murder of William Graham – another off-duty UDR member was targeted by East Tyrone PIRA. This time it was Jeffrey Lamont. Lamont served in the same platoon in 'C' Company 8 UDR as his father and was based in Cookstown. A draughtsman by trade, he cycled to work that morning, but on arriving at his offices he noticed that his boss's car was 'parked outside the office as usual, but not the way it normally was. It was at an angle, and he always parked dead straight.' He also noticed the office door was slightly open, but 'I went in ... I couldn't see what was going to happen.' Lamont put his lunch box in the kitchen, climbed the stairs to the first floor 'and that's when I got hit on the back of the head'. Knocked to the ground and half-dazed 'all I could see was a mass of masked men all round me'. Realising he 'was fighting for my life ... I kicked and fought them as hard as I could. My pistol was in my pocket, I clicked off the safety catch and started to fire.' His quick thinking saved his life. 'I fired four shots and saw them running down the stairs before I blacked out.' Coming to, he looked around only to see 'a fella come out of the back office with a sawn-off shotgun'. Lamont went for his own pistol but the IRA gunman was quicker: 'he fired and hit me in the right arm. He hit me with two shotgun cartridges at point-blank range.'[31]

He blacked out again and when he came round the gunman was gone. Lamont was lucky to survive, and keep his arm, but he ended up being medically discharged from the regiment. One of the volunteers involved was arrested in the follow up. David Wilson – another UDR soldier – remembered that 'he [the gunman] tried to get out of the estate in a taxi but was stopped by a UDR patrol. One of the soldiers that stopped him had seen a spot of blood on the ground and noticed that his backside seemed very fat. He'd stuck a towel on it where he'd been shot. He claimed he was the victim of a punishment shooting, but when they did the forensics it turned out to be a bullet from Jeffrey's pistol!' The wounded volunteer, twenty-year-old Mark Mulgrew from the Cookstown ASU, was sentenced to fifteen years.

Four months later Bill Stewart wasn't as lucky as Lamont. Another off-duty UDR man, he was shot as he drove his car near his home in Brackaville outside Coalisland. Taken to hospital he died the next day from his injuries. He was followed to the grave by his colleague Ned Gibson.

Ned Gibson, a twenty-three-year-old council bin man from the Protestant village of Coagh, worked irregular shifts so as to not set a pattern after joining the UDR some eight weeks before, but on the morning of Tuesday, 26 April he arrived at work and was told to make up the extra man on a round in Moortown near Ardboe. At the same time two masked men carrying rifles confronted local farmer Peter Devlin as he was checking his cows and demanded the keys to his nearby bungalow. Bravely, Devlin refused, after which the gunmen jumped the fence and seemed to disappear. Five minutes later the bin lorry appeared on its round to pick up the Devlin household's rubbish. The two gunmen were waiting. Seeing Gibson, they opened fire. Hit by the first rounds he fell to the ground and tried to crawl to a low wall for cover. It did him no good. One of the gunmen ran over and shot him twice in the head. A witness on the scene after the shooting said '[Gibson] was lying propped up against the wall of a house. By the time an ambulance arrived he was already dead.'

For the East Tyrone Brigade it was just another operation, the killing of an off-duty member of the Crown forces. For loyalist paramilitaries, now equipped with a whole new arsenal of modern weaponry, it was crossing a line in the sand. Gibson's murder would spark off a series of tit-for-tat killings across Tyrone that would go on for the next three years.

A week later the headlines were grabbed by twin PIRA attacks, this time not in Ardboe or Cookstown but in the Netherlands. Three RAF airmen were killed, one in a sniper shoot and two by an Under Vehicle Booby Trap – the European ASU had arrived. PIRA's move to mainland Europe almost overshadowed the first annual commemoration of their self-proclaimed Loughgall Martyrs.

Martin McGuinness led the tributes back home, doing the rounds of the graveyards for large, appreciative crowds, although rather pointedly staying away from Pádraig McKearney's, after the McKearney family's refusal to allow either McGuinness or Gerry Adams speak at his funeral, although they did attend his wake. 'The past year has seen an unprecedented campaign by the government to take out the Republican Army. As I've said, it has failed, and failed miserably.' Disappointingly for republicans, for a brigade only so recently feared for its lethality, the expected wave of attacks on and around the anniversary amounted to little more than two improvised grenades thrown at an RUC mobile patrol on the Drum Road in Cookstown. Both failed to explode.

The Brigade was rather more successful when it renewed its campaign of targeting off-duty UDR members, killing Michael Darcy in June and Raymond McNicholl at the beginning of August. In between, on 7 July, an attempt to mortar the Pomeroy RUC/Army base backfired with volunteer Seamus Woods – a member of the PIRA colour party at Tony Gormley's funeral – killed in an own goal.

To an increasing number of people, it began to look as if without the A Team, East Tyrone were now a second-rate outfit. Then there was Ballygawley.

At that time the way the British Army worked in Northern Ireland was to split regular units into two categories; five areas that were classed as especially dangerous – Fermanagh, Derry city, West Belfast, South Armagh and East Tyrone – had so-called roulement battalions deployed there for six-month tours of high-intensity operations, with the troops working continuously with only one seven-day leave period during the entire tour – no nights, days or weekends off, just ops. Troops lived in tiny, cramped accommodation, sometimes underground and usually hardened against mortar attack. Facilities were very basic with the soldiers only leaving their bunks to wash, eat, zero their weapons (test for accuracy) and go out on patrol.

For the rest of Northern Ireland, battalions were sent on two-year residential tours where married men were accompanied by families, and soldiers lived in a way more akin to normal garrison life, albeit with rotating operational duties in their assigned areas and standard local security.

In August 1988 1st Battalion The Light Infantry (1 LI) were three-quarters of their way through one such residential tour. As with all other residential battalions, 1 LI were operating a home leave policy whereby batches of soldiers went home in rotation to see family and friends for some rest and recuperation – R&R as it was known. Flights were to and from Aldergrove airport, with unmarked buses taking troops there and back from Lisanelly Barracks in Omagh. On the night of Friday, 19 August 1988 some thirty-six young light infanteers landed at Aldergrove, climbed aboard a fifty-two-seater bus with a military driver and headed off to Omagh. It was late in the evening and the bus wasn't due to arrive back at base until the early hours of Saturday morning.

Meanwhile it was getting a bit chilly lying in the grass on the hillside, and one of the men – red-haired like his brother lying next to him – said a silent prayer of thanks it was August and not December. He sent another prayer of thanks skyward for the darkness that meant they hadn't had to dig in the command wire from the firing point where he now lay, all the way down the hill before feeding it through the culvert under the road to the bomb on the other side. As it was, the darkness of the summer night was more than enough to hide the white, dual-core, twin flex wire. All they had to do now was wait. They'd picked a good spot. It overlooked the road, without standing out like a sore thumb, and there was direct line of sight to a telegraph pole they'd opted for as the aiming marker. When the bus reached the telegraph pole, he'd press the button and the bomb would go off exactly as the bus reached it. The bomb itself was a 'booster', 200lbs of homemade explosive packed around a core of deadly Semtex designed to hugely increase its killing power.

Most importantly for the volunteers there was a covered escape route back to where the getaway car was waiting, the other member of their team sitting in the driver's seat, biting his fingernails and longing to hear the blast of the explosion so he could switch the engine on and prepare to get the hell out of there along the route they'd already chosen. He wasn't armed and was wearing his normal civilian clothes – just in case. Any nosey Army or UDR patrol that appeared out of the blue wouldn't find anything other than a local claiming to be having a bit of car trouble. All three men knew each other very well and trusted each other to do their job. In a show of bravado, they called themselves 'the Untouchables', with the RUC admitting they were 'a very professional, meticulous gang'. If the bus didn't come, they'd have a choice: disconnect the trigger, roll up the command wire and take the bomb away for another day, or call it in as an anonymous tip and give the security forces the headache of dealing with it. If they were lucky, they could even look to set up a shoot on the cordon the Brits were bound to put in place around it while the bomb disposal lads were making it safe. But as the bomb was relatively easy to move – packed as it was into a car trailer – giving up 200lbs of Semtex and homemade explosive would be a bitter pill to swallow, so they'd almost certainly opt to dismantle the whole thing and save it for another day.

Back on the bus some of the young soldiers were grabbing a bit of shut-eye, still knackered from a few nights back home on the beers. Following the main A5 trunk road, they were nearing the village of Ballygawley when they passed just another telegraph pole. A split second later a massive blast blew out all the windows, ripped the metal sides away from the bus and physically threw the vehicle some thirty metres, half into the adjoining field, leaving a six-foot-deep crater on the side of the road. The sound of the explosion was heard for miles.

As the three-man ASU drove away, elated at a successful operation, Sammy Brush – himself the survivor of a PIRA assassination attempt seven years earlier – was one of the first to arrive at the scene of what he described as 'probably the worst night of my life ... There was glass, blood and bodies, and young soldiers badly mutilated but still alive. It was a scene of carnage that I would never want to witness in my life again ... All you could do was try and comfort them and give them words of encouragement and do your best for them ... It was a terrible incident, terrible to think that a human being could blow up other human beings.' The RUC night duty inspector from Omagh arrived on the scene and described it as 'like driving into hell'. Working by torchlight in the pitch dark he 'remembered one soldier who at first looked all right in the darkness, but when I looked more closely, I saw that he had been decapitated'.[32]

Eight soldiers were dead, three of whom were just eighteen, with the oldest being twenty-one. Every other passenger was wounded, most badly. Also on the scene that night was Brush's former company commander, Ken Maginnis. Maginnis had left the UDR six years earlier to go into politics and was as horrified as Brush at what he saw: 'It was horrible, just horrible, there were body parts everywhere. Those poor young lads had literally been torn to pieces.' As they cleared the surrounding area Maginnis found one of the soldiers who'd crawled away from the blast site. 'He was just sitting up in this barn like he was asleep, but when I went up to him it was too late, he was dead.' When interviewed afterwards, the mother of Jason Burfitt – one of the eight killed – said, 'he [Jason] hated that coach. All the boys knew it was an easy target. He just felt they were sitting ducks. The coach sat about the airport for so long the IRA would be able to set up an ambush.'

News of the bombing was greeted with joy in republican circles. Scout One from Loughgall made it clear in his *Irish News* interview he wasn't involved in the attack, but said as far as he and other volunteers were concerned it settled the score. 'It was eight for eight.'

For Ken Maginnis, when the clean-up was finished, he went home and personally put a call into No. 10 Downing Street to leave a message for the Prime Minister describing what had happened. His head had hardly hit the pillow when the phone rang – it was 4.40 am and it was Downing Street. The Prime Minister – famous for never sleeping more than four or five hours a night – had gotten the message and wanted to know if he could catch the first flight in the morning to London to brief her. A few hours later Maginnis and two colleagues found themselves disembarking from a plane and climbing into a waiting car which whisked them to Downing Street. Hurried into her office, the three men sat and briefed the PM on the bombing. After a few minutes she thanked them and said there were sandwiches and coffee next door. As they filed out, she turned to Maginnis and asked him to stay. Sitting down 'She said "Kenneth" – she always called me Kenneth – "do you know who did this?" I told her I almost certainly did. I gave her three names. She then asked me what she could do about it and I said, "Prime Minister, watch them, watch them day and night and wait, wait until they make a mistake, because they will, sooner or later."'

Later that day Maginnis was back in Northern Ireland shaking hands with the local divisional RUC commander. 'I said, "You're going to hate me because all your resources, everything you've got, is going to be ordered to do one job."' Maginnis knew what he was talking about. As a high-profile former UDR member and Unionist MP for the Fermanagh–South Tyrone constituency – the hunger striker Bobby Sands's former seat – Maginnis was a vocal opponent of the Provisionals and they had long viewed him as a target. Well-liked by many of his constituents – a local journalist once said of him that 'he was one of the few Unionists you could imagine enjoying a pint with in the pub' – the East Tyrone Brigade planned at least eleven assassination attempts on him, of which one in 1988 – to kill him as he travelled between his home and the offices of Dungannon town council – was the most advanced. Armed with actionable intelligence an SAS trooper was even substituted for the MP to lure PIRA into an ambush, but for whatever reason the attack never materialised. A weapons find of several assault rifles and an RPG-7 rocket launcher near his home sometime later foiled another attempt.

In truth, the ASU Maginnis believed was behind the attack was already under scrutiny, as a former RUC officer described: 'We'd been on them for a while but the bus bombing upped the ante massively ... we lifted Marty Harte and took him into Gough for questioning after the attack but got nowhere.'

Following the bus bombing the word came down from Army headquarters at Lisburn, from now on there was to be no more routine road movement of troops in east Tyrone; everything was to be done by helicopter.

Ten days after the Maginnis–Thatcher meeting, a Leyland coal lorry with a distinctive blue stripe down the side pulled over off the Drumnakilly Road near the village of the same name, onto an area of hard standing next to a boarded up two-storey farmhouse. The driver got out of his cab to see what the problem was – a flat back tyre. Cursing his luck, he set about changing it for the spare. He took his time; there was no rush. He was well-known in the area and was always on his rounds making deliveries between Carrickmore and Omagh off and around the B4 as the Drumnakilly Road was officially entitled. Jacking the truck up, he was right under the gun sights of at least two assault rifles and one light machine gun (LMG), probably more. No-one opened fire. They weren't there for him; in fact, he was one of them. This was a trap, and a very carefully laid one at that.

The night before, an IRA weapons cache had been accessed and two AK-47s and at least one pistol retrieved. The cache was under surveillance by the security forces. Acting on intelligence

– reportedly including information from an electronic bug inside a volunteer's house – a joint SAS/RUC team quietly entered the home of the coal delivery driver, who was also a part-time member of the UDR. At the same time another SAS team were dropped off and infiltrated by foot to the selected ambush site on the Drumnakilly – not far from where the same PIRA team were suspected of blowing up four soldiers from 6 UDR back in July 1983, and of killing Army Private Lyndon Morgan with a remote-controlled bomb hidden in a gas cylinder as his foot patrol passed by some four months earlier. The next morning, one of the SAS team – codenamed Soldier G – who most resembled the UDR man, took his place, dressed in his clothes and went to work, driving the Leyland lorry on the target's usual route. Reaching the ambush site well before midday, he pulled in and faked a flat, all the time acting as bait.

Then, between 2 and 2.30 pm the ASU made their move. Four armed volunteers in blue boiler suits and balaclavas burst into the home of local teacher Justin McBride on the south side of the Drumnakilly. Bundling Justin, his wife and their five terrified children into a back room, the volunteers smashed the phone, warned the family not to raise the alarm, stole the keys to their red Fiat Regatta and drove off. They didn't go far, only to the McAleer farm down the road, whereupon the volunteers repeated the process, smashing the phone, pulling down the blinds and ordering Annie McAleer to stay quiet in a back room.

Unbeknown to the waiting SAS men, the ASU had a plan of their own. Their plan was to wait for the target to fix his puncture, drive into their selected ambush site and then kill him – they had no intention of going after him. So, with Annie safely tucked up, they settled down to wait.

Then the plan started to unravel. First to arrive was the milkman who, after knocking on the door, was grabbed and put in the back room with Annie. Next was Thaddeus McAleer, back from the fields in his digger. He too was taken hostage and put in the back room. Ten minutes later a yellow Sierra parked up outside the front door. Inside were Eamon McCullough and his two children. McCullough was a salesman and had been talking to the McAleers about selling them a microwave. He'd popped in on his way past to try and clinch the deal. Instead, he found himself and his kids held prisoner in a by-now packed back room of the McAleer farmhouse. Unsurprisingly the volunteers decided enough was enough and they'd have to change tack.

So far the job wasn't going as they'd hoped, but then this type of operation was relatively new to them, as a republican source who knew them conceded. 'They were a *top country* [author's italics] outfit and mostly did their own thing; usually it was explosives, some of which they shipped to other teams.' However, this wasn't a landmine or booby trap job. This was a gun team op; this was what the A Team used to do, only they were dead.

Frustrated at their target's no-show, the PIRA team changed their plan. While one stood guard over the hostages, the other three went outside with McCullough's car keys and removed the Sierra's sunroof to give them a free field of fire. Now ready, the leader of the ASU – twenty-nine-year-old Gerard Harte – got into the front passenger seat cradling an AK-47. His younger brother Martin, aged twenty-one and with a three-month-old son at home, climbed in the back, with his brother-in-law Brian Mullin getting behind the wheel. Like his big brother, Harte the younger had an AK-47, while Mullin had a Webley .38 revolver on his lap. The fourth volunteer – reportedly a woman – would stay with the Regatta at the McAleers as the getaway vehicle.

Back at the SAS's chosen ambush site nerves were jangling. The supposedly broken-down lorry had been there for over five hours by now and the SAS trooper acting as a decoy had run out of things to check. The bonnet was up and he had been interminably fiddling with anything and everything in an attempt to make the incident look genuine. Where were the Provos?

At 4 pm a yellow Sierra appeared. It drove past the stationary lorry and slowed. The SAS decoy saw a gunman stand up through the sunroof, level his weapon and open fire. He dived 'over the hedge – it was about three foot high – but then he dropped about eight or nine feet into the boggy field below'.

The Sierra – now about twenty yards away – braked hard and Gerard Harte got out to finish the job. Both he and the car were immediately engulfed by a storm of automatic gunfire. All three volunteers were killed instantly. According to a soldier involved in the ambush, 'The last thing Gerard Harte saw before he died was this really ugly little Scotsman [an SAS trooper apparently infamous in the Regiment for his appearance] in the hedge aiming a gun at him. What a way to go, poor b****d!'

An RUC team hidden in a hedge nearby 'were on the scene in seconds ... we had three to four crews that day and a Det or Troop Liaison Officer with us.' With the scene secure, one of the RUC team 'took out some plastic spoons I'd picked up along with a black marker pen at Killymeal [8 UDR base in Dungannon] on the way through – to be honest I have no idea why I did that – and I gave them to the Troop boys who'd already been given their identifying letters [Soldier A, Soldier B and so on] and asked them to plant the spoons where their firing points were. One lad said he fired from two places so I gave him two spoons.'

After that – and as was normal practice – a helicopter quickly appeared, dropping off a green Army QRF to take control of the area and lift off the SAS team. A short time later a local priest – Fr John Cargan – took a phone call from a man identifying himself as an IRA volunteer, who told him to go to the scene. Fr Cargan later spoke to reporters about what he saw: 'It is quite horrific ... Two of them could possibly be identified but the third seemed to be fairly badly dismembered.' His description is understandable given the findings of the subsequent inquest into the shootings held some five years later, which concluded the SAS had fired 236 rounds to the PIRA team's sixteen – sheer weight of firepower at close quarters is devastating in its effects. There was little trouble linking the Ballygawley attackers to the SAS ambush, and the British newspaper the *Daily Star* splashed a headline the next day of 'Revenge! SAS Kill Three Bus Bombers'.

Drumnakilly was a bitter blow for the East Tyrone Brigade. All three men were extremely active volunteers, with Mullin – a coffin bearer at Pádraig McKearney's funeral – being 'tight with the Cappagh volunteers, and especially Martin McCaughey. They were good friends', according to one senior republican. But Harte the elder in particular was a senior member of the Brigade with a history of extreme violence. As a security force source said, 'Gerry Harte had headed up internal security for East Tyrone for a long time before going back to operations. If anyone had the finger put on them [as a possible informer] he'd take them down south [to the Republic] and work them over; electric shocks, near drowning, cigarette burns, beating the living hell out of them … torture basically, and then, if they confessed, they'd get "Cappuccino" [security force nickname for a senior member of the IRA's Nutting Squad] down from Belfast to kill 'em. Harte was a mean f***er and even his own people were terrified of him.' A senior Tyrone republican source didn't go that far, but in his own words: 'Gerry Harte was hard work.' Regardless, his team were tight-knit and effective, causing havoc in mid-Tyrone and responsible for multiple attacks. Now they too were dead, the only surviving team member waiting in vain at the McAleers.

In any army there is no substitute for experience. This goes double for a paramilitary organisation where formal training is, by necessity, limited. When the A Team were alive they could muster over half a century of experience between them from dozens of operations. Much of the rest of the Brigade were effectively a support network for them. The Harte ASU wasn't in the same league as Lynagh and Kelly's unit, but they too were a senior team who knew the ropes. Now, with so many of the Brigade's most effective operatives gone, mistakes started to creep in. On 23 November 1988 a van bomb intended for Benburb RUC station blew up prematurely and instead killed a sixty-seven-year-old Catholic, Bernard

Lavery, and his fourteen-year-old granddaughter, Emma Donnelly. That error came after the killing of Gillian Johnston back in March, when she was machine-gunned to death sitting in her car near Belleek, County Fermanagh. Mistaken for her UDR brother, her boyfriend was badly wounded but survived.

Worse was to come for the East Tyrone Brigade the day after the Benburb bomb, when UVF gunmen murdered an innocent Catholic, Phelim McNally, during an attack on his brother Francie's house on the Derrycrin Road in Ardboe. Francie was a Sinn Féin councillor and knew he was a possible target, telling the journalist and writer Kevin Toolis, 'those people [local Protestants] want to kill me. I suppose they really do hate me.' In response he'd turned his bungalow into a fortress with armoured doors and barred windows, but not long after 10 pm on the night of 24 November 1988 that didn't stop a UVF team hitting the place. Phelim McNally was in the kitchen when Francie heard 'two bursts of sustained automatic gunfire. I knew what I was going to find ... I went to the kitchen door and heard his last breath. He was dead.' Francie and Phelim were brothers of Lawrence McNally, a notorious gunman in East Tyrone PIRA for well over a decade, and a suspect in a host of attacks including the first attempt on Glen Espie's life.

The McNally hit was in revenge for the murder of Ned Gibson, the bin man and off-duty UDR soldier killed in Ardboe seven months earlier. Armed with their share of the guns bought from Joe Fawzi, a revitalised and extremely violent player was throwing its hat into the ring in east Tyrone – the UVF's Mid-Ulster Brigade.

For years the IRA's policy on loyalist killings had been one of swift and savage reprisal to demonstrate the cost of attacks on their community. Usually, off-duty members of the UDR or RUC were killed, although on occasions any Protestant civilian would do. In both cases the IRA normally claimed the dead men were, in reality, loyalist paramilitaries. The accusation was difficult to disprove as loyalist paramilitary organisations didn't routinely acknowledge their own dead but, in a dirty war between two sides that didn't wear uniforms, neither tradition was going to believe the other. In east Tyrone, Phelim McNally's murder was reciprocated three months later on 7 March 1989 in the overwhelmingly Protestant village of Coagh with a population of just over 600, two pubs, a post office, a handful of shops and one garage.

It was 4.30 pm on a quiet Tuesday at that self-same garage in Hanover Square just off Coagh Main Street. Leslie Dallas – the owner – was standing on the forecourt chatting to some friends as his two teenage children got off the school bus and headed over to say hello to their dad. A car pulled up a few yards away. Gunmen opened fire from inside. Leslie Dallas was dead before he hit the ground. Killed alongside him were sixty-two-year-old Austin Nelson and seventy-two-year-old Ernest Rankin. A relative of Nelson's ran to help: 'I knew right away it was shooting and I was afraid because there were children out playing. When I got up to the garage there were kids running around screaming and I saw Ernie lying at the side of the car. Leslie was lying in the same state. Austin was lying on his back still alive. There wasn't a mark on him 'cos they'd shot him in the back like a dog.' Nelson had been on Ulster TV the night before discussing his hobby of violin making.

In a statement to the Press after the shooting, the East Tyrone Brigade took responsibility for the killing, claiming all three were members of the UVF and that Dallas – a former European Hot Rod racing car champion known on the circuit as 'the Coagh Cowboy' – was a loyalist killer and OC of East Tyrone UVF. Dallas's family, the RUC and the UVF, denied that was the case, and the independent CAIN Sutton Index lists him as a 'Civilian' and not a paramilitary. Neither Nelson nor Rankin had any paramilitary links, and the IRA were quickly forced into admitting that both men were killed in the 'general confusion'. Local newspapers reported that the gunmen – a team made up of volunteers from Coalisland and Ardboe – were heard cheering and firing into the air as they drove away, although this is strenuously denied by republicans.

After Hanover Square, East Tyrone PIRA planned to follow it up with another killing a few days later. This time it was the turn of an ASU from Cappagh to get in on the act. On the evening of Monday, 13 March, an IRA team gathered at a house on a small estate in Galbally. Four-strong, the team finalised their plan. There would be two gunmen who would pull the triggers and do the killing. A third volunteer would drive the black Astra getaway car, while the fourth would act as back-up to pick up the guns afterwards and return them to a PIRA arms dump in Galbally. The attack would be at Granville Meats, an abattoir on the Aughnacloy Road a couple of miles southwest of Dungannon. According to former UDR soldier David Galloway, in the book *Conspicuous Gallantry*, 'There were two UDR men working at Granville Meats and they [the gunmen] tossed a coin to decide which one they would murder.' One of the gunmen was twenty-three-year-old

Dermot Moore. 'Moore worked ... [at Granville Meats] and took the afternoon off to commit the murder.' Having made their decision, the team loaded a car with 'boiler suits, a shovel, gloves – they had everything in the car but the weapons' and drove straight into a waiting VCP. Unbeknown to the gang, Galloway had seen them enter the house and, suspicious, told his patrol commander David Hogg that something was up. Setting up VCPs on the road in both directions, the car drove into Hogg's checkpoint. 'There were four of them in the vehicle, one of whom was Martin Bullock. I knew him right away ...' Bullock, thirty-eight years old and unemployed, was a known PIRA suspect, and put together with the boiler suits and other terrorist paraphernalia, Hogg was jubilant: 'I was convinced I'd caught a "team".' Calling the Ops Room, Hogg demanded the RUC come out to question the suspects and make the arrests. For whatever reason the call went unanswered. Hogg became desperate. 'I did everything to egg them [the suspects] on, even to fight. That's all I wanted them to do. If they'd started fighting then I'd have to arrest them and then the police would have had to come out. I wish I just said that they'd started fighting.' With the team refusing to take the bait, and no RUC on the way 'I held them for as long as I could and then I had to let them go.' Hogg's anger was exacerbated when 'ten minutes later Ops came back on "Have you still got those people? The RUC would like to see them."' Needless to say, Hogg's reaction is unprintable.

Undeterred by their near arrest, the ASU put its plan into effect the following afternoon. At Granville Meats, UDR Private Thomas John Hardy – known as John – had lost the coin toss. A witness described how 'I heard three shots but didn't see the gun. The lorry man fell down. I ran out, and as I did I heard a long burst of gunfire.' The gunmen 'made their getaway in the black Astra', heading towards the staunchly republican Ponderosa housing estate, 'but it [the black Astra] got bogged down in muddy ground at the junction as you turn into the Eglish Road towards the Black Lough'. Another witness saw it 'abandoned, with the passenger and driver's doors open, the engine was running and fumes were coming out of the exhaust … the terrorists had obviously done a runner'. Meanwhile, at Killymeal House in Dungannon, an off-duty UDR soldier Alastair 'Ozzie' Gordon was, by chance, at headquarters talking to his friend, David Galloway. The report on the shooting came in and the two 'jumped into a Fiat Panda [Galloway's personal vehicle] … we got there quicker than the QRF because they had to go to the scene [of the shooting] first'. Local knowledge proved invaluable as the two men took side roads to what they thought would be the likely escape route for the gunmen. Coming up to Black Lough 'there was a wooden fence to keep people out and they [the ASU] were getting over the fence to get into the water.' On foot and knowing the security force response was only minutes away, the volunteers 'jumped into the water to get rid of forensics. The three of them were drenched.' Now out of the car, Gordon drew his 9mm personal protection weapon and ran towards the soaking wet men. Gordon recognised Martin Bullock, shouted his name and told him to stop where he was while Galloway shouted they were security forces. It was a good thing he did as at that moment an Army Land Rover with soldiers from the local roulement battalion appeared at speed and with their adrenalin pumping. What they saw was a man in civilian clothes carrying a pistol.

Galloway's identification of both he and Gordon as members of the security forces may well have saved the latter from being accidentally shot. As for the PIRA team, their first thought was that Gordon was an undercover soldier, probably SAS, and they froze. As Galloway exclaimed, 'I've never seen hardened terrorists so afraid.'[33]

As police and Army units swamped the area, the ASU's support team were swept up, as 8 UDR's Major John Robinson detailed. 'Dominic Nicholl and two others were apprehended by police responding to the murder. They'd crashed their car ... having been panicked by the sirens of responding police vehicles.' Under questioning 'one admitted they'd been travelling towards Dungannon to collect the weapons used in the murder and return them to a PIRA arms hide in the Galbally area'.

That information sparked a follow-on search operation around Galbally ten days later. Day one was a wash-out, but the UDR returned the next day and this time concentrated on an isolated farmhouse. 'An elderly man lived alone on the farm; he didn't drive, had no tractor, and the house, outbuildings and land were run down. He [the farmer] chatted away, offered us tea, and was glad to see someone basically.' Senior NCO Bob McCammon – in charge of the team that day – was immediately suspicious. 'An elderly man living on his own, isolated and with no transport, was a situation we'd come across before in Coalisland, where terrorists had used an elderly disabled man's property to store explosives.' The team also saw recent vehicle tracks leading to an old hay shed. An intensive search in the pouring rain yielded big results: 'Two AK-47s, two handguns, ammunition, detonators and detonator cord, timers and grenades'. The elderly landowner 'was charged with possession of the weaponry and terrorist equipment but was subsequently acquitted on a defence of duress'.

As for the ASU itself, the security force operation on the day of the shooting nailed them. A 'search team with a tracker dog tracked their route [after abandoning the car] over the hedge, up the hill and across to Black Lough ... the weapons [two AK-47s] were in a wee clump of gorse about forty or fifty metres away'. Caught red-handed, 'Dermot Moore confessed; they couldn't shut him up in the police station, he was that scared the SAS would come and he'd be killed'. Moore was very much the junior of the two gunmen. 'It must have been his first time out. What they [PIRA] called a "blooding".' He paid a heavy price for his blooding and was sentenced to life for murder. Bullock also got life, as did Patrick McGurk, the getaway driver, and Dominic Nicholl. As Bob McCammon said with evident joy, 'It was a major success against East Tyrone PIRA.'

There was no denying East Tyrone were a wounded beast after the Hardy debacle. Killing one off-duty UDR member was scant reward for losing a bundle of modern weapons and an entire ASU from the Brigade's Cappagh stronghold. But for the people of east Tyrone going about their business it meant a quiet few months, which came to an end in mid-September with the shooting dead of Staff Sergeant Kevin Froggett in Coalisland. Froggett, a member of the British Army's Royal Corps of Signals, was up repairing a radio mast in the joint RUC–Army base when he was killed by a sniper. The signaller was what the military call a 'target of opportunity', which means there was no way PIRA could foresee the radio mast would need repairing and if so, when and how. To carry out the attack the ASU responsible would have had to collect the AK-47 from its hide, select the firing point, agree an escape plan and then carry out the attack – all in the space of less than an hour.

The killing of Staff Sergeant Froggett was a success for East Tyrone PIRA, but what it hinted at was that centralised control of the Brigade – once one of its strongest assets – was deteriorating. The Coalisland ASU had acted independently and without recourse to the chain of command in the Brigade, something it almost certainly wouldn't have done when Patrick Kelly was alive. In those days it was the A Team which dominated the Brigade; everyone else had played second fiddle and gotten used to it. But now the remains of the Brigade were adjusting to a world without the A Team. Now, the second team, as it were, were moving out of the shadows to fill the gap, but as the Hardy murder proved, that was easier said than done.

What East Tyrone needed was for its remaining senior personnel, one of whom was Liam Ryan, to hold it together and rebuild. For an operation like the Froggett shooting, the Brigade's own intelligence team wouldn't have been consulted, and the first Liam Ryan as the Brigade Intelligence Officer would have heard about it would've been on the TV or radio. As it transpired, he wouldn't have much time to reflect on the way forward for the Brigade, intelligence-wise, after the Coalisland shooting.

On the night of Wednesday, 29 November, the thirty-nine-year-old former power worker and naturalised US citizen was hosting a darts march in the Battery Bar. It'd been a good night, with a solid crowd and the till was full. Ryan had called last orders and was looking to close up, although there were still around twenty customers in the bar, finishing their drinks and chatting away. A loud crash at the front door drew Ryan out of the bar and into the hallway, four of his customers going with him to see what had happened. They were confronted by two masked gunmen. Both acted 'very coolly' with one firing bursts from an assault rifle to keep everyone's heads down while the other used a pistol to shoot Ryan at close range. Another customer who looked a lot like Ryan – Michael Devlin – was also shot dead. Having got their man, the gunmen ran back outside and apparently escaped the same way they arrived – by boat across the lough. It was a Mid-Ulster UVF hit, the loyalists claiming it as retaliation for the Coagh killings of Leslie Dallas, Austin Nelson and Ernest Rankin. They knew who Ryan was and were jubilant at having killed such a high-ranking PIRA figure. Devlin was an innocent bystander, not even a Battery regular; he'd only been there for the darts.

So far it had been a difficult year for the East Tyrone Brigade. Its heartlands had suffered, with Martin Bullock's Cappagh ASU now languishing behind bars and the Ardboe's Liam Ryan in his grave. The last PIRA stronghold to take a knock was Coalisland. With just two days to go until 1990 dawned, a six-man UDR patrol commanded by Corporal Thomas Martin was 'tasked to patrol into the town centre ... as the regular Army company that was normally there were near the end of their tour and were avoiding patrolling in the centre'. By tradition the most dangerous times for any roulement battalion in Northern Ireland was at the beginning and end of their tour, and no-one wanted to lose anyone killed or badly wounded with days to go before boarding the flight home. But, as the UDR recognised, this lack of a visible presence 'encouraged the terrorists to openly target the RUC going on and coming off duty in the station'. Corporal Martin's team were helping take up the slack and came under 'a barrage of bottles and stones from a load of kids' for their trouble. Skirting round the fracas, Martin recognised a young man standing by an open car door: 'Young Steptoe! The very man I'm looking to speak to. Come 'ere!' 'Steptoe' was the nickname of Brendan Campbell, a twenty-year-old local suspect, who promptly took to his heels. Like a cat with a ball of wool, Martin gave chase and saw Campbell bolt into a busy bar. When one of his men pointed out there were two bombs on the car's backseat, Martin knew he had his man. Calling over Ronnie Campbell (no relation to Brendan), 'a wee man from the back of the patrol who was a PTI [Physical Training Instructor] and had a punch like a fourteen-pound sledgehammer', he told him to guard the door and not let anyone out. The RUC arrived, entered the bar and apprehended Brendan Campbell. Two others were arrested in the vicinity of the car, and on seeing Campbell being hauled out shouted, 'Say nothing, Brendan! We'll be alright!'

Their optimism was short lived. All three men were charged with possession of bombs with intent to endanger life. Campbell got twenty years, and Martin Gervin, a twenty-seven-year-old joiner from Coalisland, got sixteen. The third man, Tony Doris, had the charge withdrawn. Worse was to follow for Gervin. A follow-up search operation mounted by the UDR in Coalisland centred on some stables and the large dunghill beside them. 'We got a tractor to start moving the manure out. I noticed there was a point where the tractor's wheel would keep sinking into a dip.' Using a steel pole to probe the area 'it kept hitting something solid and bouncing off, we got a spade and sure enough there was a plastic barrel'. Blowing the lid off the sealed barrel the UDR found 'three weapons; two rifles and a pump-action shotgun, along with magazines and ammunition'. Ballistic tests proved that one of the guns – an AK-47 – was the weapon used to kill Staff Sergeant Froggett three months earlier. Forensics linked Martin Gervin to the AK and he was sentenced to life for his involvement in the shooting.[34]

The bombs found in the car were identified as drogues – an improvised explosive device (IED), which consisted of a small amount of Semtex packed into a tin can with a stabilising fin, handle and a mini-parachute. The bomb was designed to be thrown above an armoured vehicle whereupon the parachute would deploy and ensure it landed the right way up, then explode downwards and destroy the car or Land Rover. As Richard Kemp ruefully admitted, 'PIRA could be quite imaginative and resourceful, especially with weapons, given the limitations they had on procuring them, and they did indeed develop quite a few; some worked, some didn't, but on the whole they were pretty good.' A drogue had been used back in January that year in Sion Mills, south of Strabane, as Detective Chief Inspector Mark Byrne explained: 'Two terrorists had been hiding on the roof of the bar [Mellon's Bar] and threw a drogue bomb at the vehicle [mobile RUC patrol]. It detonated on the roof, killing Stephen [RUC Constable Stephen Montgomery] instantly and seriously injuring his colleague.' An officer in a supporting vehicle at the time remembered, 'the revellers piled out of the pub, cheering, spitting on us and started to throw pint glasses, bottles and anything else they could find at us'. An off-duty nurse bravely offered to give Constable Montgomery first aid but was driven off by the crowd.

8

EAST TYRONE SLAUGHTERED

By 1990 the Long War was living up to its name and had been going on for over twenty years. The likes of Kevin Mallon, Brendan Hughes and Seamus Dillon were all off the scene in Tyrone, the latter two in prison and Mallon in an embittered retirement. Their successors – the A Team and the Untouchables – were all dead. The Brigade had allowed itself to be drawn into a tit-for-tat sectarian quagmire with a resurgent UVF, and had floundered. The beginning of the new decade was an opportunity for PIRA's East Tyrone Brigade to regroup and look to the future.

As security forces finds, such as the one in Coalisland and at Dungannon's Black Lough, testified, the weapons so generously supplied by Libya's Colonel Gaddafi were finally finding their way through to East Tyrone's ASUs. AK-47 assault rifles, RPG-7 grenade launchers, and the ammunition that went with them, were plentiful. But if the Brigade – and the Provisionals in general – were ever going to turn isolated attacks into a full-scale insurgency capable of forcing the

British to quit, what was needed were heavy weapons, the kind that would tip the balance in their favour. That was what the Libyan shipments were meant to be – only they weren't.

As Brotherly Leader and Guide of the Revolution, Muammar Gaddafi had pledged his support for the Provisionals' struggle and had instructed his generals to furnish them with the munificence of Libya's arsenal – but he hadn't specified from where in the arsenal the weapons were to come, and so Gaddafi's generals went to the back, right to the back, by the far wall, in the corner near the leaky pipe. The IRA's quartermasters were dismayed to find that box after box of small arms ammunition was full of rounds that were rusty, decayed and unuseable, more a danger to the gunman than the potential victim, and the RPG-7s may have looked impressive but were outdated and obselete. Far worse, however, was the state of the supposed jewels in the crown, the surface-to-air SAM-7 missiles.

Reportedly, some fifty had been included in the shipments landed at Clogga Strand, those charged with their care being under special orders to protect them with the highest level of security. The air had always been a British Army-dominated realm – even as landmines and culvert bombs put the roads in south Armagh and east Tyrone off limits to soldiers – so the reasoning was simple: start knocking helicopters out of the sky and the Brits would be forced to abandon whole swathes of rural Tyrone, Armagh and Fermanagh. The Soviet-made SAM-7s were the key. However, their debut had been in 1968, and by 1990 they were distinctly old hat. The Soviets themselves had long moved on, and were using the new generation SA-18 (aka the 9K38 Igla) by the time the Provisionals were manhandling their SAM-7s into carefully prepared bunkers. Furthermore, a large number of the SAMs were junk, their unserviced battery packs dead as dodos with no hope of being powered up.

That left East Tyrone with AKs and Semtex, neither of which could bring down a helicopter. If Patrick Kelly's successor as OC was going to rejuvenate the Brigade after so many losses he needed something else – something far more powerful – and among the boxes of assault rifles and tins of ammo there were over two dozen six-foot-long wooden crates that contained a weapon that might do the trick. These were Soviet-made DShK 12.7mm heavy machine guns. Popularised by a host of Holywood movies, the DShK is a monster. First entering service way back in the Second World War, the Dushka ('Beloved One' in Russian) and its six-inch-long bullets were designed to smash up soft-skinned vehicles and tear soldiers apart at ranges in excess of two kilometres. Gifted in large numbers to the communist North Vietnamese Army and Vietcong, a majority of the 7,500 mostly American helicopters and fixed wing aircraft lost in the Vietnam War were shot down by Dushkas, and now East Tyrone PIRA were hoping to achieve much the same result in Northern Ireland.

A plan hatched over several months was finalised over the Christmas period of 1989 and early January 1990 over cups of tea round a Cappagh farmhouse table, and then the word went out. The operation would be a come-on, with bait dangled in the hope of hooking a security force response. Brigade intelligence had noted that 1st Battalion The King's Own Scottish Borderers (1 KOSB) had taken to using a Gazelle light helicopter as top cover on some of their ops, so the idea was to lure the KOSB into an ambush and bring down the aircraft. The chosen target area was Augher in the Clogher valley, right on the border with County Monaghan. South Tyrone it is, but by a quirk of fate the area fell into the Fermanagh roulement battalion's Tactical Area of Responsibility, and the jocks of the KOSB were that battalion. The local company commander, Major Bob Andrew, was under no illusions as to the capabilities of East Tyrone PIRA. Ian Bruce, journalist and Defence Correspondent for *The Herald* newspaper at the time, visited the battalion and talked to Andrew: 'In Fermanagh, raids are usually carried out by PIRA active service units based south of the border, although there is a powerful cell of "activists" – the security forces now frown on them being called "known players" – around Clogher. And for every terrorist trained to use a gun or assemble a bomb, there are perhaps three supporters prepared to act as couriers, look-outs, and providers of transport and shelter. *Tyrone is a different proposition entirely* [author's italics]. There, the hard-core terrorists live locally. Major Bob Andrew … "They are a harder breed and very, very dangerous."'

On the afternoon of Sunday, 11 February the Brigade OC gave the go-ahead and at least a dozen volunteers swung into action. The bait was a column of vehicles manned and driven by some of Ian Bruce's most well-known 'activists', all hanging around the border in plain sight and acting suspiciously. As hoped, this was picked up and a KOSB patrol was sent to investigate. A Gazelle helicopter from 656 Squadron, Army Air Corps, was tasked to provide overwatch. There were four passengers and crew: the pilot, co-pilot, a sergeant-major from the KOSB as liaison, and a fourth man. The PIRA gun team were hidden over the border in the south, out of reach of any British patrols. At around 4.30 pm the unarmed Gazelle flew into the team's gunsights and all hell was let loose. The Provisionals later released a statement claiming to have fired some 300 rounds – although locals present at the time say it was closer to fifty to sixty – whatever the figure, the Gazelle was hit and forced to crash land, breaking apart on impact. None of the occupants were hit by gunfire and all survived, but the KOSB sergeant-major suffered serious spinal injuries in the crash. At least two heavy-calibre machine guns were used in the attack – believed to be an American-made M60 and a Dushka – as well as several assault rifles.

The operation was a huge success for East Tyrone PIRA. The volunteers involved got away scot-free, and as Ian Bruce wrote in his feature for *The Herald*, 'Helicopters are prestige propaganda targets. Only one previous aircraft, a Lynx, was brought down by gunfire in 1988 in South Armagh. It was the first casualty of its kind in the 20 years of conflict in the province.'

It looked like the re-boot of the Brigade was working. The SAM-7s weren't the miracle weapon they'd been promised, but savvy intelligence and careful planning had combined to give East Tyrone the big success they'd craved since Loughgall, possibly even bigger in propaganda terms than the Ballygawley bus bomb attack.

However, there was a cloud on the Brigade's horizon, and it was the same cloud that had produced the storm at Loughgall – informers and the SAS attacks they fed. Freddie Scappaticci and the Nutting Squad had failed to uncover the dreaded Loughgall tout, and the Brigade's own internal investigation hadn't done any better. Out on the ground with the volunteers that meant nervousness and suspicion. If a gun misfired, was it because it had been sabotaged? If they went out on an operation, would they come back alive? In the closed-off, claustrophobic world of the East Tyrone Provisionals the fear of informers was acute. Sean O'Callaghan – in Crumlin Road gaol in Belfast at the time – saw the impact for himself: 'I was being led, in the company of seven IRA members, through the tunnel from the jail to the courthouse, each of us handcuffed to another prisoner. I happened to be handcuffed to a senior and long-standing member of the IRA from Dungannon … named Henry Louis McNally. I knew him quite well from my days as an IRA operative in the mid-1970s in County Tyrone.' Named in the House of Commons under parliamentary privilege by Ken Maginnis MP as being directly responsible for the murders of seventeen members of the security forces, 'McNally was a quiet unassuming man then in his mid-forties, very canny, experienced and a long-term senior IRA man who followed his own timetable, operating in his native Tyrone for going on sixteen years, interrupted by only one spell on remand.' 'I was curious as to why this cautious man was operating so far from his normal stomping ground. I asked him, and the answer I received in that tunnel was this: "Special Branch have us in a vice-like grip in Tyrone and it is just too difficult to operate, so like a fool I finished up going to Antrim to get some kills and ended up here."'[35]

A former SB officer remembered that self-same Antrim operation with a grim sense of satisfaction. 'The landmine [planted by McNally and his team] was in a culvert under the road, and the target was a military bus doing pickups to and from Massereene Barracks in Antrim, just like at Ballygawley.' The eight-man team involved were drawn from a range of areas: 'From East Tyrone there was McNally, Gerry McGee and Sean O'Hagan, another guy from south Derry and a couple of local hoods … we were on task a wee while before that one went down.' Having foiled the bomb plot a swoop was made on the team: 'They were cruising around on the M2 motorway, waiting to hear the bang and that's when we stopped them – just one crew [three officers] in one car … we got where the bomb was mixed, where it was loaded up, everything.' Both McNally and O'Hagan were convicted of attempted murder and sentenced to twenty-three years imprisonment each, while Gerry McGee got twenty years.

Despite the 'vice-like grip' of Special Branch described by McNally, East Tyrone continued to mount complex multi-weapon attacks, which took a lot of planning and involved significant numbers of volunteers, but which seemed to lack the lethality of the A Team's earlier operations. Less than a month after the Gazelle downing, a team reported to consist of at least ten members assaulted Stewartstown RUC station, spraying it with over two thousand litres of petrol and diesel from an agricultural muck-spreader before setting the flammable mixture ablaze. A gun team then shot the station up with assault rifles and an RPG-7 for good measure – but no-one was killed or injured: 'by a complete fluke there were no police officers in the station at the time'. Disappointed at the outcome, the Provisionals then issued their usual warning to any contractors who might be minded to take on the repairs.[36]

Angered by its failure at Stewartstown, the Brigade once again targeted off-duty members of the security forces. Just four days after Stewartstown, on 8 March, Thomas Jameson, a part-time UDR soldier, was shot dead near Donaghmore while driving a mixer lorry for Henry Brothers construction, the same company the East Tyrone and Derry Brigades had been targeting for almost five years. The volunteers were hidden in a garden by the roadside and as Jameson's lorry entered the killing zone, they threw a grenade in front of it, forcing the UDR man to brake hard. The gunmen then raked the cab with automatic fire, killing him instantly. The writer, Kevin Toolis, when interviewing the leadership of East Tyrone PIRA in somewhat bizarre circumstances after Tony Doris's funeral, was told: 'These people [contractors] have been warned and they know the risks, but they will not stop. If you shoot them they will stop, just like UDR sergeant *Mr Jameson* [author's emphasis].' Toolis went on to say, 'I knew he was the UDR man's killer. The voice took pleasure from the memory.'

PIRA claimed Jameson's death was in revenge for the killing of Liam Ryan in 1989, which in itself had been linked back to Leslie Dallas's murder the same year, and that of Phelim McNally in 1988, and Ned Gibson before him – and the cycle of killing still hadn't finished. On 2 November, another off-duty UDR soldier – Albert Cooper – would be murdered at the exhaust fitting garage he managed in Cookstown, this time by a booby-trap bomb attached to a car brought in for repair by a local nineteen-year-old nurse. She would later be sentenced to life for murder. The UVF retaliated by shooting dead forty-three-year-old Malachy McIvor, an innocent Catholic civilian, at his workplace in Stewartstown six days later.

With tensions running so high between the communities that year, as the gunmen did their best to stoke fear and terror on both sides, a young British Army officer from Norfolk arrived at Belfast's Aldergrove airbase. Having already completed two roulement tours, 'Rob' – not his real name – was now a Liaison Officer between his unit and RUC Special Branch. 'We were called JCUNI – the Joint Communications Unit Northern Ireland – but everyone else still called us 14 Intelligence Company. The idea was that, badged as a comms unit, we'd be able to operate under the radar far more easily.' 'Rob' had undergone much the same incredibly tough selection process as 'Noddy' more than a decade earlier: 'I did a one-day assessment type centre with interviews, psychometric and physical tests, and if you were asked back you went to Camp 1. That was an old Second World War barracks in the Welsh borders where you were given a three-digit number and that was what you were called … there were a few hundred of us, it was January, freezing cold, no heating and we lived in Nissan huts … all they did was beast us for three weeks and cut the numbers down; loads of guys left quickly, all of them RTU'd [Returned To Unit].' 'Rob' survived and 'got a weekend off and then we had to report to another base in the borders for Camp 2, which was six-months long, but far more about learning than culling the numbers, so we did lots of weapon training including on former Soviet weapons, advanced medic training, covert surveillance, close quarter battle [CQB] and close quarter reconnaissance … we were allowed to call each other by our first names but no surnames or personal info. At the end of Camp 2 there were twelve of us left.' Those dozen could now talk to each other openly and 'Rob' discovered that 'there was one other officer and ten Other Ranks [ORs], including a submariner – the unit was tri-service – and one female'.

It was then the short journey over to Northern Ireland where 'Rob' was kept at Aldergrove as the LO for South Det that covered South Armagh and East Tyrone. 'It was potluck. I went there because there was a vacancy.' The other Dets were East and North covering Belfast and Derry respectively. 'We never worked on each other's patches; we'd be liabilities as we only knew our own areas, so the other Dets covered the cities and we were rural.' 'Rob' considered the relationship with SB to be very good: 'we worked with and to them exclusively, and they knew their stuff, especially Frank Murray who was a force of nature'. 'FT' as he was known, was a Chief Superintendent, head of the Branch, and a legendary figure who'd lost an arm, a leg and an eye in a PIRA booby-trap bomb in 1976, earning him the nickname 'the Bionic Man'. Loathed by the Provisionals, even they had to admit his effectiveness – 'Frank Murray did us real damage and I mean *real* damage.'

But the relationship with SB had its pitfalls too, as one former Operator recalled: 'The Branch pushed us hard, sometimes too hard. There was one incident especially, a weapon was being moved [by PIRA] and it went to ground in Cappagh, and the Branch wanted a drive-through to try and see if a particular car was on the high street – so we said OK and went ahead – but then they wanted another and another, and in a place like Cappagh that means exposure. We said this is getting risky. There's only one way in and one way out. Any unknown cars or unknown men driving around are clocked and raise suspicions. This is a place where all the road signs had been removed by the locals so outsiders get lost. Anyway, on the fourth drive through our Operator – "John" – was hit. A car – I think it was a Ford Escort [author: a republican source identified the vehicle as a Ford Escort XR3i] – pulled up behind him and up through the open sunroof appears this gunman with an AK-47. He popped two shots through John's rear window and into the back of his seat … he only survived because the seats and doors in our cars were armoured – the two shots were very close together; it was good grouping [British Army term for well-aimed shots].'

'John' was forced off the road, whereupon he 'scrambled for his HK [Heckler & Kock machine pistol] and returned fire. He hit the gunman in the ankle or foot and then they all made off. Next thing, we were in and got "John" out.'

In a public statement made by the then Minister of State for the Armed Forces, Archie Hamilton MP, it was claimed that an undercover agent was fired on by IRA terrorists without warning, and that the agent fired back before escaping unhurt. The Provisionals told a very different story. Not unreasonably thinking the plain-clothes soldier was in fact an undercover SAS trooper, *An Phoblacht* declared that the whole operation had been an SAS set-up which had been thwarted by an ever-watchful local ASU, who'd put in an ambush of their own and killed at least two special forces soldiers in the ensuing firefight.

What neither side reported to the Press was that the driver of the Escort was hit twice – although not severely – and the wounded IRA gunman was none other than twenty-three-year-old Martin McCaughey; hit in the shoulder, ear, stomach and leg. He'd then been spirited away across the border for medical treatment. Childhood friend and former schoolmate of the younger members of the A Team, specifically Declan Arthurs, Seamus Donnelly, Tony Gormley and Eugene Kelly, McCaughey was a well-known figure to SB, as John Shackles testified: 'Martin was one of those young guys I'd approached and tried to get to see sense. I'd stopped him at a VCP and had a quiet word you know. I told him, "Look young fella, the way you're going you're going to end up on a slab, you know what I mean", but he didn't listen.' Instead, McCaughey had got involved on the political side of the movement as well as the operational side, becoming a Sinn Féin councillor for Dungannon District having won his seat in May 1989 with campaign help from Gerry Adams himself. Ironically, incapacitated as he was by his injury, he would be disqualified for repeated non-attendance at Council meetings as he joined the ranks of those officially On-The-Run. By now a senior member of the East Tyrone Brigade, it was decided that once recovered he'd team up with an even more experienced volunteer, Dessie Grew.

Desmond 'Dessie' Grew was no Jim Lynagh, but he had a reputation. Second eldest of Patrick and Kathleen Grew's eleven children of seven girls and four boys, the family were well-known republicans from Grange Blundel who ended up settling in Charlemont on the River Blackwater, only a few minutes' walk from the McKearney family home in Moy. Despite the fact that the tiny County Armagh village was overwhelmingly Protestant – or maybe because of it – Dessie and his older brother Seamus became deeply interested in Irish history and politics and Dessie became a fluent Irish speaker as well as playing Gaelic football. In the middle of May 1976, Patrick Grew took his wife to a local dance one evening, and whilst they were out a bomb was thrown into their home by a loyalist gang. The blast left six of their children injured. They were lucky to be alive. Two further attacks that same night killed four innocent Catholics in the village. Radicalised by events, both Seamus and Dessie would end up joining the Irish National Liberation Army (INLA) – a republican paramilitary organisation like the IRA dedicated to the reunification of Ireland – before the latter switched allegiance to the Provisionals. Another brother – Aidan – would follow Dessie into the ranks of PIRA and end up sentenced to fifteen years for a bomb attack on a UDR vehicle in 1984. Two years prior to that, Seamus would be shot dead in controversial circumstances by an undercover RUC unit outside Armagh City, amid accusations of an official 'shoot to kill' policy.

Jailed in the Republic in the early 1970s for IRA membership, Dessie was released only to then serve six years in Northern Ireland for unlawful imprisonment and possession of firearms and explosives. Out again, he went south once more, and this time was arrested and convicted for armed robbery. He served another eight years and was finally let out in 1988, meeting McCaughey shortly afterwards. The British newspaper the *Daily Mail*, asserted in January 2017 that both men were members of the ASU active on the European mainland in the late 1980s. This would explain why McCaughey wasn't a member of the A Team, which would seem to be the natural place for him given his close friendship with many of its members. However, while there is no doubt Dessie Grew was in the European ASU – his brother Aidan has openly stated his older brother was 'very active in Europe; in Germany and Holland particularly' – there is no such evidence linking Martin McCaughey to the European campaign so any connection is pure speculation.

The European ASU was responsible for a number of attacks across the continent in the late 1980s and early 1990s including the three RAF killings in May 1988, an Army sergeant-major shot dead in Belgium that same August, and another soldier killed in Hanover in West Germany by a booby-trap bomb the following year.

Deadly as they were, the European ASU were also infamous for making several dreadful mistakes. In September 1989 they shot dead Heidi Hazell, a German national and wife of a British soldier as she sat in her car outside the couple's married quarter in Unna, east of Dortmund. An IRA statement said she had been shot 'in the belief that she was a member of the British Army garrison'. Barely more than a month later RAF Corporal Maheshkumar 'Mick' Islania was targeted outside the airbase at Wildenrath. Returning to his car from a petrol station shop he was cut down in a hail of bullets. Corporal Islania's wife Smita and baby daughter were also in the car at the time. Smita survived unhurt but was found by paramedics in shock as she cradled the blood-stained body of six-month-old Nivruti in her arms. Once more the IRA expressed regret and insisted they didn't know that Smita and Nivruti were in the vehicle.

In May the following year the team were at it again. Two gunmen dressed in black, wearing balaclavas and armed with automatic weapons, walked up behind Nick Spanos and Stephen Melrose after they'd left a Chinese restaurant in Roermond in the Netherlands, and shot them dead a few feet away from Melrose's wife and Spanos's girlfriend. Mistaken for off-duty soldiers from the British Army On the Rhine, they were in fact Australian tourists. The whole mess reeked of poor intelligence, no doubt caused by the lack of local eyes and ears on the ground that an IRA team would be used to having back home in Northern Ireland.

The ASU were more successful five days later when they shot dead Michael Dillon-Lee, a major in the Royal Artillery. His wife Rosalind was with him when he was killed and told a German court that she heard his attacker shout out as he pulled the trigger. 'It was a triumphant kind of a cry. I didn't understand the words. It is difficult for me now to remember the detail, but it was Irish.' Ballistics showed the AK-47 used in the Dillon-Lee killing was the same weapon that murdered Mick Islania and his baby daughter. A huge police operation ensued and picked up Paul Hughes, Donna Maguire and Sean Hick. Extradited to Germany from Belgium, the judge at their trial, Wolfgang Steffen, said, 'It is clear they are members of the IRA and trained as IRA volunteers. It is also clear they were members of an Active Service Unit.' However, that didn't stop the court from acquitting them of pretty much everything. The German authorities also issued an arrest warrant for Dessie Grew, having linked him to the ASU and its campaign, and specifically the Islania shooting where he was the chief suspect, but he was in the wind and found his way back to Northern Ireland.

Grew was thirty-seven years old by now – in PIRA terms that made him an ancient – especially for a volunteer at the sharp end. Most Provisionals who'd reached that ripe old age had either climbed the ranks sufficiently to no longer go out on operations or had quietly eschewed guns and bombs in favour of providing support such as a safe house, a car or looking after a weapon. A former British Army officer involved in intelligence said, 'going out on actual operations was normally a young man's game. By the time these guys were in their thirties they had wives and kids, and so, ok, they didn't walk away – well some did – but for the others they kind of became "semi-involved". Don't get me wrong they were still diehard PIRA, they were called "well got" in republican lingo, but they weren't going out on a Saturday night in boiler suits and balaclavas anymore.' Grew was an exception, and that made him a top target for the security forces.

Acting on intelligence, a joint 14 Company/SAS operation had been authorised on a weapons hide in an isolated farm building used to grow mushrooms off the Lislasly Road near Loughgall – close to the Mackle farm where the JCB digger for the Loughgall attack had been stolen. An Out Of Bounds (OOB) box was put around the area on Army and RUC situation maps, and from then on no patrols were allowed into the area. Special Branch believed Dessie Grew was planning an attack on an off-duty member of the security forces, as a former SB officer remembered: 'The hide was near the home of a reserve policeman and that's who they were going to attack.'

'Mary' – a Det Operator – later told Peter Taylor that she was the driver for the SAS covert team. Her job was to drop them off each night, lie up a short distance away, and then pick them up in the morning as it got light: 'You drive them in, pick them up and take them home. I would make a couple of flasks of coffee and I would have some moist baby-wipes because obviously the guys had cam [camouflage] cream all over their faces. When they came off in the morning they'd be freezing cold, gagging for a cuppa and wanting to get all this dirt off their faces. Maybe I'd have some biscuits or crisps stashed in the vehicle for them too.' She knew Grew was potentially involved. 'He'd been a terrorist for twenty-odd years … we all knew his chequered past, how many people he'd killed and how many acts of terrorism he'd been involved in.'

Tuesday, 9 October 1990 was a dark autumnal night. 'Mary' dropped off the SAS team for the seventh night in a row and then drove to her lie-up position and began the long night of waiting. By midnight she'd been there about three hours, sitting in the driver's seat, awake in the dark, listening in to the team radio net, when she heard, 'Standby, standby' – the code signal that something was happening on the ground: 'I was sitting in the van with the doors locked and the windows slightly wound down ... suddenly there was this thunderous roar of 7.62 fire [7.62mm, probably from a GPMG machine gun] going down. It's very loud and you feel the jolt. It's not like watching it on TV when you just hear a crack or a bang. This is "kerboom!"'

The priest Raymond Murray – by now a Monseigneur – received a phone call at home from the RUC asking him to attend the scene. Arriving at the shed, half-lit by police torches, Murray saw that 'the bodies were quite close to each other, maybe four or five yards apart ... I anointed the two men whilst the RUC Inspector ... shone his light on them.' It was a horrific sight. 'I remember one of them especially – I think it was Dessie Grew. There was a lot of congealed blood around his head, almost looking like black oil, with a slight sheen of red on it. The brain material out of the head was all mixed up with it.' Murray also saw the weapons: '... there were two, what I thought were Kalashnikov AK-47s, lying two to three yards from the heads of the men, and I noticed there was a pistol butt jutting out of Martin McCaughey's pocket.' Having recovered from the wounds he'd sustained in the Cappagh shoot-out,

McCaughey had teamed up with Grew and was now dead, shot a dozen times. Grew had been hit by a lot more. When Taylor asked 'Mary' about the shooting, her conscience was clear: 'They walked out of that barn carrying AK-47s, walking in the direction of the Troop guys. At the end of the day they were terrorists on a mission and they met their maker. I didn't feel sad or elated. I didn't feel anything at the terrorists' death. They chose to do it … the terrorists had a clean getaway car there as well as the operational car, and in the clean car was a bottle of whiskey. Now why would they have that? Only to celebrate the death of some innocent person they're just going out to murder in cold blood.' As with almost all fatal shooting incidents involving the security forces, controversy has dogged the outcome ever since, with the families and the republican movement claiming that no warning was given and that the two men were unarmed at the time and summarily executed. 'Mary' dismissed that idea. 'A warning is always given. The Troop, like regular forces, operate under the rules of the Yellow Card [a printed card issued to every soldier in Northern Ireland detailing the circumstances under which they could and could not open fire]. We are governed by the same body of rules as anybody else when it comes to opening fire.' Brendan Hughes was of the same opinion as 'Mary'. 'In my mind if you're out on an armed mission and you get shot that's tough. That held for both sides.'

Dessie Grew was buried in Armagh City cemetery next to his brother Seamus. Gerry Adams gave the funeral oration, calling him 'a freedom fighter, a patriot and a decent, upstanding Irish citizen'. The *Daily Mail* luridly nicknamed him 'the Widow Maker'. His death was another big blow for the Brigade, as was McCaughey's. Grew was one of the most experienced volunteers in the entire IRA, let alone East Tyrone, and McCaughey had been earmarked to become one of the unit's leading lights, but instead joined his erstwhile school mates in the republican plot of Galbally church yard.

'The jails are filling up, people are dying left, right and centre and the British are getting the better hand on us.' This is how the former republican prisoner Frankie Quinn would later describe the state of the IRA in the run-up to its landmark ceasefire, and it neatly summed up the East Tyrone Brigade in early 1991. It still had volunteers to call on but the majority were young guys with relatively little experience. The senior men, the top gunmen and bombers who could put together and carry out the kind of complex, deadly operations East Tyrone had always been known for, were getting fewer and fewer.

The three republican strongholds of Ardboe, Coalisland and Cappagh told the story. On the lough shore around Ardboe, the loss of Willie Price, and especially Liam Ryan, had left a big hole in the IRA's local set-up, but Ryan's cousin – thirty-seven-year-old Michael 'Pete' Ryan – and his long-time compatriot Lawrence McNally, were still very much on the scene. Ryan had been a volunteer since the 1970s and had carried out operations with Brendan Hughes when Kevin Mallon was the Brigade OC. He'd even been involved in the run-up to the Mountjoy gaol helicopter escape, when Hughes said, 'at the time he wasn't even of voting age but was already well on his way to becoming an IRA legend. He was small and stocky and built like a tank … we'd gone to the same school in Ardboe.'

As for McNally, he was a year older than Ryan and had been active for just as long. Back in 1972, along with two other volunteers, he'd planted 'a bomb that caused £20,000 of damage to the Rural Council Offices [in Cookstown] and on April 24th [caused] a second explosion in the area, damaging forty-seven houses'. A statement read out at his trial in 1973 said, 'Donnelly [Gerald Donnelly] and McNally were armed with revolvers and provided cover for Quinn [Patrick Quinn] while he set the bomb in the hallway of the offices.' Both Ryan and McNally had known Jim Lynagh and Patrick Kelly well, with McNally suspected of involvement in the murder of Henry Livingston in 1980, and in taking part in the Tynan Abbey attack on the Stronges. As for Ryan, the security forces believed he had been hand-picked by South Armagh's Tom Murphy to lead the flying column that carried out the dramatic assault on the Derryard Permanent Vehicle Check Point (PVCP) in Fermanagh back in mid-December 1989.

As for Coalisland it had never been the same since Kevin Mallon was sidelined. With their charismatic leader out of the picture, much of the old guard had drifted away, and much of what was left had been arrested, convicted and imprisoned. The loss of Martin Gervin and Brendan Campbell had been bad enough, but since then a slew of local youngsters had joined them behind bars, robbing the area of its next generation of volunteers. As an indication of how things were, British intelligence reports alleged that Tony Doris – he of the drogue bomb incident in December 1989 – had been appointed OC Coalisland PIRA aged just twenty. Then there was Cappagh.

Cappagh was a special case – it always had been. More akin to the 'bandit country' of south Armagh than anywhere else in Northern Ireland, the fields and farms of the land that stretched out from Cappagh Mountain were home to some of the most diehard republicans in all PIRA. A former RUC officer recalled how he 'used to go up there with my granda' shooting rabbits when I was a kid of nine and ten, so I got to know the local people and what they were like ... Later when I was in the RUC they'd be putting weapons in the bogs and wait until you relaxed a bit, and they'd notice, and then they'd whack you, just like that.'

With its long-standing aversion to any sort of external authority, and deep-seated suspicion of outsiders, Cappagh should have been as immune to penetration by the security forces as Crossmaglen, Cullyhanna and Jonesboro, except it wasn't. As Frankie Quinn conceded, 'we knew in our hearts that we were deeply, deeply infiltrated', but Cappagh had been home to half the A Team and was still the emotional home of the Brigade. Now, with the A Team long dead, a new ASU was in place with a trio of local youngsters at its heart. Aged twenty-two, John Quinn was the oldest member of the team, one of six children, Quinn's family farmed a small 45-acre plot at Cranogue. Going to primary school at St Joseph's in Galbally and then secondary at St Patrick's in Dungannon, he was friends with Dwayne O'Donnell, five years his junior but destined to join PIRA alongside him. O'Donnell himself played underage Gaelic football for Galbally Pearses GAC, (Piarsaigh an Ghallbhaile), along with twenty-year-old Malcolm Nugent. Nugent was from a well-known republican family – one of his three brothers also joined the Provos – and his best friend was his cousin, Peter McCaughey, brother of Martin. All three had a practical bent and worked for local engineering firms, which was very useful given their extra-curricular activities. Quinn had been offered the opportunity of emigrating to Australia for work but had decided to stay and continue the struggle, while Nugent gave up his job in 1990 following the death of his cousin Martin so he could become a full-time volunteer. As for O'Donnell, the 'baby' of the outfit, he had suffered a horrendous accident at work that had left him in hospital for months, only returning to work in January 1991. The three volunteers were relatively inexperienced but believed Cappagh – with no RUC station or Army base close by – provided them with a bullet-proof security blanket. However, that very remoteness also made Cappagh a target, as the loyalists had shown in 1974 when they murdered local man Daniel Hughes in Boyles Bar. It was a weakness that would once again prove deadly.

The evening of Sunday, 3 March 1991 was a clear spring night. Boyles Bar was quiet, with a few drinkers scattered around the tables and propping up the bar. One of them, allegedly, was the OC of the East Tyrone Brigade, a local man and a regular. A former RUC officer who knew the area well said, 'Boyles was probably more republican than Tally's [Tally's Bar in Galbally]. It wasn't their headquarters or anything like that – they weren't that stupid – but the local Provies would see it as a place of safety, somewhere they could go to relax, do a bit of planning.'

Around 10.30 pm a blue Peugeot 305 pulled up outside. John Quinn was driving, and with him were Nugent, O'Donnell and a fourth man, twenty-one-year-old Malachy Rafferty. Even before Quinn turned off the engine, two men wearing balaclavas opened fire from a short distance away in the car park. Quinn and O'Donnell were killed in the first salvo. Nugent scrambled out of the car and ran for his life. He only got a few yards, crossing the road before collapsing behind a nearby wall after being hit several times. A petrified Rafferty stayed hidden in the car, a decision that – along with Nugent's attempted escape – almost certainly saved his life.

The two gunmen then turned their attention to the intended target – Boyles Bar itself. Trying to force the front door they found it barred from the inside and were unable to get in. Frustrated, one of the gunmen was apparently shouting in rage even as he found a small open window high in a sidewall. It was the window of the gents' toilet. It was way too small to be a way in, so instead he stuck his gun barrel through it and pressed the trigger. By a stroke of dreadful luck, fifty-two-year-old Thomas Armstrong was sheltering in the toilets and was hit and killed, alongside a twenty-one-year-old who was wounded but survived. With no way now of getting into Boyles Bar, the two gunmen – one of whom was supposedly the well-known loyalist Mark 'Swinger' Fulton – got back into their getaway car and a third man drove them away. A second team of loyalist terrorists, parked up on the outskirts of the village, drove ahead to act as a recce vehicle so they could get clear back to Portadown. Only they didn't go to Portadown. To throw the Provos off the scent the hit team went to ground locally. 'Afterwards they laid up for the night at a nearby farm, which was what people didn't expect … there were some old UVs [Ulster Volunteers] around there.' The SB officer who divulged this information conceded it was a clever move, but dangerous. 'PIRA lashed out after that and hit the local Prods hard.'

The attack was claimed by the UVF's Mid-Ulster Brigade in a statement issued in the aftermath. 'This was not a sectarian attack on the Catholic community, but was an operation directed at the very roots of the Provisional IRA command structure in the Armagh–Tyrone area.' In truth the UVF weren't sure who they'd killed, and in the fevered atmosphere after the attack the republican media machine, under direction from Belfast, refused to claim Quinn, O'Donnell and Nugent as their own. Done to garner as much public support as possible, especially in the south, it only served to anger the families as the truth quickly leaked out that all the dead, bar Armstrong, had been PIRA. Quinn especially was well known as an active volunteer, and the vastly experienced photojournalist, Oistín Mac Bride, named him in his book, *Family, Friends and Neighbours – An Irish Photobiography*, as Martin McCaughey's driver in the March 1990 Cappagh high-street shoot-out. News that three of the four dead were PIRA was greeted with rapture in loyalist circles.

The man behind the attack was widely believed to be Billy Wright. Born in Wolverhampton in the English Midlands in July 1960 to Northern Irish Protestant parents, young Billy moved 'back home', as it were, aged four, during what was a troubled childhood, spending much of it in foster care, but it wasn't until the Kingsmill massacre in January 1976 that he turned to violent loyalism. 'I was fifteen when those workmen were pulled out of that bus and shot dead. I was a Protestant and I realised that they'd been killed simply because they were Protestants. I immediately joined the youth wing of the UVF.' Living in Portadown – the so-called 'Orange Citadel' – Wright worked his way up the ranks, serving a prison sentence and finding God on the way, as he built a fearsome reputation and earned himself the nickname 'King Rat', a moniker coined by the investigative journalist Marty O'Hagan. A polarising figure – in some ways akin to Jim Lynagh – Wright was described by a fellow UVF member as 'a serious individual, intense; he didn't play practical jokes like Johnny Adair did [Adair was a senior commander in the UFF]'. While acknowledging their historical grievances Wright didn't agree that Catholics in Northern Ireland were a downtrodden minority: 'I grew up living alongside nationalists and let me tell you there were rich nationalists and poor nationalists, just like there were rich unionists and poor unionists, no difference.' An admitted hardliner since Kingsmill, in a 1995 interview he expanded on his own radicalisation: 'I was in the H Blocks standing next to a republican who was on the blanket and the sight of him, the stench of urine and excrement, it was unbelievable [Wright had himself spent six months on the blanket until ordered to quit by his UVF superiors], and I thought that a movement that can inflict that much pain on its own people, what would it do to mine?'

By the early 1990s he was a leading figure in extreme loyalism and was on the verge of taking over from Robin Jackson as OC of Mid-Ulster UVF. His father David struggled to accept what his son had become: 'I didn't know then of his UVF involvement. I've never had so much as a parking ticket in my life and the only club I ever belonged to was a catalogue club where you paid a few bob a week for a pair of trousers. He was clever and well-read. Theology, Irish history, you name it he could talk about it. He could have taken any route he wished … he didn't drink, smoke or gamble. I knew very little about his social life but I thought he had put prison and all that behind him.' It was Wright himself who laid claim to the Boyles Bar attack, later boasting to the British *Guardian* newspaper, 'I would look back and say Cappagh was probably our best.' He went on to say: 'I genuinely believe that we were very successful, and that may sound morbid, but they [East Tyrone PIRA] know we hammered them into the ground and we didn't lose one volunteer. Indeed, members of the security forces had said that we done what they couldn't do, we put the East Tyrone Brigade of the IRA on the run … East Tyrone were decimated, the UVF wiped them out and that's not an idle boast.' John Shackles didn't agree but conceded the Boyles Bar attack was a bad day for East Tyrone PIRA: 'Getting hit at home and hit that hard, that's a tough one to take.'

Unsurprisingly the Boyles Bar incident has been a source of controversy ever since. Wright's allusion to the supposed satisfaction of the security forces at the result gave additional oxygen to the oft-repeated charges of collusion between them and the UVF, with Peter Taylor echoing republican claims that the only way the loyalists could have gotten in and out of Cappagh without being stopped by the security forces would have been with the latter's assistance – and more damningly that only the security forces could have supplied them with the intelligence on the ASU itself. In contradiction of that accusation, according to the highly respected Conflict Archive on the Internet (CAIN) the three volunteers had only made the decision to go to Boyles Bar 'on the spur of the moment' and therefore couldn't have been the UVF's intended target. In which case the attack was probably planned as a repeat of the

1974 atrocity: a sectarian assault to demonstrate that not even a republican heartland like Cappagh was safe.

Even that wasn't the end of the claims and counter claims surrounding the incident. Senior figures in the UVF later insisted to the likes of Peter Taylor that Wright wasn't responsible for the attack at all and was taking credit – as they saw it – that rightly belonged to others: 'the men who carried out Cappagh were not from Portadown [Wright and his Mid-Ulster UVF team] – nowhere near it.' But as these claims tended to come after Wright had split from the UVF they carried more than a whiff of an internal feud about them. Interestingly, the SB view was that 'Belfast UVF could claim it was them, but it was Mid-Ulster who did it.' The former loyalist prisoner Clifford Peeples is adamant: 'as for Cappagh ... it was Mid-Ulster UVF, and Billy Wright was Brigade Commander Mid-Ulster UVF, end of story'.

Peeples also says, 'all this talk of collusion is nonsense. Ask the police, ask the Army what they thought of us. They detested us and would never help us.' Johnny Adair concurs with his erstwhile comrade: 'the police, the security forces in general hated us, no question'. Richard Kemp's view is more nuanced. 'I intensely disliked the Protestant paramilitaries. We were the security forces not them. Was there collusion? I never knew of any personally, and definitely not at any official level, but at an individual level I'm sure there was, yes.' It's a difficult judgement not to agree with. Robin Jackson served in the UDR for a short time; Robert McConnell, Harris Boyle, Wesley Somerville – all UDR – John Weir and Billy McCaughey, RUC Special Patrol Group – all members of the notorious Triangle of Death loyalist killing machine known as the Glenanne Gang. Even the owner of the farm from which the squad drew its name – Jimmy Mitchell – was an officer in the RUC Reserve. However, in the case of the Boyles Bar attack, a former senior UVF commander commented ruefully, 'so when South Armagh blew up the Gibsons [Chief Justice Maurice and his wife Cecily] on the border with the South it was good intelligence, but when we hit the Provos in Cappagh it was collusion – really?'

Regardless of the media furore, the real impact from Boyles Bar was in the hearts and minds of the Provisionals and the communities they drew their support from. The killing of Quinn, Nugent and O'Donnell right in the middle of what was meant to be PIRA's most secure fortress shook the East Tyrone Brigade to its core. If a UVF hit team could saunter in, wipe out an entire ASU and get away scot-free, then the world had turned. In short, if Cappagh wasn't safe, nowhere was.

The Brigade was now under intense pressure to hit back and hit back hard, and everyone was braced for the inevitable. No-one had to wait long. Just over a month later, on the evening of 9 April, thirty-one-year-old builder Derek Ferguson was sitting watching television with two of his children in their temporary mobile home on the Aughaveagh Road in Coagh. At the time Ferguson was renovating a house in the Tyrone village. Ferguson's cousin – the Unionist MP for Mid-Ulster the Reverend William McCrea – remembered him as a man 'who minded his own business and had one great goal in his young life – the building of a new home for his wife and four children'. That goal was ended when a ten-man PIRA team fired through the trailer window, killing him instantly. Ferguson's seven-year-old son raised the alarm by telephoning relatives and saying, 'Bad men have shot my daddy.' A statement by the IRA claimed Ferguson was an employee of their sworn enemy: Henry Brothers construction – which was true – and that as a close friend of the 'Coagh Cowboy' Leslie Dallas he was also a member of the UVF – a claim denied by his family. The CAIN Sutton Index lists him as a Civilian and not a paramilitary.

The next-door villages of Protestant Coagh and Catholic Ardboe – combined population of under a thousand – had been the scene of a number of lethal incidents already during the war, with Derek Ferguson's murder simply the latest. Allister Harkness knew the reality all too well. 'I was born and grew up in Coagh … the village bordered the … Ardboe, a known republican stronghold. Several PIRA attacks had been carried out in the area, both on military and police patrols, against the local RUC station, and on off-duty members of the security forces.' Harkness was particularly wary having served in 8 UDR himself: 'the threat remained at the highest level during my service … and after I left'. He was right to be concerned. Having left the UDR and gone back to working full-time in a kitchen factory in Coagh, Harkness was married with two children 'and [had] an old beat-up car leaking oil, which was all I could afford, when a policeman called at the house. It was a Thursday and I thought it was something to do with this old car and I was wondering what I was going to do if he put it off the road.' Harkness was wrong about the visit. 'He said I was to go immediately to Dungannon RUC station where someone would meet me.' His biggest fear on the journey was 'that the old car wouldn't make it' but he became really concerned when 'at the station they were waiting for me and I was ushered in without stopping at the checkpoint'. Taken to an empty office he was told 'to go back home, a police officer would stay with me, and I was to have the wife – she worked in Cookstown – and our children go to her mother's, where there'd be … protection'.[37]

What Harkness wasn't told was that Special Branch had intelligence that he was the target of a planned assassination led by Michael 'Pete' Ryan. Along with his long-time comrade-in-arms Lawrence McNally, Ryan intended to kill Harkness as he was setting off for work. Apparently, Derek Ferguson's death hadn't been enough to even the score for Boyles Bar, and East Tyrone had resolved to do more. Harkness was no random target either; according to republican sources, during his service in the UDR he had become a hate figure for local Catholics due to his alleged bigotry and harassment.

Warned off on the Thursday night, Harkness kept to his routine for the next few days, all the time carefully shadowed by his assigned undercover policeman. A former RUC officer involved in the operation recalled, 'we recce'd it [the target area in Coagh] for quite a while, and a couple of nights before the op I was standing with a policewoman on the path under the bridge there, checking we were OK'. Then, on Sunday evening, a red Vauxhall Cavalier was stolen in the nearby village of Moneymore. The Operators watching Ryan and McNally confirmed it was them and identified a third man involved in the theft: Tony Doris, the alleged OC of Coalisland PIRA. This would've been news to the RUC involved: 'We didn't know it was Ryan or McNally or whatever. The way it worked was that we were given just enough information to make the job work, but not the kind of information that would expose us to the danger of committing perjury in court.' Another RUC officer involved told the author Colin Breen, 'we'd got the heads up that three IRA men from the East Tyrone Brigade were planning to murder a UDR soldier [Harkness had actually left the UDR some time previously] and we were there to throw up a cordon to try and save the man's life if they showed up'.

With the Cavalier stolen and stashed it was assumed the hit would take place the following morning and the decision was made to substitute a look-a-like SAS trooper for Harkness as the intended target, just as at Drumnakilly back in 1988.

The following morning the PIRA team – with Doris driving – headed off to Coagh, all the time followed and watched by the Det. In the village itself the ambush was put in place. 'Police and Army were in place in good time and a member of the SAS was undercover posing as the intended victim.' An eight-man SAS team boarded the back of a red Bedford lorry which was then parked up on Coagh's narrow Main Street where it enters the village over the bridge across the Ballinderry River – the border between Counties Londonderry and Tyrone – a few hundred yards from Leslie Dallas's old garage. Close by was the point where Harkness would park up to wait for a friend to take in to work. The human decoy drove Harkness's car and pulled over in the usual place.

At 7.30 am the Cavalier with the gun team on board drove over the bridge onto Main Street, passing by the Bedford lorry. As the car slowed, Ryan and McNally – the shooters – had their windows down and brought up their weapons to open fire. The decoy trooper saw them, dived out of Harkness's car and vaulted a wall.

The ambush was sprung. A storm of automatic fire engulfed the Cavalier. Tony Doris was hit immediately and lost control of the Cavalier, which careened into a parked VW Golf. An RUC officer at the scene said, 'I believe that the terrorist car ... was hit some two hundred times before it burst into flames.' An Operator remembered, 'There was a massive fireball and smoke hundreds of feet in the air ... it was like watching a James Bond movie.' At least one RUC witness found the whole incident traumatic. 'The thing that always struck me about the operation was ... the level of commitment and the dedication of the terrorists to their cause. One of the gunmen was shot and wounded ... and was on fire, but he managed to get out of the ... vehicle and crawl up the street. Whatever was driving him, he still obviously felt that ... he could get away.' Whether the dying man was Ryan or McNally the policeman didn't know: 'There was nothing that could be done to save him ... and eventually he just lay down and died. All three terrorists died.'[38]

Two weapons were recovered from the scene and forensically tested, with the results linking them to four murders, 'including one killing that had taken place in a garage only two hundred yards from where they'd been intercepted'. That had been the killings of Leslie Dallas, Austin Nelson and Ernest Rankin back in March 1989.

Once more the RUC, the Det and the SAS had combined in the destruction of an East Tyrone PIRA team out on an op, and one that included two of its deadliest members and last remaining veterans.

For Allister Harkness the news was a blessed relief. 'On the Monday morning someone drove my car and a three-man PIRA ASU murder gang that were waiting along the route I would have taken were shot dead ... I never had an inkling that

I was being targeted for assassination by PIRA. I never noticed or spotted anything unusual.' Unsurprisingly the former UDR soldier thanked his lucky stars: 'I owe my life to the security forces to whom I am very grateful.'

As for the reaction in PIRA, one Tyrone republican told Ed Moloney, 'After McNally and Pete Ryan, that was it, we had nobody left.' For the first time since the long war had been declared, there was murmured whisperings among IRA men in Tyrone of 'war weariness'.

For Tony Doris's family it was a time of sorrow. Living on Coalisland's Meenagh Park estate, the Doris's were a well-known republican family, but Kathleen Doris had been filled with dread when she realised her son had joined the Provisionals, as she told the writer Brendan O'Brien. 'You know they're going to die if they join the IRA. They have a life expectancy of one to two years.' On the wall behind her as she spoke to O'Brien were the tricolour flag and the military-style gloves and beret from Tony's paramilitary funeral.

The Coagh ambush was another bloody marker in the war in east Tyrone, and one that carried a stark warning for the Brigade. It was clear the security forces had excellent intelligence to pre-empt the attack, and while PIRA immediately began an internal investigation that reportedly included dragging a suspected informer south of the border for interrogation, other sources suggest that the technical side of surveillance was just as responsible for providing the vital information.

For the Provisionals Coagh also threw up a number of other serious questions. Ryan and McNally had joined PIRA in the early 1970s and had decades of experience between them. But the fact that these two well-known and senior volunteers were carrying out an operation with seemingly little or no support network in place – bar Tony Doris as their driver – is puzzling. Where was the getaway car and driver? Why wasn't a recce team working with them, clearing the route and warning them of any danger? Why wasn't the gun car stolen that same morning so removing the chance of the owners reporting it as such? None of these questions were answered for an operation that looked half-baked at best and seemed to have been lacking in just about every department.

However, as if to prove it could still bite as well as bark, the Brigade looked to make a statement of intent, and once again chose a local man to make its point. On 5 August – two months after Coagh – the Provos shot dead Eric Boyd, a forty-two-year-old former UDR soldier, as he left work on the Altmore Road near Cappagh. As they had done with Leslie Dallas and Derek Ferguson, PIRA declared the victim was a member of the UVF – and a senior one at that – a claim his family denied, as the families usually did. Ten days later it was the turn of another former UDR man, Ronnie Finlay, murdered on the farm where he worked on the Brocklass Road near Sion Mills. This was West Tyrone PIRA's turf. An RUC officer involved in the investigation told the author Colin Breen that 'his wife and children had just dropped him [Ronnie Finlay] off at work. It turned out a six-man IRA team had taken over the farmhouse during the night, holding the family at gunpoint while they waited for Ronnie to arrive for work at around 8.30 am. The terrorists stepped out of the house and opened fire just as Ronnie got out of his car. His wife [Kathleen] reported hearing a noise just as he'd closed the car door but she didn't think it was a gunshot … [then] she could see that he was trying to keep himself upright on his feet.' Getting out of the car Kathleen Finlay thought her husband had been suddenly taken ill when 'there was this burst of automatic fire and she knew they were under attack'. She told the officer afterwards, 'All I can remember is being back in the car and trying to force my children down onto the floor to protect them. Andrew, my youngest, clung to me and I thought I've got to get them to the farmhouse for protection.' Carrying Andrew, Kathleen Finlay tried to reach the supposed safety of the farmhouse but 'this gunman confronted me and told me to get back'. Doing as she was told, she then had to stand there as the gunman 'stood at my right-hand side with his gun trained on me and then they just pumped Ronnie with automatic fire with the children there'. When it was over, she 'walked about three quarters of a mile for help, my legs were all punctured with shrapnel, streaming with blood'.[39] The PIRA team then ran across the neighbouring field and were safely in Donegal.

For the RUC the frustration was palpable, with one officer remembering, 'That whole Provisional IRA unit were known to us; they were mostly from one family.' The same officer recalled with not some small satisfaction that the reported ringleader of the attack and head of the local ASU, 'nicknamed Snake', was later shot and badly wounded by another off-duty UDR target, this time one who was able to react and fire back. 'Snake' was convicted of attempted murder before being released under the terms of the Good Friday Agreement. Ronnie was the second Finlay to be killed by the Provisionals, his brother Winston – a former UDR soldier turned RUC reservist – died four years earlier in 1987: 'arriving home with his wife after visiting relatives, he got out of the car and was opening the garage door when he was shot'. That was in Ballyronan, County Londonderry, and given Ronnie's killers had fled into Donegal, the ASU responsible may have been from the Derry or Fermanagh Brigades; however, as the Army veteran Lieutenant-Colonel Bob Goodin remarked, 'as the Provisionals didn't keep any records it's very difficult to tell'.

By now the façade of invincibility that had so long cloaked the East Tyrone Brigade was badly cracked and would be further eroded by their loyalist foes. With Robin Jackson out of the picture, loyalist paramilitaries were increasingly targeting known republicans and their families rather than the uninvolved mass of Catholics. Responding to what they saw as a deliberate policy of 'ethnic cleansing' with the killings of the likes of Boyd and Finlay, they took their revenge by killing Pádraig Ó Seanacháin, a member of Sinn Féin, shot dead by a UFF sniper as he went to work in Killen near Castlederg on 12 August, and Sean Anderson – a former republican prisoner – killed in his car on the Loughbracken Road near Pomeroy on 25 October 1991. The security forces pointed the finger at Ó Seanacháin as being behind a number of booby-trap bomb attacks in the preceding years including those that killed the off-duty UDR soldiers Victor Foster and William Pollock in Tyrone in 1986, along with Desmond Caldwell, an innocent Protestant civilian mistaken for an off-duty RUC officer and blown up in the cab of his lorry at work. Ó Seanacháin was belatedly acknowledged by the Provisionals as one of their members in 2002. But at the time the message from loyalists was clear – Tyrone is now vulnerable – as a former senior UFF commander made clear with evident relish. 'With the rise of Sinn Féin we could now see who was involved. We had the

Lebanese guns, and now for the first time we could hunt them – we could hunt the Ra [IRA].'

The new year brought east Tyrone no reprieve. On 3 January 1992 loyalist gunmen walked into the McKearney family butcher's shop in Moy and shot Kevin McKearney and his uncle John at point-blank range. Kevin – brother to Séan, Tommy and Pádraig – died at the scene. John lingered on in hospital, finally passing away on 4 April. Both men were innocent civilians, selected for execution solely on account of their family name. For most of the preceding two decades and more, IRA policy and practice following loyalist sectarian attacks had been clear: immediate and deadly reprisal, but by 1992 times had changed and the Belfast leadership of the organisation were keen to dampen down any talk of revenge as they looked longer term to a possible political solution to the war. This was not what the East Tyrone Brigade wanted to hear, nor were they much interested in the nuances of the emerging political situation. Their answer was Teebane.

On the morning of 17 January a bomb team lay in wait on the Cookstown to Omagh road. They'd spent the early hours digging in a roadside bomb with 1,500lbs of homemade explosives packed into a number of plastic barrels. Once in place the team laid out a command wire from the bomb back to the chosen firing point approximately a hundred yards away – then they waited. It was a typical January morning and before they knew what was happening, a thick blanket of fog covered them and the road. Visibility was dreadful and there was no way the bombers could make out their target. They made the decision to abort and try again that night.

And try again they did. Around 5 pm that afternoon

headlights appeared from the direction of Omagh. The bomb team got the signal – this was it. Waiting until the vehicle slowed down as it reached the Teebane crossroads, they detonated the device. The explosion was ear splitting and heard at least ten miles away. The target vehicle was a Ford Transit van the PIRA team believed belonged to their old enemy, Henry Brothers construction, being used to transport workers home from a job for the security forces. They were only half right. It was indeed full of workers going home after a day's labour on a military base, but it actually belonged to another company, Karl Construction, based in Antrim. It didn't really matter. The van was torn apart. The side nearest the blast disappeared, along with the men sitting along it in the back. The remainder of the van was sent tumbling along the road for at least thirty yards, throwing out the bodies of the dead and injured. There'd been fourteen men inside – including the forty-four-year-old driver Oswald Gilchrist – all of them working on rebuilding Lisanelly Barracks in Omagh. Only six survived, all of them badly wounded, many suffering life-changing injuries. The other eight died; seven at the scene and Oswald Gilchrist in hospital four days later. All the victims were Protestants in what was very much seen by unionists as a nakedly sectarian attack, and the worst of its kind since the Kingsmill massacre back in 1976.

Claiming responsibility, the East Tyrone Brigade said, 'the IRA reiterates its long-standing call to those who continue to provide services or materials to the forces of occupation to desist immediately. Since 1985 the IRA has adopted a policy of taking military action aimed at ending Britain's cynical use of non-military personnel for the servicing and maintenance of British Crown Forces' bases and installations.' One survivor described how 'I looked around and all I could see was fire.' The blast had brought down the overhead power lines: 'I have experienced getting an electric shock, but fire was coming out of my eyes.' Helped by another survivor he said, '"Get me up", and part of my kneecap came off but I knew my leg was there and I thanked God that I was alive.' Another victim was twenty-five-year-old Gary Bleeks from Cookstown. He'd worked in England for a time, lost his job, moved back home and found work with Karl Construction. He lived with his grandmother, Mrs Elma Oxteby: 'We waited in suspense from 6 o'clock. Didn't know till ten. We rang the hospitals. He wasn't admitted and we knew if he wasn't admitted then he must be dead. And a woman came yesterday and told us her daughter held his hand till he died [a car was behind the van when it was hit and it's assumed this lady was in it]. She asked him where he was from and he said Cookstown ... it was a comfort that we know there was somebody with him, that he wasn't dying on his own.'

Jay Nethercott remembers Teebane with real bitterness: 'That job was done on the express orders of the Brigade OC at the time. He didn't even tell hardly anyone else in the Brigade they were going to do the job, let alone Belfast. They mixed the explosives in a nearby farm – the farmer didn't really have any choice but to agree – but later on two of his sons died in a car accident and he was grief stricken and said it was the sins of the father come back to haunt him.'

Gerry Adams put out a statement saying Teebane highlighted 'the urgent need for an inclusive dialogue which can create a genuine peace process'. His real views are impossible to know with certainty but with the British Prime Minister John Major loudly condemning Sinn Féin, promising more troops on the streets and publicly reassuring unionists that the IRA would never change British policy, he could be forgiven for cursing the hard-liners in Tyrone. Not that there was a great deal of communication between Belfast and Tyrone at the time. The Falls Road Think Tank Adams had set up in the early 1980s to act as his inner circle and a sounding board for his ideas on the movement's future was almost entirely comprised of Belfast men, with just one representative each from Derry, Donegal and Monaghan, and not a single man from Tyrone. Kevin McKenna was still the IRA Chief of Staff, but with the deaths of Lynagh and Patrick Kelly at Loughgall, his influence on the Brigade was not what it was.

Money had now once again become a major sticking point for republicans, with much of the available cash channelled into politics rather than the war. Volunteers were meant to receive a weekly allowance: £20 for a married man, half that if single, with a one-off payment of £100 to the dependents of any volunteer arrested. Sometimes the money was paid and sometimes it wasn't. South Armagh was still the wealthiest IRA unit, cross-border smuggling proving as lucrative as ever, but elsewhere cash was tight. The Libyan shipments were meant to have removed the need for the organisation to buy any more weapons, but the Gardaí were becoming more effective at finding IRA dumps, unearthing more than 800 guns and over 300,000 rounds of ammunition between 1985 and the early 1990s. Much of what was found was in Donegal and the other border counties, despite the majority of the main arms caches being centred on Limerick in Munster, and, of course, the security forces in Northern Ireland constantly chipped away with almost a conveyor belt of finds steadily reducing the IRA's arsenal. That arsenal was still substantial though, with the Provos in possession of more than 600 AK-47s, some forty RPG-7s and over three tons of deadly Semtex. East Tyrone in particular were set on using it.

In fact the weapon East Tyrone really wanted to use was the monster-sized DShK heavy machine gun they'd been supplied from the Libyan haul, and which was now safely tucked away in a hide under the control of Coalisland PIRA. The town had always been a republican stronghold, and Kevin Mallon had built up a formidable local organisation in the area before his sidelining by the leadership in the mid-1980s. The elevation of Tony Doris to OC was meant to help reinvigorate the local ASUs – of which there were two – and his involvement with Pete Ryan and Lawrence McNally was part and parcel of that build-up. The subsequent deaths of all three men had been a major blow for both Coalisland and Ardboe PIRA, and led to a new generation taking the reins in the former.

At the heart of the new Coalisland unit were two school friends: Kevin Barry O'Donnell and Sean O'Farrell. O'Donnell, known as Barry by one and all, came from a militant family who'd insisted he was christened on that most auspicious of republican dates – Easter Sunday. He knew Tony Doris well and had joined PIRA aged nineteen, before heading across the water to England where he enrolled as an agriculture student in rural Shropshire. Combining his studies with his duties as a volunteer, O'Donnell was under surveillance by the police when he became involved in a high-speed car chase through north London in May 1990. In the boot of his car were two

AK-47s. Stopped and arrested, he was tried at the Old Bailey in 1991 where his defence hinged on convincing the jury of twelve men and women, good and true, that he had found the weapons in his car, and, being in a state of shock at their discovery, had driven away in haste to find somewhere to dump them. On the stand he said to the jury, 'I don't support the IRA. I come from a devout Catholic family … they do not support the taking of life.' They acquitted him on the major charge of possession with intent. Finding him guilty on a lesser charge, he was sentenced to time served and set free. He went straight back to Northern Ireland and re-joined the ranks of the East Tyrone Brigade.

Safely at home in Coalisland, O'Donnell lost no time in renewing his friendship with Sean O'Farrell. O'Farrell was a fitter welder for a local building supplier in the town and had been involved in PIRA for several years already. Even before his friend Barry's madcap chase round London he was a suspect for the security forces, believed to be hiding weapons in at least one cache near his home according to local UDR sources: 'I was the Search Adviser [formal trained role leading on planned searches] at the time [Christmas 1989] … I was tasked into Dungannon and was told by the police and the Commanding Officer that they wanted to do a search in Coalisland at the back of Sean O'Farrell's house.' The resulting operation uncovered the AK-47 used to shoot Kevin Froggett as he repaired the local base's radio mast and put Martin Gervin away for life. Back together once more, O'Donnell and O'Farrell were soon arrested in May 1991 and charged with possession of an assault rifle and an RPG-7 warhead. The charges were later dropped and both men were released.

With Tony Doris now dead, twenty-one-year-old O'Donnell became the *de facto* leader of PIRA in Coalisland, and he and O'Farrell came up with a plan to hit the security forces, avenge Tony Doris's killing and put East Tyrone back on the map, all at the same time. The plan centred on the joint RUC/Army base in the centre of town. Detested by local republicans as the most visible symbol of British imperial rule, the base was fortified with anti-rocket wire fences, thick walls and protective sangars. O'Donnell and O'Farrell wanted to hit it, and hit it hard.

Unlike the under-resourced Coagh attack on Allister Harkness the previous year, O'Donnell intended to mount a far more sophisticated operation this time round. In an echo of the type of assault launched by the A Team of old, there would be two teams, one in a support role acting as the eyes and ears, and the other as the gun team itself – both of Coalisland's ASUs were going to be busy. One ASU would first carry out a diversion to draw away any security force units in the area, while the other mounted the precious DShK onto the back of a stolen lorry. The lorry would then drive to the target and reverse up so that the gun faced the entrance and the sangar that protected it. That sangar was usually manned by RUC officers on a rotational basis. The lower half of the sangar was brick but at head height it was darkened glass, hardened against bullets – normal bullets anyway, but not the hand-length shells from a 12.7mm DShK. They could penetrate the glass and kill everyone inside. O'Donnell would be the shooter, with O'Farrell in the back of the lorry with him as his loader.

The driver would be twenty-year-old Patrick Vincent, second child of Danny and Rose Vincent. His parents had no idea he was a volunteer or that on the evening of 16 February 1992 he was going out to rendezvous with the other members of his ASU in the car park of St Patrick's Roman Catholic church in the village of Clonoe just outside Coalisland.

Alongside Vincent in the cab would be Peter Clancy. Aged just nineteen and working as a fitter welder for a Cappagh firm, Clancy had already been injured in a previous operation but had returned to active service as soon as he was able. There would be two more volunteers at Clonoe: Aidan McKeever and Martin Woods. Neither would be armed; their job was to drive the getaway car.

As darkness fell the plan went into operation. First, a takeaway delivery order was called in to a Chinese restaurant in nearby Cookstown. When the driver arrived at the given address with the food he was held at gunpoint and told a bomb was being put in the back of his van. He was then ordered to drive to Cookstown RUC station and abandon the vehicle outside where it would be blown up. Terrified, the delivery man headed off towards Cookstown as ordered. On seeing a VCP he stopped and told the soldiers about the bomb. The soldiers got him to safety, called it in and set up a cordon around the van. But it was all a hoax designed to draw the security forces away from the real target.

As the diversion was unfolding, the stolen lorry with the DShK bolted on the back was driven to the church car park. Also on the way to St Patrick's was Sean O'Farrell. Sergeant John McLaughlin of 1st Battalion the Queen's Lancashire Regiment (1 QLR) was leading his multiple on patrol south of Coalisland when he received a radio message from 8 UDR Operations Room placing the area he was in Out Of Bounds with immediate effect. 'On checking my map I realised that I was in the middle of this area so I informed the Ops Room that I would move my troops east and tell them when I was out of the area so a helicopter could pick us up.' He later told an inquest what happened as he and his men moved east: 'About 1630hrs … whilst we were moving … towards Cloghog Hill, a member of my team told me that Sean O'Farrell was the passenger in a car travelling towards him. I told the soldier concerned … to stop the vehicle and await my instructions. I then informed the Ops Room … and asked what they wanted us to do. I was instructed to search, log all details and send all information to the unit Int [Intelligence] cell … Nothing was found during the search … the vehicle … sped off towards Coalisland.' By coincidence 1 QLR had also been involved at Loughgall.

By now it was past ten in the evening and with the volunteers mustered at the church car park, everyone took up their positions and headed off into Coalisland some two miles away – the recce car taking the lead and behind them the lorry driven by Patrick Vincent with O'Donnell, O'Farrell and Clancy aboard. Arriving outside the joint Army/RUC base, Vincent drove a few yards past it and then reversed so the DShK was facing it. O'Donnell then let fly, spraying the front sangar and the base entrance with tracer ammunition at point-blank range. The DShK is too heavy to have the rapid-fire rate of smaller machine guns, but even so dozens of rounds riddled the target. Job done, the ASU made its getaway, the recce car leading, its hazard lights flashing in triumph and the gun team waving an Irish tricolour flag off the back of the lorry. But instead of taking the shortest route back to the Clonoe car park, the two vehicles turned left up Annagher Hill towards the fifty-house Meenagh Park estate, and then slowed down. This was where Tony Doris had lived. In tribute to him the gun team then fired their weapons into the air and shouted, 'Ra! Ra! Up the Ra! [IRA] That's for Tony Doris!' Having made their point, the two vehicles headed to Clonoe along a back road.

Arriving in the church car park at around 10.45 pm, the gun team began to dismount the precious DShK from the lorry, while McKeever and Woods waited in the getaway car. Everything had gone to plan, and O'Donnell could congratulate himself on mission accomplished. At that point a flare was fired into the air, lighting the scene.

According to the security forces a warning was shouted out. When the gun team didn't immediately surrender, at least ten SAS troopers waiting in ambush positions opened fire. Vincent died in the cab of the lorry, Clancy a few yards away and O'Donnell by the back wheel. Clancy was hit ten times and O'Donnell just twice. Sean O'Farrell made a run for it but was killed before he got to the road. McKeever and Woods tried to escape in the getaway car but ran into a waiting cut-off group which peppered the vehicle with automatic fire – the car crashed into a hedge and the two were lucky to survive, wounded but alive.

A former British soldier explained what had happened. 'It was an informer. He warned RUC Special Branch about the attack. The security forces knew all about it – they knew who was going to be involved, they knew about the lorry, they knew about the DShK – everything.' Crucially the security forces also knew the front sangar was the main target. 'The policemen who would've normally been in the front sangar had been pulled out and were safe in the back of the base, but the PIRA boys couldn't see that as the protective glass was tinted so they couldn't see inside.'

There is no evidence linking the two, but on 12 August 1992, the body of twenty-two-year-old Coalisland PIRA volunteer Robin Hill was found at Beechmount Gardens, west Belfast. Hill's hands were tied, his eyes were taped shut and he was wearing a white boiler suit. He'd been shot twice in the back of the head. His family refuted the PIRA claim that he'd been an informer.

The entire Clonoe operation had been carefully planned by the security forces. With Operators from the Det watching the suspects, the SAS ambush team had taken up position around the church car park even as the ASU neared their target. The original idea was to hit the gun team in Coalisland itself but no suitable place was found and the risk to civilians was too great, so the SAS commander – a senior NCO who'd begun his military life in the Parachute Regiment – had opted instead to target the car park. However, after the attack on the base, the ASU's diversion to drive past the Doris house had almost thrown the whole plan into disarray. With the volunteers not returning straight back to the car park, and seemingly heading off in another direction, the SAS commander was put under immense pressure to abandon his plan and chase after the gun lorry. But he'd stuck to his guns and told everyone to stay in position and wait. Thereafter it had been textbook, all except for the gas tank next to the church being hit by a stray bullet and burning down part of the building.

In the aftermath, the republican media machine kicked into action straightaway, claiming that another four-man ASU involved had returned fire and escaped unhurt after wounding at least one SAS trooper, and that an unidentified eyewitness saw one of the volunteers executed after trying to surrender. A Catholic priest asked to attend the site in the aftermath, inadvertently stoking the flames, as a retired RUC officer explained: 'There were just two crews – only six of us – and we were laid up nearby and when we heard "Bodies Down" we ran to take over the cordon, get the Troop away and preserve the scene for evidence. We brought the priest in [Fr Kieran McKeone] and walked him round, and he walked right by an AK [AK-47] stuck barrel down in the grass, and the Dushka was still hanging off the back of the lorry. He gave the last rites to all the boys, but he still told everyone there were no guns, but hey, it was dark.'

Rumours also circulated about the attack itself, with one being that it had all been a publicity stunt rather than a serious operation, with claims that the whole thing had been filmed for propaganda purposes. A former RUC officer doubted that scenario but was nevertheless puzzled about the attack. 'Did senior or even middle management in the Provies know beforehand about the job, I doubt it. It seemed more like an act of bravado to me.'

Behind the scenes, the East Tyrone Brigade went into shock. Coalisland PIRA still hadn't recovered from the death of Tony Doris the year before and now it had lost an entire ASU. At a stroke the most active remaining gun team in the Brigade were gone. O'Donnell and O'Farrell were young but they were experienced, and their deaths left a gap that no-one stepped up to fill. As for the Clancy family, Peter's father Leo told reporters he'd only found out his son was a volunteer a year earlier when he'd been admitted to Monaghan Hospital over the border with shrapnel in his foot after a bomb he was planting went off prematurely. He'd pleaded with Peter to get out, offering to get him a job in Dublin or even a ticket to America, but he refused. Patrick Vincent's parents were even more distraught, with his mother not only turning down the IRA offer of a paramilitary funeral but stating openly that 'as far as we are concerned our son was not involved with the IRA, but they are claiming him. We are sure he was pressurised.'

In a postscript to the incident, the getaway driver Aidan McKeever received a three-year suspended sentence in return for pleading guilty, only to later sue the British government for his injuries, receiving a £75,000 settlement years afterwards.

9

THE LONG WIND DOWN

'East Tyrone had a proper reputation. I'd already been a platoon commander on a Fermanagh tour, but Tyrone was meant to be much more dangerous – a far greater threat.' This was how the Intelligence Officer of an incoming east Tyrone roulement battalion felt in 1993. Setting up shop in Dungannon, however, he soon realised that all was not as it seemed: 'On arrival I soon realised that SB had the whole area pretty well sewn up. What was clear early on was that shoots – especially the big multi-weapon team shoots that East Tyrone were well known for – were out. PIRA couldn't persuade any of the local players to pick up a gun and go on that sort of operation. All of them – and there were still a lot of them – were worried, and I mean really worried, about intelligence being leaked and then they'd either end up dead or doing life.'

Clonoe marked a real turning point for East Tyrone PIRA. A former SB officer said with no little satisfaction: 'After Clonoe they knew they had a problem – a real problem ... the saying at the time was that if you stopped a car full of loyalist terrorists, three out of four would be touts, but if you stopped a car full of republicans you'd be saying "Maybe he is, or maybe him and no more", but having said that you'd be surprised just how many there were and who they were.'

However, the Brigade didn't disappear, or stand itself down, and it was still committed to fighting the war, but it changed the way it fought. The era of the kind of deadly close-quarter operations that the likes of the A Team, the Harte brothers, Dessie Grew, Martin McCaughey, Pete Ryan and Lawrence McNally, all specialised in, was gone. As a young British intelligence officer declared, 'from then on it was mortars – and particularly attacks on bases – that was the main threat, so we changed the way we fought too. It was far more about endlessly patrolling the towns where our bases were, so Dungannon, Cookstown, Pomeroy, Coalisland and so on.' He wasn't wrong. From mid-1992 up to the ceasefire in 1994 the Brigade mounted a dozen mortar attacks across Tyrone, mostly using their latest 'wonder weapon' the Mark-15 Barrack Buster.

East Tyrone pioneered the new mortar, announcing its arrival on 5 December 1992 by firing one at Ballygawley's rebuilt RUC station. The Barrack Buster itself was a bit of a monster, measuring a full metre long and made from adapting the domestic gas cylinders that were common on pretty much every farm across the Tyrone countryside. Its range was greater than the Mark-13, but still short – only about 150 metres – but it packed a punch, with around 150lbs of homemade explosives in its 36cm-wide tube. Given its weight it was usually mounted on a suitable vehicle and driven into place – at Ballygawley that meant a tractor parked up near the village's health centre. The attack itself was a failure, the bomb hitting a tree by the station wall and landing harmlessly in an adjacent field. The British bomb disposal team called to the scene to make the device safe were able to examine it at length and send it away for analysis.

Not put off by their lack of success at Ballygawley, PIRA used the Mark-15 again against the RUC stations at Clogher, Beragh, Caledon (twice), Dungannon, Fintona, Carrickmore and Pomeroy, as well as the British Army's Permanent Vehicle Check Point (PVCP) on the border at Aughnacloy. For the Brigade's volunteers, the advantages of the Barrack Buster were manifold, of which the most important was the lack of personal risk when they used it. Driving a mortar into place and then setting a timer before speeding off in a getaway car was a relatively safe option, and not a single volunteer was shot dead by the security forces while doing it. But if the mortar was a safer option for PIRA's volunteers, it was also safer for the security forces with the mass casualties of the 1985 Newry mortaring never again replicated in what in some ways was coming to resemble a sort of phoney war.

In fact, deaths in Tyrone were now far more likely to be the result of loyalists rather than the IRA, with Mid-Ulster UVF continuing to target republicans and their families. In early September 1992 it was the turn of Charles and Teresa Fox, murdered in their own home on the Listamlat Road near Moy. The Foxes were selected because their son Patrick – a Provisional volunteer – had just been imprisoned for possession of explosives, and they were related by marriage to the McKearneys. A UVF gun team stormed into the house and shot fifty-three-year-old Teresa in the kitchen. Her husband was gunned down in the room next door, dressed in his pyjamas. Their bodies were found the following morning by their daughters as they called at the house when their parents didn't answer the phone. The Unionist MP Ken Maginnis condemned the murders and called them 'a blasphemy before God'.

Further attacks left Patrick Shields and his son Diarmuid dead in their grocer's shop at Lisnagleer near Dungannon, and mother of five Kathleen O'Hagan, killed at home in Greencastle in August 1994 after a UVF gang forced their way into the house. Mrs O'Hagan was seven-months pregnant at the time. The Shields were targeted because Patrick had been an IRA member in the 1970s, but having left the organisation years previously he had remained in contact with Kevin Mallon – not a fact many would be privy to. As for O'Hagan, her husband Paddy was a former republican prisoner who'd served eight years for possession of a weapon.

The vz.58 assault rifle used in the Fox murders – and most of the others besides – was finally recovered by soldiers from 'A' Company 1st Battalion Royal Anglians in Greystone near Dungannon after the killing of seventy-six-year-old Roseanne Mallon in May 1994. Ms Mallon was watching television in her sister-in-law Brigid's house on the Cullenramer Road in Castlecaulfield when a loyalist hit team parked up outside, ran round to the back of the bungalow and opened fire through the living room window. The pensioner was hit multiple times in her arms, legs, head and body and was killed instantly. Her 'crime' was that her nephews, Martin and Christopher, were both members of the East Tyrone Brigade, with Martin Mallon – a senior volunteer – convicted nine years earlier for possession of explosives. The murder weapon was from the shipment purchased from Joe Fawzi; its stock had been removed and the letters 'T' and 'UVF' engraved on the rear plate. Ballistic tests linked the rifle to as many as twelve murders and two attempted murders across east Tyrone and south Londonderry over the preceding four years including the 1991 Boyles Bar attack in Cappagh and the shooting of Liam Ryan in the Battery Bar in 1989.

By now, East Tyrone may have been relegated to less riskier stand-off attacks on security force bases, but it was still determined to hit back against those it deemed a threat to its own community. Consequently, on Monday, 11 January 1993, barely a week after the Shields attack, the Brigade shot dead Matthew Boyd, a sixty-year-old Protestant, as he drove his car along the Donaghmore Road outside Dungannon. In a statement to the Press the Provisionals claimed that Boyd – a former B-Special – 'had a long involvement in the UVF dating back to the 1970s ... we will execute those involved in sectarian killings'. Boyd's family denied any such involvement and CAIN lists him as a Civilian.

Three months later the Brigade struck again, this time in Cookstown, employing an under-vehicle booby-trap bomb to kill David Martin, a thirty-three-year-old former member of the UDR. Once more PIRA claimed the dead man had links to loyalist terrorists, and once more the family denied it. Renewed claims from loyalists that the Provisionals were engaged in a calculated programme of ethnic cleansing of Protestants in border areas resurfaced as gunmen from both sides continued to wage a brutal internecine war.

In truth, the war in Tyrone had changed irrevocably. PIRA kept up a steady stream of operations over the next few years;

two horizontal homemade mortar attacks on RUC patrols in February 1997, another intercepted near Caledon with the PIRA volunteers escaping on foot, the shooting in the face of a female RUC officer in the same town – she survived – and the throwing of a bomb into Coalisland RUC station in late March that same year and the subsequent wounding of one of the volunteers involved – another member of the Doris clan, this time nineteen-year-old Gareth, cousin of the late Tony Doris. More landmines, more IEDs, most of them victim-operated, such as one in January 1994 intended for an unwary Royal Irish patrol (the UDR having been disbanded and merged with the Royal Irish Rangers to form the Royal Irish Regiment in 1992). 'It was a pretty large device, around 400lbs, triggered by a pressure pad made from an old front door. PIRA had seen patrols there before having a brew-stop [hot cup of tea] so put the bomb in place to catch them out.' No patrols had taken the bait until the local farmer happened along one evening to herd his sheep into the old building. 'We got the call out and when we arrived by helicopter the derelict building had literally disappeared. Two civilians had been injured – the farmer and his girlfriend, who was with him at the time.'

The next morning found the troop cordon looking out at dozens of sheep with most of their wool burnt off in the blast, but still happily chewing away at the grass. In the follow-up operation an Army patrol found another VOIED as they were called (Victim Operated IED), again utilising a front door as an improvised pressure pad buried into the soft earth and covered with turf, linked to a number of beer kegs packed with homemade explosives and hidden behind a low wall by the roadside. The patrol commander was on his first tour in

Northern Ireland: 'It was a route clearance, so ATO [bomb disposal] could drive their gear in and clear the site of the first explosion, and I remember we'd literally just been landed on the ground by the Puma [helicopter] and as we started the route I looked over this wall and there they were – a row of beer kegs all connected together with the white twin-flex the Intelligence guys told us they [PIRA] liked using. I used a hand signal I'd agreed beforehand with the RUC guy with us and he came over, saw it and we moved off. After we'd moved away I called it in as an Op Clean and set up a snap rummage to make it look like we hadn't seen anything, but I guess as I was pretty green and it was my first tour they probably thought I was mistaken, so they didn't opt to put the Det on it and we just had to clear it as a second device. To be honest we'd been on non-stop ops for days and I was so tired I didn't think about it blowing up and killing me – all I wanted was a few hours' sleep.'

Times had certainly changed. A former Scots Guards officer, who'd earlier served in West Belfast, remembered his time in east Tyrone with little affection. 'Without doubt, Cookstown was the worst, most miserable six months of my life. By '94 there was no real sense of threat from East Tyrone PIRA. It was nothing like Belfast in '92 with RPG Alley, the Ballymurphy etc. It just felt like another God-awful rural tour, tramping round the cuds.'

Frankie Quinn – caught in possession of a massive 1,000lb bomb in 1988 and sentenced to sixteen years – was in the Maze Prison at the time. He remembered the arguments between prisoners from different parts of the IRA, primarily those from Belfast – the majority – and the relative few from East Tyrone and South Armagh. 'We were saying the armed struggle's failed, it can't win,' Quinn explained in an interview he gave. 'The armed struggle had to stop. We'd dump weapons, call the ceasefire, and then go into talks.' Those from 'Belfast [IRA] and all these other people were saying we needed to fight on', says Quinn. 'All these other people – who are now standing up on stages – couldn't be convinced. We had arguments with them.'

Emotions ran high in summer that year as Quinn recalled. 'Some of the people at, let's say, the top table, got very emotional, but most of the rest of us knew it was coming and accepted it and said yeah, it's good. That's fine … We weren't able to achieve our goal any longer through military struggle and we needed to adopt another approach.'

It's incredibly difficult to tell exactly what was going on within the ranks of the IRA leadership at the time unless you were one of them – and even then, it was probably a hard ask. Some reports state that of the various brigades, South Armagh was against a ceasefire – contrary to Quinn's recollections – while East Tyrone and Fermanagh were unsure. Belfast was divided. Peter Taylor has said that the RUC Chief Constable at the time, Sir Hugh Annesley told him that East Tyrone had said no to a ceasefire and wanted to go back to the war, almost certainly along with South Armagh. Other reports said that the Army Council vote on the ceasefire had been five to two for the agreement, and even hinted that one of the two dissenting voices had been none other than Kevin McKenna himself. If true that would have been astounding. The ceasefire was a fundamental part of the Adams/McGuinness programme of moving towards a political solution to the war, and McKenna had always been an Adams loyalist, despite his long-running personal feud with McGuinness. Crucially though, there were no splits, and on Wednesday, 31 August 1994 PIRA's Army Council announced a ceasefire.

The announcement was met with mixed emotions in the Scots Guards Right Flank Company ['A' Company in other British regiments] in Tyrone: 'There was a huge change in "posture" as they called it when the ceasefire came in at the end of August. All of a sudden we went to wearing our berets and not our helmets [viewed by the military as less threatening to civilians]. We had to keep our patrolling hours up but didn't want to provoke the locals so we ended up flying out and patrolling areas that were perfectly safe and hadn't seen any soldiers in years – they all came out of their houses and asked what was wrong. After a while it was just rolling from tea stop to tea stop for days until the boys started to ask what the f**k we were doing there … and they had a point.' The only incident of any note – if it could be called that – was during a night patrol: 'We were atop this hill and looked down onto a road where a car had pulled up and the headlights kept flicking on and off. It was a very quiet out of the way spot and I absolutely thought this was a weapons drop or something like that, so we set up and waited for the other vehicle to show, and when it didn't I sent one of my jocks down to take a look. He tapped on the driver's window and inside were a young couple having it away. They'd gone there for a bit of privacy, but his backside kept on knocking the light switch on the steering wheel. We sent them on their way, looking very sheepish.'

On Easter Sunday 2017, as part of the annual republican commemorations, Gerry Adams was the main speaker at the showpiece event in Carrickmore. Standing before a crowd of the faithful, Adams paid homage to Tyrone's place in militant republican tradition and especially the part played by the East Tyrone Brigade. 'Tyrone's contribution to the fight for Irish freedom is incomparable, not just in our generation but going back over many generations … This includes the fifty-six IRA volunteers of the Tyrone Brigade and the three Sinn Féin activists who laid down their lives in the most recent phase of struggle.' The point Adams made about the blood price paid by East Tyrone was apt; nowhere else had the toll been so high or so concentrated in such a short space of time. In the five years from 1987 to 1992 the Brigade lost twenty volunteers killed. During that same period the Belfast Brigade lost two, and Derry not a single one. Tyrone's sister brigade, South Armagh, only lost ten dead in the entire war.

Why the East Tyrone Brigade in particular suffered so badly is an oft-asked question, to which there would seem to be no simple answer. But there would appear to have been a set of circumstances unique to the Brigade, which, together, combined to prove almost fatal to its existence. Indeed, its own deadly nature and accompanying reputation came to work against it. From the early days of Kevin Mallon, Brendan Hughes and Sean O'Callaghan, East Tyrone made its mark and that brought it to the attention of the security forces. South Armagh undoubtedly did the same, but there were crucial differences between the two.

The biggest difference was the makeup of their local populations. South Armagh is almost wholly Catholic, of whom a significant percentage are pro-republican. That meant support for the security forces was limited and there was no chance of raising a local UDR unit or staffing the police stations with men and women from Crossmaglen or Cullyhanna. The security forces in south Armagh were, therefore, necessarily outsiders and struggled to build the sort of knowledge-based intelligence picture that was the norm in east Tyrone. There, large numbers of men and women from Dungannon, Cookstown, Coagh, Caledon and Aughnacloy stepped forward and provided a critical bulwark against the Provisionals, despite the enormous risks their service entailed. Tommy McKearney's highlighting of the local dimension to the security forces' response to the Provisionals is basically true. Any student of the type of insurgency warfare fought in Northern Ireland knows that to win, the insurgents had to radicalise the population into providing at least passive support, removing them as a prop from the existing administration and creating an 'us against them' scenario that becomes a self-fulfilling wheel of atrocity followed by reprisal and so on, until those in charge realise the game is up. The fact that PIRA were never able to get even remotely close to that situation in east Tyrone is both a tribute to the service of people such as Glen Espie, Jay Nethercott, John Shackles and the hundreds like them, and a failure of the Provisional leadership as a whole to appeal beyond their heartlands.

A second reason why the East Tyrone Brigade suffered such a hammering was British policy itself. Despite the non-jury Diplock courts, and the undoubted success of the RUC in arresting, charging and convicting suspects, the collapse of the supergrass trials, and then the Maze breakout in particular, seemed to suggest the judicial system could not defeat PIRA on its own and a more muscular approach was needed. With the crowded streets of Belfast and Derry totally unsuitable for such muscular operations, the options were Fermanagh, east Tyrone or south Armagh. The latter two were the cockpits of violence at that point, especially when the death of Séamus McElwaine effectively beheaded Fermanagh and brought it – to an extent – under East Tyrone's wing. In a straight choice between Tyrone and Armagh, the vital intelligence needed to launch lethal operations was far more plentiful in Tyrone – in south Armagh the security forces lacked the vital intelligence that was available in east Tyrone from Special Branch's long list of informers, and that put a target on the back of the East Tyrone Brigade.

The Brigade didn't do itself any favours either. True or not, actions such as the killings of eighty-six-year-old Norman Stronge and his son James as they sat watching TV, and Ned Gibson as he emptied the bins in Ardboe, looked nakedly sectarian to both Protestants and many Catholics, and caused genuine anger among both communities. One former RUC officer claimed, 'They [the majority of Catholics] didn't like us much, but they grew to hate the Provos who they saw increasingly as bloodthirsty hooligans.' Clearly this was far from a universal view among the county's Catholics, but as the RUC – and Special Branch in particular – became more effective, that increasingly meant a steady stream of individuals willing to supply information, and more than anything else it was that information flow which crippled East Tyrone PIRA.

Richard Kemp – who served two years in an intelligence role in Army headquarters in Lisburn and then later worked in the Cabinet Office covering the situation in Northern Ireland – was clear as to the importance of the RUC in the fight with

PIRA: 'The RUC played the major role in winning the conflict, no question – they couldn't have done it without the Army, but especially in the latter stages of the war it was an intel war and that war was won by the RUC and particularly RUC SB, without a shadow of doubt. The Army played a part, MI5 played a part, but it was SB's victory. Towards the end, with a few exceptions, the IRA couldn't mount an op because SB had so thoroughly infiltrated them.'

A former battalion Intelligence Officer from the time echoed Kemp's opinions: 'They [SB] were very careful with sources, very rarely did they let anything slip and they were very professional. Their intel was incredible. They seemed to know down to the hour almost when something was going to happen. There was one time when they'd asked for an Ops Company [Operations Company – non-special forces brigade asset used for high-profile operations] heli drop-off at a certain location to be moved from 0300hrs to 0400hrs instead, but there was a cock-up and the op went in at 0300, and the RUC guy almost kicked my f**ing door down at 0310 shouting, "what the f**k? Tell them not to touch anyone and stay where they are."' However both men were also careful to temper their praise with a broader view. 'Overall though, we never really trusted SB as they played their cards so close to their chest and they made it plain they never really trusted us, and that made working together hard.' Kemp in particular was careful not to beatify the entire RUC: 'As far as the individual coppers were concerned their quality was variable, like police or the military anywhere. Some were very good, some were very bad, but the good ones were in the majority and they kept whittling away at PIRA.'

That whittling away had a corrosive affect on the East Tyrone Brigade. Never a mass movement – even in the 1970s – the Provisionals decision to opt for an ASU-cell strategy suited the insularity and clannish nature of east Tyrone republicanism, but also made it incredibly vulnerable to attrition. Numbers are impossible to quote accurately given the secrecy of the organisation, and also the differing roles within it – not every volunteer was a gunman or a bomber – but it's safe to say the Provos could always be counted in the hundreds rather than the thousands. As the 1970s came to a close, the sheer number of informers was in danger of sinking the IRA as the courts filled up the cells with dozens of men convicted for very long stretches. For an organisation without a deep well of recruits, this was a very dangerous situation and the Provisionals desperately tried to halt the flow of information to the security forces by killing those found informing. In the nine years up to Loughgall, PIRA killed no fewer than twenty-four alleged informers – mostly in Belfast in point of fact – but even the horrors of torture, public shame and death at the hands of the Nutting Squad had little effect, Loughgall being a case in point. All sides – for their own reasons – talked down the idea of one or more informers having been involved in the SAS ambush, but the whiff of the tout was enough to cast a debilitating black cloud over the East Tyrone Brigade that had every volunteer looking over their shoulder from then on.

In truth, the number of volunteers arrested, charged, convicted and imprisoned always significantly outnumbered those killed on operations, and for that growing number of men, being locked up was no small matter. There was no discretionary sentence reduction to free up space in crowded jails – ten years could mean ten years – and it meant spending a large portion of your youth locked up, staring at the walls, only seeing loved ones at visiting times. Self-help education programmes and learning Irish along with fellow inmates only went so far, as Henry Robinson, an Official IRA former prisoner acknowledged. 'There were always courses, and groups you know. You could do lots of that, and it was good, and some did them and some didn't, but you were still behind the wire you know.' The Ardboe volunteer Brendan Hughes was emphatic about what his jail time was like. 'I did time hard. My family did time hard ... I literally couldn't do one more minute in jail. I've had more than enough.'

That was a common sentiment, and one that greatly contributed to reducing the Provos in number from near a thousand at the beginning of the 1980s to somewhere between 250 to 350 across the entire north in 1987. That wasn't supporters, that wasn't local auxiliaries – those prepared to drive a car, keep a lookout or turn a blind eye – but those few prepared to pull a trigger or detonate a bomb. The East Tyrone Brigade was one of the strongest of PIRA's units at that point, having perhaps as many as fifty to sixty of those active volunteers. Henry Robinson's view of the Brigade at that time is chilling. 'It was the Provisionals' killing machine.'

Then came Loughgall. At Jim Lynagh's funeral Gerry Adams defiantly declared that 'Loughgall will become a tombstone for British policy in Ireland.' In reality it was East Tyrone PIRA's death knell. There are those who argue the opposite is true, saying recruitment went up in the aftermath, pointing to the fact that in the two years before Loughgall, the Brigade killed seven members of the security forces and actually increased that figure to eleven in the two years following Operation Judy. They also point out that according to data collated by the weekly IRA *War News* column in *An Phoblacht*, East Tyrone accounted for almost the same percentage of Provisional operations in 1988 as they had in 1986, but these claims hide the distorting impact of the eight soldiers killed in the Ballygawley bus bombing, and the downward trajectory of the Brigade thereafter to the point where by 1993 fewer than one in ten PIRA attacks were carried out by East Tyrone. The unit that had once been a byword for the deadly efficiency of its operations was now a shadow of its former self, and that spiral began at Loughgall when the British realised what the Provisionals already knew: that the fields, lanes and hedgerows of east Tyrone and neighbouring north Armagh were a perfect killing ground. For the security forces that meant they could utilise the skills of 14 Company and the SAS with less chance of collateral damage, hence Drumnakilly, Grew and McCaughey, Coagh and Clonoe. Anthony Hughes's family have every right to disagree with that statement.

The fact remains that in a paramilitary organisation like PIRA the small number of older, more experienced members wield enormous influence, particularly when it comes to passing on the baton to the next generation. So when the SAS opened fire at Loughgall and wiped out the A Team in a matter of seconds, they not only annihilated those at the top of the tree, like Lynagh, Kelly and McKearney, but also those destined to take their place in the future. To illustrate the point, the average age of the A Team at Loughgall was almost twenty-four, with three men in their thirties; at Clonoe five years later it was just twenty.

Unlike anywhere else – excepting Belfast – east Tyrone was also a key battleground between the Provisionals and the loyalists, especially the UVF. Clifford Peeples explained why the UVF focused on east Tyrone and not the neighbouring bandit country of republican south Armagh: 'South Armagh wasn't open. Loyalists have no network there, no structure. There just aren't any loyalists, so you can't get anyone in and out, but east Tyrone is different; there are pockets of loyalists, in Stewartstown, in Cookstown, in Coagh, a spine of loyalists throughout the county who can see what's going on, so intelligence-wise you have people on the ground, people who are sympathetic to you and that makes all the difference. So there's people you can ask to hide a weapon, mind a car and so on.' This meant the UVF could exert significant pressure on East Tyrone PIRA, partly through its tit-for-tat sectarian murder strategy, but also with far more targeted attacks such as the ones against Liam Ryan and Boyles Bar, that further shrank the Provos ranks and wore away the sense of safety in its heartlands. Just as importantly, the loyalists inexorably drew the Brigade into a brutal and bloody sectarian campaign that did nothing but lead the Provisionals down a blind alley; a blind alley that more or less ended with the deaths of Billy Wright and Mark Fulton, the former in late December 1997, shot dead in the Maze Prison of all places, by three other inmates from the Irish National Liberation Army, and the latter in Maghaberry Prison from suicide five years later while awaiting trial. As Brendan Hughes acknowledged, 'It was a dirty war. When we set out we thought we could finish it, but we were only skirmishing around the abyss before we fell in.'

Hemmed in, the political path looked increasingly rosy to Provo high command and the fate of the East Tyrone Brigade became the cautionary tale that helped smooth the way for the peace process. No less a character than Kevin Mallon – once East Tyrone's commander and now a retiree in Dublin – joked, '[Gerry] Adams simply stood there in the enveloping mess and acted as if he had planned it all along – and then it just came to seem that way.'

East Tyrone is relatively quiet now. There aren't the peace walls of Belfast or the murals of Derry to alert the visitor to its recent bloody history, neither are there the Troubles tourist trails that do such a brisk trade in Northern Ireland's two largest cities. There are memorials of course; the volunteer statue in Cappagh, the granite pillar at Teebane, the 8 UDR commemorative monument in Dungannon churchyard, and endless graves in churchyard plots, rarely visited except by the Tyrone National Graves Association (the republican ones anyway) and the families, for whom the past is still very real.

One such family is the McKearneys. Speaking to an American journalist in 1998, seventy-year-old Maura McKearney made her views crystal clear: 'The IRA should have stopped what they were doing twenty-five years ago. It would have left so many homes so much happier.' She should know. Her family was ravaged by the war, and so was her village of Moy. With a population of less than 1,500, it typified the brutality of the struggle in east Tyrone. Seventy per cent Protestant in 1969, its quiet streets became stained with blood. The UVF struck first, murdering the Mullens, an innocent Catholic couple in their farmhouse in the summer of 1973. Two years later they struck again, this time shooting another

Catholic couple dead, whose bad luck was to bear the surname McKearney – although they were no relation to Maura and her family. The following year the tiny neighbouring village of Charlemont – home to the Grews – was to bear the brunt. The same night the Grews were bombed out of their house, four Catholics were killed in bomb and gun attacks on two pubs, prompting immediate IRA retaliation. Two brothers – Protestants – Robert and Thomas Dobson, were shot dead at their work, an egg-packing factory in Moy's Dungannon Street near the McKearney family's butcher's shop. More were to follow. George McCall – a former UDR solider – was shot dead by a three-man ASU from the East Tyrone Brigade in August 1977 while out walking, and Fred Lutton – an ex-RUC officer – was killed two years later while working at The Argory, a National Trust stately home. Moy then had two years of peace before PIRA struck again. This time it was the turn of John Donnelly, an off-duty UDR soldier, as he sat drinking in the Catholic-owned Village Inn on 16 April 1981. 'The IRA gunman walked in and shot my brother point-blank. He wasn't masked. People saw who he was, a Moy boy. But none of the people in the bar would tell the police.' Donnelly's sister Edie also lost her husband William, gunned down at a cattle market in Ballybay, County Monaghan for being an ex-UDR member. Remarkably, given its recent history, the guns would then fall silent in Moy for an entire decade, until Robin Farmer came home from university for Christmas. Working in his ex-RUC father's shop, nineteen-year-old Robin was shot dead by a gunman from the Irish National Liberation Army. In the tit-for-tat merry-go-round it was the UVF's turn in 1992, murdering Maura McKearney's son Kevin and her brother-in-law John in the family shop in January, and then shooting dead Charles and Teresa Fox in their home in September. In all, twenty-two people were killed in or near Moy during the war. As a local Protestant shopkeeper, Derek McMullen, told *The Los Angeles Times*, 'The real trouble in this country is that we've too many Protestants and too many Catholics and too few Christians.'

The visible signs of the Troubles in Moy are few. There are no paramilitary murals, no kerbstones painted in the colours of the Union Jack or Irish tricolour. The small RUC station is no more, and the same is the case for almost all the security force infrastructure across Tyrone, built with so much treasure and protected by so much blood. Coalisland RUC station, once universally derided as 'the ugliest building in Northern Ireland' was torn down in 2016, *Northern Ireland World* reporting that local Sinn Féin Councillor Dominic Molloy welcomed the news of the demolition, saying that it removed 'an eyesore' from the centre of the town. 'This will be welcome news to local people as it tidies up the derelict site and will provide affordable social housing in an area where there are great housing pressures ... Hopefully, the town centre will be allowed to return to what it once was, and new life breathed into it.' Likewise Castlehill barracks in Dungannon is now deserted, the fences, watchtowers and sleeping accommodation clad in mortar-proof protective concrete long since removed. All that stands there now is the original farmhouse, Killymeal, and that is fast collapsing into the earth from which it sprang – the haunt of online bloggers and website hosts looking for some vestige of what once stood there. Even Loughgall RUC station is gone. Blown up once more by a huge 1,000lb van bomb on

5 September 1990, it was rebuilt, only to close for good in August 2009. Eighteen months later it was sold off for private development, the building demolished and a clutch of mews houses built on the site. The irony of a brutal, vicious conflict that had a measure of its roots in the unequal and unfair allocation of housing to those in need, finally ending with the building of large numbers of homes on former security force land, is unique.

APPENDIX A

EXCERPT FROM A JANE'S DEFENCE REVIEW REPORT (AUGUST 1996) ON THE PROVISIONAL IRA AND ITS STRUCTURES

Some analysts estimate the current strength of the IRA at about 400 hard-core activists, with perhaps a similar number of 'auxiliary' or 'second-line' activists who can be called on in a crisis. Many of these volunteers may not necessarily be full-time but may work at other occupations. There is believed to be a hard core of about forty middle-ranking members of the IRA who make operational decisions. The day-to-day running of the IRA is conducted by a seven-person Army Council. Members of the Council always include the Chief of Staff, the Adjutant General and the Quartermaster General. The General Army Convention (GAC) is the supreme authority of the IRA and meets on comparatively rare occasions. According to the IRA Constitution, the GAC is to meet once every two years unless a majority deem it better for military reasons to postpone a meeting. Delegates to the GAC include IRA members selected by various units within the organization as well as the members of the Army Council. The GAC selects a twelve-member Army Executive which meets at least once every six months. One of the key roles of the executive is to select the members of the Army Council. It is also the role of the executive to advise the Army Council on all matters concerning the IRA. The planning and implementation of Army Council decisions are carried out by the General Headquarters (GHQ) Staff, which acts as the link between the Council and Northern and Southern Commands. Each Command has its own Commanding Officer, Director of Operations and Quartermaster. The operational arm consists of cells known as *Active Service Units* (ASUs) each with usually five to eight members, sometimes more. Occasionally, special teams are assembled by the Army Council/GHQ Staff for special operations. There is a women's section known as *Cumann na mBan.*

ENDNOTES

CHAPTER ONE

1. *Daily Telegraph*, Obituary, 22 September 2005.
2. O'Callaghan, Sean, *The Informer*, p. 81.
3. McCluskey, Fergal, *The Irish Revolution, 1912–23: Tyrone*, p. 89.
4. Brock, Michael and Eleanor (eds), *H.H. Asquith 'Letters to Venetia Stanley'*, p. 109.
5. Churchill, Winston S., *The World Crisis, Vol. 1: 1911–1914*.
6. McCluskey, *The Irish Revolution*, p. 59.
7. Ibid., p. 106.
8. Townshend, Charles, *The Republic: The Fight for Irish Independence, 1918–1923*, Penguin, 2014.
9. McCluskey, *The Irish Revolution*, p. 115.
10. Flynn, Barry, *Soldiers of Folly: The IRA Border Campaign 1956–1962*, p. 151.
11. O'Callaghan, Sean, *The Informer*, p. 46.

CHAPTER TWO

12. O'Callaghan, Sean, *The Informer*, p. 56.
13. Leask, Anthony, *Conspicuous Gallantry*, p. 40.
14. Hughes, Brendan, *Up Like a Bird: The Rise and Fall of an IRA Commander*, p. 181.

15. Leask, Anthony, *Conspicuous Gallantry*, p. 38.

16. Interview with Freya Clements, *The Irish Times*, 31 August 2019.

17. McKearney, Tommy, *The Provisional IRA: From Insurrection to Parliament*, p. 117.

18. O'Callaghan, Sean, *The Informer*, p. 245.

CHAPTER THREE

19. Hughes, Brendan, *Up Like a Bird*, p. 292.

20. Leask, Anthony, *Conspicuous Gallantry*, p. 47.

21. O'Callaghan, Sean, *The Informer*, p. 32.

22. Denmark, Edward, *Not for Queen and Country*, p. 130.

23. Matchett, William, *Secret Victory: The Intelligence War that Beat the IRA*, p. 12.

24. Peter Sherry would later unwittingly lead the British police to a safe house in the Queen's Park area of Glasgow in June 1985, where he was arrested along with the Brighton Bomber, Patrick Magee. Sherry received a thirty-year sentence for terrorist offences.

25. Conway, Kieran, *Southside Provisional: From Freedom Fighter to the Four Courts*, p. 138.

26. Urban, Mark, *Big Boys' Rules: The SAS and the Secret Struggle Against the IRA*, p. 175.

CHAPTER FOUR

27. Urban, Mark, *Big Boys' Rules*, p. 183.

CHAPTER FIVE

28. Leask, Anthony, *Conspicuous Gallantry*, p. 172.

29. Breen, Colin, *A Force Like No Other: The Real Stories of the RUC Men and Women Who Policed the Troubles*, p. 98.

CHAPTER SIX

30. Rennie, James, *The Operators: On the Streets with Britain's Most Secret Service*, p. 221.

CHAPTER SEVEN

31. Leask, Anthony, *Conspicuous Gallantry*, p. 202.
32. Breen, Colin, *A Force Like No Other: The Next Shift*, p. 162.
33. Leask, Anthony, *Conspicuous Gallantry*, p. 217
34. Ibid., p. 196.

CHAPTER EIGHT

35. O'Callaghan, Sean, *The Informer*, p. 245.
36. Leask, Anthony, *Conspicuous Gallantry*, p. 148.
37. Breen, Colin, *A Force Like No Other: The Next Shift*, p. 11.
38. Ibid., p. 15.

SELECT BIBLIOGRAPHY

Adams, James, Morgan, Robin and Bambridge, Anthony, *Ambush: The War Between the SAS and the IRA*, Pan, 1988

Asher, Michael, *The Regiment: The Definitive Story of the SAS*, Penguin, 2018

Barthorp, Michael, *Crater to the Creggan: The History of The Royal Anglian Regiment 1964–1974*, Leo Cooper, 1976

Breen, Colin, *A Force Like No Other: The Real Stories of the RUC Men and Women Who Policed the Troubles*, Blackstaff, 2017

Breen, Colin, *A Force Like No Other: The Next Shift*, Blackstaff, 2019

Breen, Colin, *A Force Like No Other: The Last Shift*, Blackstaff, 2021

Brock, Michael and Eleanor (eds) *H.H. Asquith 'Letters to Venetia Stanley'*, Oxford, 1982

Bruce, Paul, *The Nemesis File*, Blake, 1995

Burke, David, *Kitson's Irish War: Mastermind of the Dirty War in Ireland*, Mercier, 2021

Churchill, Winston S., *The World Crisis, Vol. 1: 1911–1914*, Bloomsbury, 2015.

Conway, Kieran, *Southside Provisional: From Freedom Fighter to the Four Courts*, Orpen 2014

Coogan, Tim Pat, *The IRA*, Harper Collins, 2000

Coogan, Tim Pat, *The Troubles*, Arrow, 1996

Denmark, Edward, *Not for Queen and Country*, Pharoah, 1998

Dillon, Martin, *The Trigger Men: Assassins and Terror Bosses in the Ireland Conflict*, Mainstream, 2004

Edwards, Aaron, *UVF: Behind the Mask*, Merrion Press, 2017

English, Richard, *Armed Struggle: The History of the IRA*, Pan, 2012

Flynn, Barry, *Soldiers of Folly: The IRA Border Campaign 1956–1962*, Collins, 2009

Geraghty, Tony, *The Irish War: The Military History of a Domestic Conflict*, Harper Collins, 1998

Geraghty, Tony, *Who Dares Wins: The Story of the SAS 1950–1982*, Fontana/Collins, 1983

Harnden, Toby, *Bandit Country: The IRA & South Armagh*, Hodder & Stoughton, 2000

Holland, Jack and Phoenix, Susan, *Phoenix: Policing the Shadows: The Secret War Against Terrorism in Northern Ireland*, Coronet, 1996

Hughes, Brendan (with Douglas Dalby), *Up Like a Bird: The Rise and Fall of an IRA Commander*, Time Warp, 2021

Ingram, Martin and Harkin, Greg, *Stakeknife: Britain's Secret Agents in Ireland*, O'Brien Press, 2004

Kelley, Kevin, *The Longest War: Northern Ireland and the IRA*, Zed Press, 1982

Kennedy, Liam, *Unhappy the Land: The Most Oppressed People Ever, the Irish?*, Merrion Press, 2016

Leahy, Thomas, *The Intelligence War Against the IRA*, Cambridge University Press, 2020

Leask, Anthony, *Conspicuous Gallantry*, Helion, 2020

Mac Bride, Oistín, *Family, Friends and Neighbours: An Irish Photobiography*, Beyond the Pale, 2001

Matchett, William, *Secret Victory: The Intelligence War that Beat the IRA*, Matchett 2016

McCallion, Harry, *Undercover War: Britain's Special Forces and Their Secret Battle Against the IRA*, John Blake, 2020

McCluskey, Fergal, *The Irish Revolution, 1912–23: Tyrone*, Four Courts, 2014

McKearney, Tommy, *The Provisional IRA: From Insurrection to Parliament*, Pluto 2011

McKittrick, David and McVea, David, *Making Sense of the Troubles: A History of the Northern Ireland Conflict*, Viking, 2012

Moloney, Ed, *A Secret History of the IRA*, Allen Lane, 2002

Mulroe, Patrick, *Bombs, Bullets and the Border: Policing Ireland's Frontier: Irish Security Policy, 1969–1978*, Irish Academic Press, 2017

O'Brien, Brendan, *The Long War: The IRA and Sinn Féin*, Syracuse University, 1999

O'Callaghan, Sean, *The Informer*, Bantam, 1998

Parker, John, *Death of a Hero: Captain Robert Nairac GC, and the Undercover War in Northern Ireland*, Metro, 1999

Potter, John, *A Testimony to Courage: The Regimental History of the Ulster Defence Regiment*, Leo Cooper, 2001

Rennie, James, *The Operators: On the Streets with Britain's Most Secret Service*, Pen & Sword, 2016

Ryder, Chris, *The Ulster Defence Regiment: An Instrument of Peace?*, Methuen, 1991

Stevenson, Jonathan, *'We Wrecked the Place': Contemplating the End to the Northern Irish Troubles*, Free Press, 1996

Taylor, Peter, *Brits: The War Against the IRA*, Bloomsbury, 2002

Taylor, Peter, *Families at War: Voices from the Troubles*, BBC Books, 1989

Taylor, Peter, *Loyalists*, Bloomsbury, 1999

Taylor, Peter, *Provos: The IRA and Sinn Féin*, Bloomsbury, 1997

Tiernan, Joe, *The Dublin and Monaghan Bombings*, Joe Tiernan, 2006

Toolis, Kevin, *Rebel Hearts: Journeys within the IRA's Soul*, Picador, 1995

Townshend, Charles, *The Republic: The Fight for Irish Independence 1918–1923*, Penguin, 2014

Urban, Mark, *Big Boys' Rules: The SAS and the Secret Struggles Against the IRA*, Faber & Faber, 1992

Van der Bijl, Nick, *Operation Banner: The British Army in Northern Ireland 1969–2007*, Pen & Sword, 2017

White, Robert W., *Out of the Ashes: An Oral History of the Provisional Irish Republican Movement*, Merrion Press, 2017

INDEX